# Contents

# Index of Tasks

# INTRODUCTION

This book is about teaching juniors. It is for teachers of children aged from seven to 11 years, although it contains much that is relevant across the whole primary age range, and beyond, reflecting the fact that teaching and learning are continuous processes throughout the school years.

The book focuses on the key issues related to teaching junior-age children. It is divided into units, each unit exploring a major theme and related sub-themes. The units fall broadly into three sections. The first units focus on the *context* of teaching and learning in the classroom (Units 1–6), then comes a consideration of the *content* of teaching and learning (Units 7–14), finally aspects of the *assessment* of teaching and learning are explored (Units 15–19). For the sake of clarity each unit is self-contained, but they are often inter-related and cross-referenced since teaching involves coping with many varied task demands, including the ever-fluctuating needs of children.

Within each unit there are suggested *tasks* to carry out in the classroom, as the opportunity arises, or during teaching practice. These tasks often involve activities with children and discussion with colleagues, since much of the professional development is or should be a sharing process. There is also an emphasis on self-evaluation throughout the book, based on the view that development in teaching often comes through reflection on our own practice.

Wherever possible the text is confined to fairly short blocks, and information is presented in the form of *tables* or *figures* for ease of reference. The aim has been to assist teachers and students-in-training to use the book selectively to fulfil their own needs as part of their busy professional programme. The book serves two purposes. Firstly it is a comprehensive classroom-based reference book, particularly related to meeting the needs of the National Curriculum. Secondly it is a handbook of practical activities, offering 70 or more tasks designed to improve classroom skills in a conscious and systematic way.

References and suggestions for further reading will be found at the end of the book, together with a glossary of National Curriculum terms that appear in the text.

This book does not seek to propound one particular view or philosophy of teaching. There are no ready-made lesson plans or recipes for instant success. Reference is made to a wide range of research and theory related to primary teaching, and ways are suggested which can help in the analysis and development of practical teaching skills. But there are no golden rules applicable to all teaching, for there is no perfect lesson, and no perfect teacher.

# Unit 1

# THINKING ABOUT TEACHING

How to express the quality of his teaching? A thorough mastery of his subjects, an inexhaustible sympathy for the scholastic underdog, a unique ability to make unexpected connexions and to mix in an always fresh and eye-opening way the stuff of lessons with the stuff of life, an effortless humour, a by no means negligible gift for dramatization, a restless and doubting temperament that urged him forward ceaselessly toward self-improvement in the pedagogic craft ... To sit under Mr Caldwell was to lift one's head in aspiration.

John Updike *The Centaur*

Some teachers one never forgets. Their influence and our memory of them remain with us throughout our lives. Such teachers have the capacity to enhance, or to blight, our understanding of what it is to be alive, of our potential for living in and learning about the world. Are there teachers like Mr Caldwell who remain in your memory? Or perhaps teachers like Mr Gradgrind who gave you a particularly hard time? In thinking about teaching and our professional development we are not engaged in any small undertaking but one that will have far-reaching consequences, and that can illuminate the lives of those whom we teach.

## Task I  Remembering a teacher

1  Call to mind a special teacher in your life.
2  Write a short account of your memories of that teacher, and explain why that teacher was special.
3  Find out what others remember about a special or favourite teacher in their lives.

4    Compare your findings. What do they tell you about particular teachers and
     about the impressions they leave?

The teacher is the most valuable resource in any classroom. Valuable in the
sense of being the most effective facilitator of children's learning, as well as
being the most expensive item in any classroom. The teacher is high in value,
and in power of authority. Part of this authority is invested by society to care
for, and mediate the curriculum for, each child under her control. She also
has professional authority invested in her by children which derives from her
knowledge, skill and training in teaching. There is also her personal authority
which she establishes for herself through her 'presence', her confidence and
her personal qualities.

Teaching has a public, as well as a personal or private, aspect. It is made
up partly of legal responsibilities, and partly of a personal commitment to all
that is entailed in being a teacher. Teaching, with its many responsibilities,
can be viewed in different ways, for example as:

- a task
- a job
- a career
- a profession
- a role
- a vocation
- a way of life

How do you view teaching? What is it for you that makes teaching worthwhile?

# Why teach?

What makes primary teaching worthwhile for most teachers is first and
foremost the children. Teachers tend to find them more honest, spontaneous,
enthusiastic and amusing than adults. Herbert Kohl found that 'they were
purer, more open, and less damaged than I was ... they could dare to be
creative where I was inhibited; they could write well because they didn't
know what good writing was supposed to be; they could learn with ease,
whereas I was overridden with anxiety over grades and tests.' Teachers like
helping children to learn, seeing the breakthrough when suddenly 'the penny
drops' and the child says at last, 'Oh yes, I've got it now!' It is reassuring too
to be liked and needed by children, to be the key person in their lives at
school.

Teaching juniors can be varied, stimulating and creative. No two days are ever the same. With 20 or 30 unpredictable personalities in the class the job need never be boring. In the words of one teacher, 'the children help you to stay alive'. Children are exploring their world for the first time, and the teacher too can share in their discoveries, problems and findings out. Part of the excitement of teaching is sharing in the vitality and exploratory energy of children.

Satisfaction can also come from working with other teachers at school, developing joint plans and policies with colleagues and being part of a teaching team. The staffroom can be an 'essential source of friendship, company and conversation'. Self-esteem can grow from a sense of professional competence, enhanced by positive feedback from colleagues, from children and from parents, and contribute to a justifiable pride in a job well done.

Teaching can be a source of self-fulfilment. It can also be the cause of much frustration and dissatisfaction. When teaching is not going well teachers may blame themselves for their own perceived inadequacies. External factors can make it more difficult to teach effectively. Such factors include working in schools with inefficient administration or poor communication, or lacking essential resources such as books, paper or equipment. Large classes and disproportionate numbers of disruptive or disadvantaged children makes it hard to provide the individual help that is necessary. Excessive levels of external control can also lead to frustration and a diminished sense of professionalism.

Teaching can exact a high personal cost from teachers, especially if they are committed to doing a good job. One head summed up the teacher's vocation as 'Give, give and give again'. Some teachers are more or less in a permanent state of tiredness due to the relentless day-by-day pressures of the job, teaching a variety of lessons all day without a break, preparing and marking in the evenings and at the weekend, and collecting resources and teaching ideas while on holiday. No wonder many ask themselves whether the stress of teaching is worth what is seen as a meagre reward.

Being a teacher involves many dilemmas and contradictions: being both rewarded and frustrated in the classroom, being both stimulated and exhausted, feeling in control of things as well as failing, finding the job creative and satisfying as well as tough and draining. The teacher has to be egocentric in the sense of knowing who she is and where she is going, as well as selfless in trying always to put the children first. No wonder teachers can find it both the best and the worst of jobs.

## TABLE 1 Some positive and negative aspects of teaching

| Sources of satisfaction | Sources of dissatisfaction |
| --- | --- |
| *Pleasure* in the enthusiasm and responsiveness of children | *Stress* in dealing with discipline and behaviour problems |
| *Variety* in every day being different and varied | *Exhaustion* due to workload and lack of non-contact time |
| *Reward* in seeing children learn | *Frustration* in dealing with large classes and underachieving children |
| *Creative stimulus* of lesson planning | *Relentless demands* of preparation and marking |
| *Opportunities to learn* alongside the children and in professional development | *Repetitiveness* of much teaching activity |
| *Sense of community/teamwork* with other colleagues | *Sense of isolation* in the classroom |
| *Autonomy* and independence in one's own class teaching | *Imposition* of schemes of work and learning materials |
| *Social value* of playing key role in local community | *Low esteem* due to lack of support from community or Government |
| *Effectiveness* is making things happen, achieving important results | *Failure* to achieve hopes for one's children and oneself |
| *Flexibility* in job opportunities and location | *Being stuck in a rut* with little prospect of change |

## Task 2  Analysing your response to teaching

Draw up a balance sheet of your own sources of satisfaction and dissatisfaction in teaching.

Try to place your responses in order of priority or importance.

Think of, or discuss with others, ways of increasing your sources of satisfaction, and overcoming some of the sources of dissatisfaction.

Teaching is not a simple matter. It is hard work. But for many of us the effort makes sense, for it gives one the opportunity to help children grow, and to play a positive and caring role in their lives. It is not like driving a car which is learnt once and for all, but is in a constant state of development and refinement. It takes experience, including frustration and failure, to develop one's skills. We all need to reflect on and learn from our defeats as well as our successes. We all need to think about and review what we are aiming for in our teaching, what we are doing and why we are doing it.

# What aims do you have?

What knowledge, skills and attitudes do you hope a child will have developed by the time he or she leaves your class? The Schools Council research on the aims of teaching (Ashton et al, 1975) identified some 172 aims for primary teachers. The Junior Project researchers (Mortimore et al, 1988) identified the following range of aims that teachers had for their children:

- *Aims relating to personal development*  Qualities that teachers hope to develop in their children include self-respect, self-confidence and self-discipline. The development of 'a healthy self-image' is a frequently mentioned aim, as was reliability. Others included 'being self-critical', 'accepting criticism as well as praise' and developing a sense of humour.
- *Social and moral aims*  Such aims may focus on abstract qualities like 'caring' and 'sharing', or 'being sensitive to the needs of others'. They may express the hope of developing children's attitudes to others in their group, class or school, or in the wider social world.
- *Cultural aims*  These relate to developing an awareness of the environment, a sensitivity to the natural world, and a need to conserve what is of value within it.
- *Curriculum aims*  These include knowledge and skills related to particular subject areas within the school curriculum, for example communication skills, numeracy or ability to learn through scientific observation.
- *Autonomy*  In the Junior Project over half the teachers mentioned 'autonomy' as an aim for their children. This might entail the ability to work on one's own, to be curious, independent and willing to express one's own opinion.
- *Cognitive aims*  These include the ability of children to think for themselves, to be critical and creative in their thinking and to develop problem-solving skills.
- *Religious and spiritual aims*  Such aims are common not only to teachers in church schools, but to all interested in fostering spiritual development and knowledge of major world faiths.

 ## Task 3  Identifying your aims for children

List the aims that you have for the children in your class. What are your top ten aims?
Compare your list of aims with those of colleagues, or those listed in a school prospectus or curriculum policy.
Keep your list of aims to review at a later date.

The traditional mode of organisation in primary schools is through class teaching. The junior teacher is primarily a class teacher, associated with a group of children for an academic year, getting to know them as individuals, with their own interests and needs. A class teacher is immersed in classroom life, creating a world in her own image, and coming to identify with her own class in the same way that headteachers identify with 'their' schools. The classroom becomes the creative hub of the teacher's life, and a 'home from home', a source of inspiration for her and for her children. It is in the classroom, with the children, that our thinking about teaching children should begin, for it is they who lie at the heart of the enterprise.

# Unit 2

# SEEING HOW CHILDREN LEARN

> The most important single factor influencing learning is what the learner already knows. Ascertain this and teach him accordingly.
>
> D P Ausubel *Educational Psychology* (1968)

Children are sent to school in order to learn. Each child brings to school her or his own personal experiences and inherited characteristics. The children that make up a class are a collection of very different individuals. The teacher's task is to cater for the needs of differing children, and to do this she will need to find out, and go on finding out, as much as she can about each child – about what they are like and how they learn.

One of the problems for the teacher will be that in any given class the children will be at various stages of maturity and ability. Different aspects of the developing child will contribute to his or her own special profile of abilities and characteristics at any particular age.

A child's physical attributes will affect him or her in a number of ways. The child who develops early may have various advantages which contribute to a sense of self-confidence. Children born late in the school year, summer-born children, can be at a disadvantage. A child who is physically unusual, such as a very fat child, may attract comment from others which damages self-esteem.

The development of a positive self-image is closely related to the child's sense of physical, social and emotional wellbeing. Teachers need to be sensitive to the child's social relationships – to help him cope with the ways others treat him, while at the same time encouraging him to be sensitive to the feelings and reactions of others. A child tends to respond and live up to the expectations that others, principally those at home and school, have of him. If a child's parents or teachers demonstrate their high expectations and

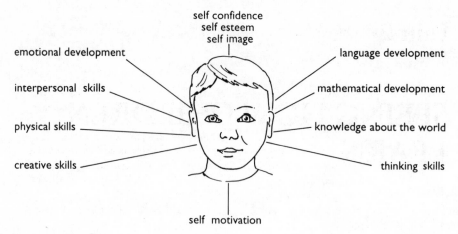

self confidence
self esteem
self image

emotional development

interpersonal skills

physical skills

creative skills

language development

mathematical development

knowledge about the world

thinking skills

self motivation

*Figure 1  Some aspects of the developing child*

confidence, then the child is more likely to achieve them. Success will help to reinforce the child's sense of confidence when faced with the next situation.

Children are at an immature and emotionally vulnerable stage of development. They are learning about their place in the world, largely through trial and error. Many of the mistakes children make are due to their limited experience. It is easy to overestimate their experience and underestimate their intelligence. We need to build on a child's experience to help him in the process of learning.

Questions to consider about the process of children's learning include:

● How do children learn best?
● What context for learning do children need?
● What motivates children's learning?
● How can you find out about your children's learning?
● What different learning styles do they have?
● What do they think of themselves as learners?

# 1  The learning process

Learning can be defined as the process by which knowledge, skills and attitudes are acquired or extended. Learning is not to be confused with simply the completion of tasks. A child may complete a task correctly and have learnt or gained nothing from it. Or the child may have learnt something quite different from what the teacher intended. Such incidental learning can be very productive, or it can be faulty and cause later problems.

---

## TABLE 2 How children learn

Children learn best through:

- *making connections* – connecting new knowledge to what they already know
- *meaningful experience* – rich and meaningful experiences that encourage enquiry, discovery and enjoyment
- *talking things through* – thinking aloud and discussion with others
- *writing things down* – thinking through writing, expressing ideas and experience
- *creative expression* – exploring and communicating through art, design, craft, dance, drama, music
- *praise and recognition* – praise for success, effort and progress
- *challenge and expectation* – continual challenge and expectation of high standards of achievement
- *responsibility and self-assessment* – to be responsible for and to evaluate their own learning
- *mediation of others* – support in learning from teachers, parents, other adults and children
- *stimulating environments* – contexts that provide a stimulus for learning at school, at home and in the community

---

Children bring their own ideas and experiences to the learning situation. These may be unconnected, intuitive, half forgotten or only partly learnt. They need help in making their ideas explicit, in bringing out what they know, and in sharing and comparing ideas with others.

Learning involves change in ideas, concepts or ability, either through addition or modification. Children need experiences to help them explore and extend what they know, and to evaluate what they do. They need opportunities to apply knowledge and understanding in different contexts, and help in assessing the outcomes of their learning. Table 2 shows some ways of achieving this.

## 2 The context for learning

The teacher provides the context for learning in the classroom. Two of the basic elements a child needs for effective learning in the classroom environment are security and challenge.

Like adults, children feel secure in an environment where they can make sense of the situation and can confidently predict what will happen. For this the child needs to know:

- what the teacher expects of him/her
- how to win the teacher's approval
- what the child may/may not do
- where the child may/may not go
- what the child may/may not use
- when the child may/may not do certain things
- how the child can succeed in tasks

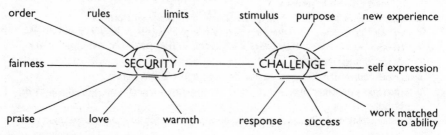

Figure 2 Security and challenge

A child who is taught by a teacher who is unpredictable or frightening will feel a sense of insecurity and be preoccupied by this instead of learning. The teacher needs to work towards providing security for the less confident, and challenge for the child who is confident, and then to motivate their best efforts. (For more on establishing a secure context for learning, see Units 3–5. For ways of offering challenge to children, see Units 6–14. See also Figure 13, 'Modes of Learning', p 102.)

# 3 Motivation

Part of the challenge of teaching is to try to find ways of motivating every child in the class. The following are some ways in which children may be motivated:

Figure 3 Sources of motivation

- *Inner needs*   Children have a number of inner needs, including the needs for love, recognition within a group and a sense of self-worth. Tasks will be motivating if they help towards satisfying children's social, emotional and other needs.
- *First-hand experience*   Children's experience is limited and they are keen to extend it when their interest is aroused. Offering them first-hand experience in seeing and doing can stimulate questioning, thinking and learning. Such experience can include stories, objects, audiovisual aids and computer work.
- *Desire for mastery*   Children seek to understand and to master their environment, to solve problems and meet challenges. The teacher's task is to present opportunities for children to work out ideas and tackle problems that are within their capacity.
- *Competition*   Most children are competitive and teachers can take advantage of this natural urge. The trouble with competition is that children tend to become focused on winning rather than learning. They will try to take short cuts, such as cheating, and may end up as losers. However it can be a powerful motivator of extra effort, and is especially useful if it becomes a matter of beating one's own previous performance.
- *Helping others*   A child needs to know something well before helping others with it. Teaching someone else, such as a peer or younger child, can be a valuable means of practice, purpose and motivation in learning.
- *Incentives and rewards*   Rewards can be very motivating. Wherever possible rewards should be linked to progress and effort. Rewards can be *tangible* (stickers, stars), *symbolic* (marks, ticks) or *social* (praise, recognition or positive comment by the teacher for effort, such as 'That's good, you're working really hard', or for achievement, such as 'You've done very well at this'). Children are more likely to renew effort if it is positively reinforced.
- *Target setting*   Teachers often set targets for children, for example, 'I want you to finish this in 15 minutes'. Targets are rarely motivating, however, unless children are committed to them. Helping children to choose and set realistic goals for themselves can be good for motivation and self-appraisal.
- *Technological aids*   such as computers and other audiovisual aids can offer interactive satisfaction what will motivate children's learning.

Unfortunately, what motivates one child will not necessarily motivate another. Some children (convergers) tend to want to find the 'right' answer, and prefer a learning environment which offers order and structure. Other children (divergers) prefer a freer and more experimental environment in which they can use their imagination and initiative. Some children depend on teacher recognition, others are more independent and self-motivated.

Teachers need to develop a variety of teaching approaches to suit the varied learning styles of children. It is important to find out what the individual needs of children are, but how do you do it?

# 4  Finding out about children

Most teachers of juniors know a lot about the children they teach. The process of getting to know the individual needs of children can often begin before teaching them. The following are some of the ways of finding out about children already in the school, or coming from a feeder school:

*1 Study the child's records*
- Look at levels of attainment in curriculum areas.
- See if there are any physical or health problems.
- Identify any children with learning difficulties.
- Note any special home circumstances that might affect the child, such as journey to school, siblings, one-parent families, non-English speaking background (languages spoken etc).

*2 Talk with child's previous teachers*
- Ask for information on previous learning experiences, eg topics covered, work attempted and achieved.
- Ask about teaching approaches which may or may not have worked.
- Ask about children with special educational needs.
- Ask about any children with problems, the high-fliers and underachievers, and those with particular skills or interests.

*3 Visit the children, if possible before you teach them*
- Talk with the children about what they have been doing.
- Look at their work, note any that is outstanding, and any showing problems.
- Identify children about whom you wish to know more.
- Note anything unusual about individual children, eg left-handedness.

Once the child is in your class, you will have many opportunities to see how she or he is learning. Ways of finding out more about children are shown in Table 3.

Preliminary observations and information gained about your children should enable you to identify at least three broad groups – the most able, the average for the class, and those with low ability or learning problems. Task 4 may help you check on what you know from your early observations.

## TABLE 3 Ways of finding out about children

*Observing*
- in an informal way, looking at the child at work and play
- as a participant in a child's learning activity, assessing what she or he is doing
- in a systematic way, eg with a checklist of things to look for and assess

*Talking*
- to children: asking questions and inviting them to tell you about their learning experiences, their successes and failures
- to parents and other significant adults in the child's life
- to professionals involved in the child's education

*Testing*
- by setting children tasks, such as Standard Assessment Tasks (SATs)
- by 'pencil and paper' tests
- using self-assessment by children themselves (see Unit 15: Assessing pupil progress)

## Task 4 Making preliminary observations

1  List the children on a chart such as the following, to provide a framework for future planning and investigation:

| Very able children | Children of average ability | Less able children |
|---|---|---|
|  |  |  |

2  Go through the register, checking up on what you know about each child. It will help you focus on the individual needs of children, and help you assess in your planning whether you are taking sufficient account of the most able and least able children.
3  Try writing the names of the children in your class from memory. Note which order you have listed them in, and who you found hard or impossible to remember! What does the order tell you about children who are most memorable, and for what reasons?

In any grouping of children by ability there is a danger of labelling and stereotyping children, and allowing this to colour your expectations of them too much. Children can turn out on further observation to be very different from your early ideas of them. It may be helpful to start a file with a page for each child relevant to your teaching. Gradually you will gain a fuller and more composite picture of each child, particularly having talked to his or her parents or guardians. Your observations should help you in identifying the needs and particular learning style of each child.

# 5    Learning styles

Aspects of a child's learning style include:

- *cognitive response* eg visual, auditory or kinaesthetic
- *social response* eg solitary, collaborative or attention seeking

One way of assessing the variety of children's responses to learning is to look for:

- *visual learners*, who like to see what they learn and who respond best to tasks which involve demonstrations or looking at illustrations
- *auditory learners*, who like to hear what they learn, and often prefer direct forms of teaching such as being given verbal instructions
- *kinaesthetic learners*, who like to be physically involved in what they learn, to feel what they are doing, to construct models and manipulate materials.

Most children learn readily through all these styles, but sometimes a child will learn best through a strongly preferred style. We need to provide opportunities for children to process their learning in a variety of ways, and to utilise their preferred style in any area of weakness.

The ORACLE study (Galton et al, 1980) looked at different social styles of learning and classified children's responses under four broad headings:

- attention seekers
- intermittent workers
- solitary workers
- quiet collaborators

Teachers will readily recognise children who fall into these groups and their many subdivisions. For example, solitary workers include the 'hard grinders', children who work continuously on set tasks, and 'easy riders', who work slowly and tend to procrastinate such as by looking for lost books, remaining 'stuck' for a long while on a problem etc. It can be easy to overlook the solitary workers and quiet collaborators in a class. Often there is a need to slow down the hard grinders and help them focus on the quality of their work, and to speed up the easy riders, seeking greater quantity. The child who is happy to repeat work previously done before is an example of a solitary worker who may need closer monitoring. Ted Wragg has described how his own daughter completed the same work card three times rather than 'bother' the teacher or 'waste time' waiting in a queue. Some children may regularly find a particular way of working easier or more difficult. We need to be aware of the differing responses of children and to look for patterns of strength and weakness. The better we get to know our children the more successful we can be in matching our teaching to their learning. Part of getting to know children will be to find out how they see themselves as learners.

# 6  Finding out how children see themselves

In trying to understand children as individual people and as learners it is helpful to build up a 'biographical' picture of the child. This can be achieved by looking up school profiles, seeing samples of work, talking to parents, but most importantly through personal contact with the child. Presenting the child with open-ended opportunities to write, draw, talk or otherwise communicate about him- or herself will help you to understand the child's needs and interests. Discussion or writing about favourite reading, hobbies, TV programmes or school experiences can be very revealing. How do your children see themselves as learners?

To see how children view themselves at school they could be asked to compile and complete a 'Me at School' survey, such as the one in Task 5, to provide a basis for further discussion.

## Task 5 'Me at School' survey

Name........                Date........

|  | Always | Usually | Sometimes | Rarely | Never |
|---|---|---|---|---|---|
| I am happy at school | ☐ | ☐ | ☐ | ☐ | ☐ |
| I am worried about school | ☐ | ☐ | ☐ | ☐ | ☐ |
| I am keen to learn at school | ☐ | ☐ | ☐ | ☐ | ☐ |
| I am not interested in work at school | ☐ | ☐ | ☐ | ☐ | ☐ |
| I find it hard to concentrate on work at school | ☐ | ☐ | ☐ | ☐ | ☐ |

| | | | | | |
|---|---|---|---|---|---|
| I get into quarrels at school | ☐ | ☐ | ☐ | ☐ | ☐ |
| I am well behaved at school | ☐ | ☐ | ☐ | ☐ | ☐ |
| I bully other children at school | ☐ | ☐ | ☐ | ☐ | ☐ |
| I am helpful and kind to other children at school | ☐ | ☐ | ☐ | ☐ | ☐ |
| I am naughty at school | ☐ | ☐ | ☐ | ☐ | ☐ |
| I would rather work on my own at school | ☐ | ☐ | ☐ | ☐ | ☐ |
| I prefer to work with other children at school | ☐ | ☐ | ☐ | ☐ | ☐ |
| I try my best at school | ☐ | ☐ | ☐ | ☐ | ☐ |
| My teacher thinks I work hard | ☐ | ☐ | ☐ | ☐ | ☐ |
| My teacher thinks I am well behaved | ☐ | ☐ | ☐ | ☐ | ☐ |

This self-evaluation task could be adapted to cover curriculum subjects or other aspects of learning, for example using a five-point scale:

Good ◄─────┼─────┼─────┼─────┼─────► Bad

Although the teacher is the central figure in any classroom, as children get older their place in the peer group becomes more and more important to them. Patterns of friendship in the class can be used to group children and to support their learning. The status of a child with her or his friends and within the class group can have a powerful effect on a child's self-image. You may wish to find out about the friendship patterns in your class and to use this information in creating a positive learning atmosphere. A sociometric analysis such as the one in Task 6 may help you develop greater awareness and sensitivity to class friendships.

## Task 6  Identifying class friendship patterns

To construct a sociogram of friendships:

1   Each child can be asked to write down, confidentially, the names of the three children who she or he would most like to play with or sit next to in class.
2   Having collected the data, chart the friendship groupings by linking names where friendship is reciprocated with a double arrow ◄───►, and with a single arrow ───► where the choice is not reciprocated.
3   This should enable you to identify:

- stars – the favourite children in the class
- isolates – the children rarely or never chosen
- pairs – children who are mutual choices
- groups – three or more children who are mutual choices

By becoming more aware of the cognitive and social aspects of children's learning we will be better able to take account of their needs when planning classroom activities and appropriate styles of teaching.

*Note*:  For more on encouraging self-assessment in children see Robert Fisher (1991) *Recording Achievement in Primary Schools* (Blackwell).

# Unit 3

# DEVELOPING A TEACHING STYLE

> It took me years to realise that instead of trying to be like other teachers I should have been trying to be more like myself.
>
> Teacher of juniors

There are nearly as many ways of effective teaching as there are teachers. At the beginning of your career you tend to draw on models of teaching you have seen, influenced by knowledge gained in your initial training. With experience you become more aware of your own strengths and limitations, and clearer about your own preferred ways of working. Many teachers, especially early in their careers, have few models of teaching to draw on. So it is valuable at all stages to see how other teachers teach and organise their classrooms. Gradually, over time, every teacher develops a teaching style that is uniquely their own.

Table 4 shows some of the elements that make up your own style of teaching.

The ability to form good relationships with children is an essential part of primary teaching. This ability is partly a matter of skill, of knowing the right words to say at the right time, and partly a matter of attitude, of showing children that you care about them and have confidence in their ability to learn. What relationship do you want to establish with your children? Do you see your role as an educator only, or are you also involved with children as people? The relationships that develop between you and the children in class will directly affect the atmosphere that is created in your classroom.

In the Junior Project one teacher was described as: 'A very cheerful person, smiling a lot and chatting with interest and animation to the children. The teacher is obviously interested in them and cares about them. The teacher teased them and allowed them to tease her.' Of another teacher it was observed that there was: 'No sign of a warm relationship with the children

---

## TABLE 4 Elements of teaching style

*Professional skills*
- interpersonal skills, relating/motivating/communicating etc
- classroom management
- planning and preparation
- matching tasks to children
- assessment and record keeping

*Professional knowledge*
- how children learn and develop
- awareness of curriculum developments
- current educational debate
- recent classroom research
- new materials for teaching and learning

*Professional attitudes*
- personal qualities, enthusiasm/energy/confidence/flexibility etc
- personal values and beliefs
- personal relationships with colleagues etc
- professional and life goals
- self-awareness and self-appraisal

---

beyond (the) bounds of the classroom. The teacher ignored all small talk initiated by the children. Good manners, behaviour and hard work were all that was important.'

Relationships with children can be analysed along a continuum from intimate, implying close emotional involvement, to platonic, implying an approach which is distanced and detached. (See also Unit 19, pp 243–254.)

## Task 7 Analysing relationships with children

1 Where along the continuum would you wish to establish your relationships with children?

intimate  platonic

2 What words would you use to describe the relationships you wish to form with children in your class?
3 Which children do you find easy to form relationships with? Why?
4 Which children do you find most difficult to form relationships with? Why?

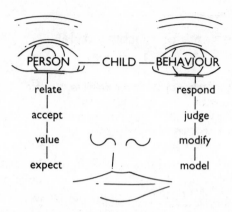

PERSON —— CHILD —— BEHAVIOUR

| relate | respond |
| accept | judge |
| value | modify |
| expect | model |

*Figure 4 Relating to the child*

The relationship that psychologist Carl Rogers advocated for children's psychological health was one of 'unconditional positive regard', but it is doubtful that a teacher's regard can be maintained without it being conditional in some way on children's behaviour. Perhaps there is a 'positive regard' we can have for children as people, and a more conditional regard for their behaviour – 'I like who you are, but I don't always like what you do.' This distinction is illustrated in Figure 4.

There is a danger, well documented in research, of teachers being over-personal when telling children off – 'You are a *naughty* boy/girl' – rather than focusing positively on the way they should have behaved – 'You must take your turn like everybody else.' We may need to condemn the action of the child, but not the child him- or herself. In that way self-esteem and good relationships stay intact, and the child can see you are being fair.

Children generally have a clear idea about the quality of relationships and of teaching in their classroom. Being 'fair' is usually high on their list of priorities. They tend to like teachers who are strict rather than domineering, who are kind, consistent, efficient at organising their teaching, patient with their problems, have a sense of humour and are not boring. 'Softness' is invariably seen as a sign of weakness. Moodiness is also disliked, and children will be quick to see when you are in one of your 'moods'.

Task 8 is designed to give you some feedback from children on how they regard you as a teacher.

## Task 8 Investigating the way children see you

At the end of a period of time, such as a term, with your class, ask the children to rate you as their teacher on a scale such as the one below:

'Most of the time my teacher is ...'

| Unfair | 1 2 3 4 5 | Fair |
|---|---|---|
| Soft | 1 2 3 4 5 | Strict |
| Unkind | 1 2 3 4 5 | Kind |
| Boring | 1 2 3 4 5 | Interesting |
| Serious | 1 2 3 4 5 | Fun |
| Moody | 1 2 3 4 5 | Not moody |
| Impatient | 1 2 3 4 5 | Patient |

Try to find out from time to time what children think about aspects of classroom life and their work. It may be that your pupils' views about the success of your teaching and their learning may differ from yours. Classroom life is full of complexities, contradictions and undercurrents of feeling. Teachers have many dilemmas and difficulties to face, for example that their liking of some children may not be reciprocated. The way you respond to demands, dilemmas and daily decisions will depend very much on the values and aims that underlie your teaching.

What are the major dilemmas which have to be faced? Table 5 shows some of the common dilemmas in teaching. Your response to these and other dilemmas are not simple options, but call for careful judgements which you will need to monitor and evaluate continually. The decisions you take will reflect the way your teaching style is developing or is adapting to the needs of the situation.

## TABLE 5 Common dilemmas in teaching

| | |
|---|---|
| Planning carefully in advance | Responding to changing circumstances |
| Organising children as a class | Organising children's work individually |
| Keeping control of children's work | Offering children control over their work |
| | |
| Focusing on one topic/subject/activity | Planning a variety of activities |
| Aiming for quality in school work | Aiming for quantity in school work |
| Maintaining formal relationships | Being relaxed and informal |
| Concentrating on curriculum achievement | Concentrating on personal/social education |
| Developing individual skills/self-reliance | Developing social skills/groupwork |
| Using competition to motivate | Fostering cooperation between children |
| Allocating time/resources equally | Focusing on children with special needs |
| Liking a quiet working atmosphere | Allowing noise and bustle in the classroom |
| | |
| Giving or encouraging homework | Keeping work within lesson time |
| Encouraging parental involvement | Maintaining professional independence |

Your chosen way of working will depend not only on what you see as important for children, but also on your strengths and limitations. It may also depend on your personality and professional experience. As we get older we generally become more confident and competent. We tend also to become less flexible and more fixed in our style of teaching. Over time our style may be changing in ways of which we are hardly aware. Hence the need to constantly reflect on our aims and practices, and to take account of the experience of other teachers.

The concept of 'teaching style' has become part of professional vocabulary following research into classroom practice during the 1970s. Neville Bennett (1976), for example, defined style by identifying a number of different types of teaching behaviour which can be listed under the headings of 'progressive' and 'traditional'. Table 6 is a summary of these characteristics.

The terms 'progressive' and 'traditional' are used rather loosely by parents, governors and the media, and have come to symbolise deep conflicts that exist about the methods of teaching. The HMI Survey (1978) labelled these two styles 'exploratory' and 'didactic', and they have also been called

---

## TABLE 6 Characteristics of progressive and traditional teachers

| Progressive | | Traditional | |
|---|---|---|---|
| 1 | Integrated subject matter | 1 | Separate subject matter |
| 2 | Teacher as guide to educational experiences | 2 | Teacher as distributor of knowledge |
| 3 | Active pupil role | 3 | Passive pupil role |
| 4 | Pupils participate in curriculum planning | 4 | Pupils have no say in curriculum planning |
| 5 | Learning predominantly by discovery techniques | 5 | Accent on memory, practice and rote learning |
| 6 | External rewards and punishments not necessary, ie intrinsic motivation | 6 | External rewards used, for example grades, ie extrinsic motivation |
| 7 | Teachers give high priority to social and emotional development | 7 | Teachers give highest priority to academic attainment |
| 8 | Little testing | 8 | Regular testing |
| 9 | Accent on cooperative group work | 9 | Accent on competition |
| 10 | Teaching not confined to classroom base | 10 | Teaching confined to classroom base |
| 11 | Accent on creative expression | 11 | Little emphasis on creative expression |

Adapted from Bennett, N (1976) *Teaching Styles and Pupil Progress* 'informal' and 'formal' approaches. The ORACLE and other studies have shown that purely progressive or traditional teachers are quite rare. The great majority of teachers use *mixed styles* incorporating different elements of formal (traditional) and informal (progressive) styles.

The ORACLE study analysed teaching styles and put them into four broad categories – individual monitors, class enquirers, group instructors and style changers.

## Individual monitors

These teachers organised work mainly on an individual basis, with little group or class teaching. They therefore spent much of their time monitoring individual progress, largely telling children what to do or marking their work. They were under pressure to cope with the high level of individual interactions needed in large classes.

## Class enquirers

This group engaged in more class teaching, with an emphasis on questioning, problem solving and the discussion of ideas with children. Theirs was a more teacher-managed approach to learning, with less individual or small-group work.

## Group instructors

These teachers spent more time than others on organising group work. They tended to structure the work of the group carefully before allowing children to engage in activity or discussion themselves. Spending less time on individual interaction allowed them more time to 'instruct' groups through asking questions and offering information.

## Style changers

About half the teachers observed changed their style of teaching during the school year to suit varying forms of organisation in the classroom. They could generally be classed in one of three ways:

1 *Infrequent changers*, who changed their style occasionally to suit the particular needs of their class, becoming more or less informal to suit the children involved.
2 *Rotating changers*, who rotated the work of different groups of children

during the course of a day or week, each group working on a different activity or area of the curriculum. This approach requires high levels of teacher management and supervision.

3  *Habitual changers*, who made frequent changes between class and individual work whenever they felt it necessary. A flexible approach, but sometimes not allowing much time or concentration on any one activity.

The ORACLE study found that there was no best style, although the style more clearly related to pupil achievement in maths and language was that of the 'class enquirers', that is those teachers who did more speaking to all the children in the class and who questioned them about the task in hand. Research has found that some formal teachers generate high levels of achievement and personal development in their children, and some do not. Similarly some informal teachers are successful and others are not. Teaching style alone does not explain differences in pupil achievement and development, which, as the Junior Project shows, can vary greatly between schools and between classes of comparable children. The more successful teachers, whether formal or informal, achieve success through providing their children with *more opportunities to learn* and successfully motivating their learning efforts. How is this success achieved?

## Task 9 Reflecting on your teaching style

In reflecting on your teaching style, and the strategies you use in the classroom, you may wish to:

1  Identify the problems/dilemmas that you find most challenging about teaching (see Table 5).
2  Consider what you think are the characteristics of your teaching style (see Table 6).
3  Think about the emphasis you give in your teaching to *class* enquiry, *group* organisation and *individual* monitoring (cf the ORACLE study).

Discuss with colleagues possible strategies that may help you in developing your teaching style (see also Task 67, p 244).

The Junior Project identified the following factors associated with effective teaching and learning, whatever the teaching style:

• *Teaching that is consistent*
Consistency in teacher approach is important within the classroom and the school. Teachers need to work with colleagues in following a com-

mon policy throughout the school. Pupils benefit from teacher loyalty to their school and continuity of staffing.

- *Teaching that is structured*
  Children benefit when their school day is given structure by teachers, when there is always plenty of work for them to do, and when they are allowed some freedom of choice within an organised framework.
- *Teaching that is intellectually challenging*
  'In those classes where pupils were stimulated and challenged progress was greatest' (p 252). Such teachers communicated their interest and enthusiasm, encouraged creative imagination and problem solving and stretched the children's thinking through higher-order questions and statements.
- *Teaching that is work centred*
  A feature of effective classrooms is that they are work-centred environments, characterised by the industry and independence shown by the children.
- *Teaching that is focused*
  Children tend to make better progress when lessons are organised around one particular curriculum area, rather than sessions which mix different topics or activities. Varied levels of work need to be planned within the one curriculum area to suit the needs of different children.
- *Teaching that is interactive*
  Effective teachers aim for maximum communication and interaction with children, in class teaching, group and individual work.
- *Teaching that is assessed and recorded*
  Assessment of what is taught and learnt, carefully recorded by the teacher, is an important aspect of professional planning.
- *Teaching that is a partnership*
  Effective teachers do not work alone, but in partnership with colleagues and with parents.

The following chapters look in closer detail at how these characteristics of effective teaching can be put into practice and adapted to suit your own individual style of teaching.

# Unit 4

# MANAGING A CLASSROOM

> How do I cope with a large class of children of mixed abilities, with limited space and resources, without any help in the classroom?
> Student teacher

The way a teacher organises the work of a class is a very personal matter. There are many successful ways of working, and each has its strengths and drawbacks. No one way of working will suit everyone.

The good teacher is always looking for better ways of organising the learning of children, and seeking the best use of time, space and resources, including her own teaching skills and the children's capacity to respond. Figure 5, and this chapter, consider some important elements in managing a classroom.

## 1 Using time

Research shows that some teachers consistently inspire higher achievements from comparable children than other teachers. How do they do it? One common factor that emerges from classroom studies is that achievement is influenced by the amount of time children spend on appropriate learning tasks. Some children have far more extended learning opportunities than others. Making the most of learning opportunities depends on the way teachers and children use their time in the classroom.

### Teacher time

Teachers spend only a proportion of lesson time actually engaged in teaching. Many teachers routinely spend more than 25 per cent of their time on

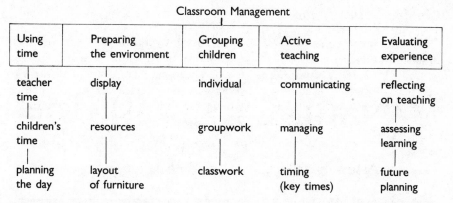

Figure 5 Some aspects of classroom management

low-level tasks like giving out materials, sharpening pencils, looking for lost books and responding to a host of trivial requests. Under the pressure of incessant demands it is easy for a teacher to be diverted from the task in hand by a stream of interruptions and requests. Without realising it, teachers can end up using their time in class quite differently from how they believe they should be using it. Classroom studies often show differences between what teachers *think* they are doing and what they actually do.

Good organisation – the time spent on organising children, space and materials – is the necessary foundation for good teaching. But the more it eats into teaching time, the more it becomes a problem to be solved. One way to monitor how you use time is to record the ways you are using it in a checklist or time log. Keeping a time log should help you identify priorities and see which activities are using too much time.

## Task 10 Devising a time log

1  Compile a checklist of particular activities such as: talking to the class, organising groups, explaining to individuals, checking work, responding to queries, disciplinary comment, listening to individuals, mounting work, marking etc.
2  Keep the list beside you morning and afternoon, and tick off when you deal with any of the matters listed. Record if you can how long you spend on these activities, using a timer. A student or colleague might help you in this task.

Looking at how you use time will also involve studying how children use their time in class.

## *Children's use of time*

Children too can be encouraged to keep a record sheet on how they use their time. How much time do they spend talking (with whom?), working (with whom? at what?), waiting for the teacher, reading, writing etc? Ask them to make a list of activities and to discuss these with others. They will need either to work out a way of recording the length of time spent on each activity, or to score the number of occasions they engaged in each activity.

## Task 11  Assessing children's use of time

Using categories that you or they devise, get your children to study and record their use of time. Discuss ways of representing results, for example graphically. Try to predict outcomes and draw conclusions from the study.

Use the results to discuss with the children how far each feels she or he is using the time properly. Discuss whether the children work best in long or short spells. What would cut down the number of interruptions? How could they become more independent, less reliant on you the teacher for minor requests? What personal goals might they set themselves to improve their pattern of working?

Effective use of time requires thoughtful planning for teacher and child.

## *Planning the day*

The time children spend actively learning depends on various organisational factors. Included in these are the established classroom routines, which can help or hinder the time children spend 'on task'. The following are some daily routines with questions to help you evaluate procedures and to consider possible improvements. The table can be extended to include other routine activities.

## Task 12  Appraising your classroom routines

| Routine | Analysis |
|---|---|
| Entry | Do children enter in an orderly fashion? |
| Registration | Are the children gainfully occupied? |
| Going to the toilet | Does the routine encourage independence and work well? |

| Asking for help | Do children know how to get help? |
| When tasks are finished | Do children know what to do next? |
| Changing for PE/Games | Does the process take the minimum of time and fuss? |
| Tidying up | Are routines efficient and properly shared? |

. . . . . . . . . . . . . . . . .
. . . . . . . . . . . . . . . . .
. . . . . . . . . . . . . . . . .

Routines are important in helping to develop a sense of community with clear expectations for each child. But in planning the day we need to beware of *routinisation*, boring children with a monotony of preordained activity, for example through over-reliance on published materials, worksheets and mechanical exercises. We need to plan for a mixed diet of activity to include fresh stimulus, variety and the interest of the unexpected. Questions to ask about your daily plans include:

- Is there a planned highlight for each day?
- Is there variety between active and passive tasks?
- Is there variety between individual, group and classwork?

## 2 Preparing the environment

The classroom is a prepared environment for learning, and children have much to learn from the way you organise space, materials and resources. The physical setting and display of work can have an important influence on the mood of the classroom. What atmosphere do you wish to create?

Questions to ask about the way you prepare your classroom setting include:

- *Is it pleasing aesthetically?*
  Do the children draw pleasure from what surrounds them? Have they the opportunity to see pleasing pictures and to handle objects of interest?
- *Does it set high standards of presentation?*
  Do classroom displays set standards you wish to see reflected in children's work?
- *Does the working environment function efficiently?*
  Are tools and resources well stored, with ease of access for children, and clear rules about how things are used and returned?
- *Are classroom displays stimulating?*
  Do displays stimulate children's thinking and questioning? Are children encouraged to respond to what surrounds them? Are displays changed at regular intervals?

- *Does the layout of furniture facilitate children's learning?*
  Are there sound educational reasons for the layout chosen for desks/tables? Have you tried alternative layouts? Do you vary the layout for differing lessons, purposes or groupings?

## Task 13 Classroom layout – an analysis of alternatives

Draw a large-scale plan of the space available in your classroom, for example on squared paper.
Cut out card shapes, drawn to scale, of the furniture in your class.
Investigate different ways of organising the classroom layout.
The children can of course help you in this exercise.

Question to ask: Is there one best layout for all activities, or should the layout be varied to suit different activities?

Most teachers keep the desks or tables separate from the rest of the furniture, roughly in the middle of the room, with cupboards, display areas and shelving placed round the outside of the room. Many create distinct work areas, for example reading or book corners, art and craft area, project displays, or less often an area for writing, maths, science, music or other activity. The majority of teachers have their own desk placed where they can survey the whole class, a few dispense with a special desk altogether.

Whatever the classroom arrangement, teachers with more tidy rooms tend to be judged more favourably by adults and children than those with messy rooms. Pupils in neat rooms were rated by others as happier and better behaved than those in untidy rooms. However accurate these findings, they underline the need to take care of your physical environment, to make sure your classroom creates the impression and influence you want.

## 3  Grouping children

Children need to be grouped in ways that support their learning. Tables are often grouped together to encourage conversation, cooperation and collaboration between children, and to facilitate work on a large scale. Rows of desks or tables tend to encourage a more work-centred environment for individuals or pairs of children. The Plowden Report (1967) argued that grouping children together gave them 'opportunities to teach as well as learn', but the ORACLE survey showed that most children sitting in groups were involved in non-collaborative individual work and that most of their talk was not task-related. Recent research (Wheldall and Glynn, 1989) suggests that children spend more 'time on task' seated in rows, but that the work is not necessarily of better quality than work done in groups.

Seating and grouping arrangements do not have to follow one pattern. They can be varied according to the activity so that children experience learning in a variety of contexts – individual, group and classwork. Each form of grouping has its own rationale, advantages and limitations.

## Individual work

Setting individual work is useful in developing the ability to work independently and autonomously. It is ideally suited for quiet working periods when children need to concentrate on the task in hand. The teacher, however, can only give a limited amount of attention to each child, often having to explain the same point on several occasions. The Junior Project found that when children spent most time on individual work they received on average only 11 individual contacts with the teacher per day, and many, especially quiet children, much less.

## Groupwork

Groupwork helps develop social and language skills, where children can listen to and learn from each other in a collaborative setting, for example in brainstorming, problem solving and in creative work. Children should have opportunities for working in a wide range of groupings, including:

- pupil with teacher/adult
- pairs
- small groups of varied size and mix
- larger groups
- whole-class groups
- groups larger than a class

Criteria used in forming groups could include:

- random – convenience groups (but beware boy/girl divides)
- mixed ability – helping children to teach and learn from each other
- similar ability – useful for matching learning tasks to ability
- interest – children working together on chosen topic
- friendship – good for social interaction but may become divisive

- age – own class or larger parallel class groupings
- mixed age – providing the opportunity to work across age ranges; especially useful for very able children

## Classwork

Working as a class is useful for building a sense of community, for listening to instructions and reviewing work, and for activities like story, singing, music, PE and games. The Junior Project found positive effects on pupil progress when teachers spent more than a quarter of their time in communicating to the class as a whole. The benefits included spending more time in task-related discussion, encouraging the interplay of ideas, asking more 'probing' questions, and encouraging children to share and solve problems.

Task 14 suggests a method to help you analyse the group structure of tasks, to help achieve the best balance for you and your class.

## Task 14 Grouping children – planning an analysis

Devise a matrix such as the one given below to note the groupings used for different lesson activities in the class:

| Lesson/activity | Individual work | Whole-class work | Groupwork (type of group) |
|---|---|---|---|
|  |  |  |  |

Whatever the chosen grouping of children, the key factors in pupil progress are:

- amount of *teacher communication* with pupils about the content of work rather than routine matters
- high levels of *pupil industry*, whether as individuals, in groups, or as a class

The Junior Project noted that communication was difficult and pupil progress slow in classes with high levels of noise and pupil movement. To achieve high levels of teacher communication and pupil industry without undue noise and movement requires active teaching.

# 4  Active teaching

The role of active teaching presents many management challenges. Figure 6 shows some of the key elements in active teaching.

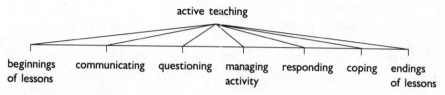

Figure 6 *Active teaching*

## *Beginnings of lessons*

Beginnings are important in that they set the tone for what is to follow. At the start of each session the teacher will need to be in the classroom before the children to ensure an orderly entry. The children's attention will need to be gained, their interest stimulated, activities planned and expectations clearly communicated. Table 7 is a checklist of questions related to gaining and maintaining the attention of the whole class.

---

**TABLE 7  Gaining attention: a checklist for self-evaluation**

- Do you stop all activity in the class or do you try to speak through noise or movement?
- Do you use a clear signal to the children that you want their attention?
- Are you in a position where all can see you?
- Do you know and use individual names when referring to children?
- Do you emphasise key words when you speak?
- Do you persist and insist that your instructions are carried out?
- Do you use positive praise when children attend well?

Example: '*Listen* class. Put everything down, I want to talk to you. Jane, you as well. Put your ruler down. *Everybody* quite quiet and still. *Good*, most of you are ready. Jane, quickly please. Now that you are *all* listening, I have something to tell you . . .'

---

Attention depends on being motivated and stimulated. In what ways do you seek to stimulate children's interest? How often do you try a fresh stimulus? What kinds of stimulus have you found most successful? A good stimulus is generally one that:

- relates to children's interests and experience
- challenges them to think and investigate
- stimulates their curiosity

Examples of sorts of things that can arouse interest include news items, strange objects, artefacts, models, posters, poems, stories, tapes and videos.
  If children are inattentive, strategies to try include:

- asking a question    – 'What is going to happen ...?'
                        'What am I going to write next ...?'
                        'What do you think this is?'
- focusing attention   – 'I want you to look at ...'
                        'I want you to listen very carefully to ...'
- varying the stimulus – 'I've got something (new) to say/show you/for you to do ...'
- involving the children – 'I want someone to help me ...'
                        'I want you all to ...'
- setting clear targets – 'You have got five minutes to ...'

## Communicating with children

In order to set the scene for learning, it is essential, whatever the activity, that each child understands what is involved and how to go about it. There must be a shared understanding of the task and of what your expectations are. Guidelines for the information that children need to know are given in Table 8.
  Children learn more when their tasks are well presented and their efforts are supported by effective teacher communication. The art of good communication is to 'talk to' rather than 'talk at' others, whether it be to children or adults. Good communication evokes a positive response. But how is it achieved? Important elements include:

1  being prepared
2  being clear
3  being simple
4  being vivid
5  being natural

# TABLE 8 Setting the scene: the information children need

| | |
|---|---|
| *What* they are to do. | Type of task, what and how much to do. Amount of choice. What happens when they finish. |
| *Why* they are doing it. | The purpose of the task, and who they are to share the results with. |
| *When* they are to start and finish. | Length of time allowed for tasks. |
| *Where* they are to work. | The work area, seating arrangements, and what movement is allowed. |
| *Who* they will work with. | Whether alone, with a partner or group. Cooperation or competition? |
| *How* they are to get help. | Whether to ask partner, group or teacher. How to request teacher's attention. |

## 1 Being prepared

This principle covers every aspect of a teacher's work and lies at the heart of effective class management. Being prepared means focusing on four factors, at the outset and at each stage in the lesson:

- material – planning what is to be said
- audience – thinking about the needs of the group
- setting – preparing resources, methods of delivery, follow-up activity
- speaker – clarifying one's aims, being aware of one's skills, knowledge and attitudes

Make a plan of the lesson/communication on paper, or in your head, covering the main points you wish to make. The essential point of the plan is to identify your central aims and objectives – what you really want to communicate. Being well prepared will help you maintain the momentum of the lesson and avoid distractions, over-long pauses or interruptions to the flow, and so sustain interest.

## 2 Being clear

Aim to be clear rather than vague or rambling. Emphasise key words and ideas. Repeat if necessary, or check the children understand by asking them to tell you. Fit your ideas into a coherent pattern or framework. It was said of George Bernard Shaw that his head contained a confusion of clear ideas. What you say should have structure and sequence, one idea leading on to the next. One way out of a muddle (yours or theirs) is to go back to first principles. What is *important* in what you want to say? What is the clearest and simplest way of saying it?

### 3 Being simple

'Simplify! . . . Simplify!' urged Thoreau. Simplicity is a close relation of clarity. The ability to speak simply about difficult matters is the mark of a gifted teacher. It is possible to introduce any concept to any child at any age, using the appropriate language. But to be simple is no easy thing. Being simple is not being simplistic or over-simplifying. To present a complex problem in a simple and coherent way takes skill and hard work. But it is the simply expressed instruction, plan or procedure that is likely to be best remembered.

### 4 Being vivid

The principle of vividness enters all good teaching. The word 'vivid' means 'full of life'. Vividness means bringing to life:

- the speaker, by showing signs of warmth, enthusiasm and lively interest
- the subject, by bringing it alive and giving it meaning

'Enthusiasm' comes from the Greek, 'being inspired by the divine spirit'. It consists in delight in what is happening, and a determination to create something from it. Not always easy on a Monday morning or a wet Friday afternoon!

The most vivid of elements is the visual. 'A picture is worth a thousand words', said Kung Fu-tse. An actual picture or diagram, supported by words, or a word picture to summon images in the mind, or a story, can enliven any subject matter. Humour can add sparkle and vitality, and contribute to the sense of community in the class.

### 5 Being natural

Success has been defined as grace under pressure, a good definition of effective class teaching. Communicating in a natural, relaxed way is not easy under the pressure of organising large numbers of children. Being natural includes being vocally relaxed, and allowing the expression of natural emotions to colour (but not cloud) our speech. Interest, curiosity, joy, sorrow and anger are natural expressions of emotions we need to share with children from time to time. Telling them how you feel will encourage them to share their feelings with you. Help them to understand you, as you try to understand them.

### Non-verbal communication

Messages are not only verbal. We communicate through movement our fears and feelings, whether we are confident or dithery, pleased or bad-tempered

TABLE 9 Developing classroom confidence

| Aspect of communication | Practice |
| --- | --- |
| Eye contact with individuals | Act with 'uncooperative friend', facing and eyeballing him/her before speaking your message. |
| Eye contact with group or class | Read a poem while making visual contact with (scanning) all children. Repeat looking at individual children. |
| Gesture and tone of voice | Repeat poem or story using expressive gesture and varied tone of voice. |
| Voice projection | Breathe slowly and deeply from the diaphragm. Test your voice – is it clear, firm and relaxed? Recite a dramatic passage or poem, using a range of voices, soft and loud. |

and so on. Our physical messages can draw attention to what we say, or distract from it.

We use *eye contact* to signal beginnings and ends of communication, and to control children's behaviour. When we call for full attention from children we can confirm and maintain it through eye contact with each child. Other aspects of non-verbal communication include facial expression, bodily movement (such as head or hands), tone of voice, proximity and physical touch. We need to be confident in our use of physical signals, so that they reinforce rather than obscure our verbal messages. Table 9 suggests exercises in non-verbal communication.

## Questioning

The ORACLE study showed that most teacher talk was devoted to supervising set tasks, and very little time was spent in asking questions which required children to think for themselves. The Junior Project showed that good pupil progress required intellectually stimulating teaching. They found evidence that 'the more time teachers spent asking questions, the greater the positive effect on (pupil) progress'.

Questions can serve many important functions. Socially they can help develop relationships through positive interaction. Psychologically they can motivate response. Educationally they can stimulate children's thinking and help in the assessment of their knowledge and understanding, as summed up in Table 10.

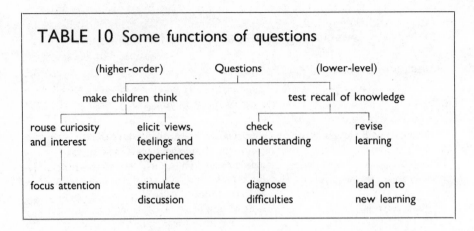

TABLE 10 Some functions of questions

|  | (higher-order) | Questions | (lower-level) |  |
|---|---|---|---|---|
|  | make children think | | test recall of knowledge | |
| rouse curiosity and interest | elicit views, feelings and experiences | | check understanding | revise learning |
| focus attention | stimulate discussion | | diagnose difficulties | lead on to new learning |

It is useful when framing questions to distinguish two broad kinds – lower-level, less demanding questions which test knowledge, and the more demanding, higher-order questions which challenge children's thinking. Lower-level questions tend to elicit quick answers, and typically begin with 'What ...?' 'Who ...?' or 'Where ...?'. Higher order questions invite extended answers, and often begin with 'Why ...?' or 'How ...?'. Both types of question are important, lower-level questions being valuable in setting the stage for, or following up, higher-order questions.

Questions can be directed towards individuals, groups or the class as a whole. To sustain attention, teachers often add a child's name, for example: 'Who can tell me whether a spider is an insect?'. Pause. 'Sharon?'. In asking individuals, we need to be aware of the danger of ignoring certain children. Research shows that teachers tend to have locational 'blind spots', some asking more frequently those sitting at the back, or front, or sides, or certain groups such as boys or (rarer) girls.

## Task 15 Analysing your questioning technique

Ask a colleague or student to help monitor your questioning technique, for example by recording on a class seating plan or checklist:

- who answers you and where they sit
- the number of higher-order and lower-level questions
- which groups answer, eg boys or girls

Analyse afterwards the balance you achieved in the questions you asked and the spread of children who answered.

Questioning is also an effective means of summoning a child's wandering attention, and bringing him or her back on task: 'What do you think about it, Jean?', 'Do you agree with that, John?'. We need to allow sufficient 'wait time' for answers, not always demanding a quick response but encouraging children to take time to think. We need to ensure that everyone has heard the child's answer, repeating it when necessary. We need sometimes to allow a range of answers, and encourage others in the group to think and judge between the alternatives given.

In asking questions it is important to choose the right language for the age and ability, and to stir their thinking (what the experts call making a 'positive cognitive intervention'). What question would you ask eight- to nine-year-olds in explaining the characteristics of insects? Research into the approach of different teachers showed that the teacher who obtained the best learning response from children began with one question: 'Is a bird an insect?'. The class compared, analysed, evaluated: their thinking was stirred!

## Responding to children

In responding to children's answers, the techniques of *prompting* and *probing* can help to encourage children to think and say more. Prompting involves giving hints to help children. Probing takes the form of seeking further information, or inviting the child to expand on her or his answer or to explain the meaning more clearly. In responding to answers which may be partly correct, or incorrect, we need to acknowledge which part is correct, and if there are fair chances of success to prompt an improved response.

Responsiveness means taking an active interest in the children and in what they are doing. It means *active listening*, attending to what they say and offering verbal cues – 'Really? What happened next?' – which say you want to hear more. Even when not directly talking with children, the good teacher is always 'out there' in the classroom, not wrapped up in his or her own inner thoughts, but monitoring what is going on. What are some of the signals to look for when monitoring the class? Table 11 lists some (p 42).

## Managing classroom activity

A number of important skills in the management of classroom activity have been identified by Kounin (1970) and other researchers. These include 'withitness', 'overlapping' and 'pacing'.

- *Withitness* describes the teacher's ability to scan the whole class while engaged in a particular classroom activity. Teachers who are 'with it'

---

### TABLE 11  Signals to look for when monitoring a class

- **Posture**      Are the children turned towards or away from the object of the lesson?
- **Gaze**         Are the children looking at or away from the object of the lesson?
- **Expression**   Do they look interested or bored, involved or withdrawn, sleepy or awake?
- **Activities**   Are children engaged in something relevant to the lesson? Is their talk task-centred or not?
- **Responses**    Do the children make appropriate responses to your questions?

---

have 'eyes in the back of their heads'. They are aware of everything going on in the class and so can anticipate trouble and help where needed.

- *Overlapping* describes the skill of doing two or more things at once. Most teachers work under such pressure that they must think and do more than one thing at a time. The typical teacher makes more than 1000 interpersonal interchanges with children in any one day. Judging, decision making, intervening, monitoring and communicating are necessary activities which teachers need to blend, combine and overlap.
- *Pacing* is another important skill. It is easy to forget the clock and suddenly find it is playtime, lunchtime or hometime. Once activities have been introduced there is a need to maintain motivation and to keep children 'on task'. This can take the form of reviewing activities from time to time to remind children of key aims and to reinforce good efforts. Allow time at the end for children to share their experience and reflect on their learning. In the words of the old saying, you may need to 'Tell 'em what to do, tell 'em while they are doing it, and tell 'em when they've done it.'

## Coping with crises

*The best laid schemes o' mice an' men gang aft a-gley.*

Crises and disruptions can occur in any classroom at any time, whether it be a wasp flying through the window, a sudden nosebleed, unexpected accident or 'flare up' of temper. In times of crisis do you 'cry' or seize the opportunity? How did you respond to your last classroom crisis? How would you respond next time? The following are some aspects to consider:

- Did I minimise the disturbance?
- Did I maximise reassurance to the children concerned?
- Did I allow time to consider the best response?
- Did I communicate positive expectations to the children about what to do or how to behave?
- Did I follow up afterwards, perhaps to find out the cause or to thank those who helped?

---

**TABLE 12  Evaluating your classroom management – summary checklist**

- Do you know the children as individuals, their names, personalities, interests and friends?
- Is the physical environment of the class well prepared?
- Have you agreed clear rules and routines with the class?
- Do you continuously monitor, observe and scan the classroom?
- Are your lessons well planned and smoothly flowing?
- Is there sufficient variety and challenge in the learning activities?
- Do you consistently follow up on the quality and completion of work?
- Do you model the standards of work and courtesy that you expect from pupils?
- Do you clearly communicate your expectations, the help available and options open to children?
- Do you analyse and learn from your own classroom management experience?

---

For more on classroom organisation and ways of evaluating it see Unit 19, pp 243–254.

Table 12 presents some questions which may help you in evaluating aspects of classroom management.

## Endings of lessons

The timing of activities depends on the skilled judgement of teachers and their sensitivity to children's responses. If they become bored or too excited and distracted, it is wise to regain the initiative, to review and maybe to redirect or end the activity. Points to consider at the ends of lessons include:

- early warning about the end or change of activity
- clear instructions about clearing up
- praise for what children have done well

- a review of achievement and effort
- orderly exit or transition to the next activity

Try to end on a positive note. Send them on their way whenever possible with 'a song in their hearts'. It will make them feel good, and you, too.

my teacher

# Unit 5

# PROMOTING DISCIPLINE AND GOOD BEHAVIOUR

'Oh, you have to keep order if you want to teach,' said Miss
Harby, hard, superior, trite.
Ursula did not answer. She felt non-valid before them.
'If you want to be let to *live*, you have,' said Mr. Brunt.
'Well if you can't keep order, what good *are* you?' said Miss
Harby.
'An' you've got to do it by yourself' – his voice rose like the bitter
cry of the prophets. 'You'll get no *help* from anybody.'

D H Lawrence *The Rainbow*

Times have changed since teachers like Ursula Brangwen, in *The Rainbow*,
had to cope with classes of 55 11-year-olds in Board schools at the beginning
of the century. But the problems and frustrations experienced by Ursula in
trying to keep a class under control will be familiar to many young teachers
in schools today. Problems of discipline are perennial and they return to
haunt the world of most teachers.

In this country, and abroad, there has been growing concern about standards of behaviour and school discipline. The teacher's ability to control
pupils is widely regarded as the single most important factor in achieving
good standards of classroom behaviour. Parents worry about the inability of
teachers to maintain the necessary well-ordered environment for learning.
Teachers complain about the levels of verbal and physical aggression that
children bring with them into school. According to union surveys the majority of teachers believe that violent behaviour from children is on the increase
and that indiscipline has become commonplace in schools. In response to this
growing disquiet the government commissioned an independent research
enquiry to be carried out by a committee led by Lord Elton. This national
survey on discipline in schools, the Elton Report, was published in 1989.

Task 16 Questions on discipline

The Elton Report into discipline in schools asked teachers the following five questions. What answers would you give from your own experience?

1 What are your routine experiences of discipline, both in the classroom and around the school?
2 How serious do you think the problems of discipline are in your school?
3 What particular pupil behaviours do you find difficult to cope with?
4 How are you trying to deal with difficult pupils and difficult classes?
5 What action might best be taken to help with problems of discipline in your school?

The Elton enquiry found that physical violence against teachers was rare, particularly in primary schools. The real problem was the 'continuous stream of relatively minor disruptions' caused by children bickering, shouting and jostling in and out of class. Teachers are more likely to be worn down by an endless stream of petty annoyances than by the occasional major upset. Although only a small minority of children cause disruption the cumulative effect can be very great, and can be an enormous strain on the teacher's energies. The continuous struggle to instill discipline can make teaching a frustrating and debilitating experience.

Table 13 lists different types of pupil behaviour which primary teachers reported having to deal with during lessons, and frequency of occurence (Elton Report).

 Task 17 Monitoring pupil behaviour

Make a copy of the Elton Report pro-forma (Table 13), leaving space for items you may wish to add. Observe your class during one day, or one week, and tick each time a particular behaviour occurs. You may wish to add the initials of a child by each tick to monitor individual behaviour. Discuss your findings with a colleague. Were any unexpected?

## Steps to effective discipline

The first step to effective discipline is to apply the principles of good classroom management (see Unit 4) to your teaching. Although there are personal differences in teaching style, there is a high degree of agreement between teachers about the main features of good practice. There is also general

# TABLE 13 Pupil behaviour in the classroom

Percentages of primary teachers reporting that they had to deal with different types of pupil behaviour during the course of their classroom teaching the previous week.

| Type of pupil behaviour (listed by frequency of occurrence) | Reported frequency with which dealt with during lessons: | |
| --- | --- | --- |
| | At least once during week (%) | At least daily (%) |
| Talking out of turn (eg by making remarks, calling out, distracting others by chattering) | 97 | 69 |
| Hindering other pupils (eg by distracting them from work, interfering with equipment or materials) | 90 | 42 |
| Making unnecessary (non-verbal) noise (eg by scraping chairs, banging objects, moving clumsily) | 85 | 42 |
| Physical aggression towards other pupils (eg by pushing, punching, striking) | 74 | 17 |
| Getting out of seat without permission | 73 | 34 |
| Calculated idleness or work avoidance (eg delaying start to work set, not having essential books or equipment) | 67 | 21 |
| General rowdiness, horseplay or mucking about | 60 | 14 |
| Verbal abuse towards other pupils (eg offensive or insulting remarks) | 55 | 10 |
| Not being punctual (eg being late to school or lessons) | 53 | 11 |
| Persistently infringing class (or school) rules (eg on dress, pupil behaviour) | 50 | 13 |
| Cheeky or impertinent remarks or responses | 41 | 6 |
| Physical destructiveness (eg breaking objects, damaging furniture and fabric) | 16 | 1 |
| Verbal abuse towards you (eg offensive, insulting, insolent or threatening remarks) | 7 | 1 |
| Physical aggression towards you (the teacher) | 2.1 | 0 |

Source: The Elton Report (DES, 1989)

agreement that if lessons are well organised and well delivered this will help secure good standards of behaviour. Guiding principles include:

- *know children as individuals* – their names, personalities, interests and friends
- *plan lessons to maintain pupil interest*, being enthusiastic and using humour to create a positive environment
- *be flexible* and prepared to take advantage of the unexpected
- *continually observe* and scan the behaviour of the class
- *model the courtesy* you expect from children
- *emphasise the positive*, praise good behaviour as well as work
- *agree clear rules* for classroom behaviour, and explain why they are necessary
- *be sparing and consistent in use of reprimands*
- *be sparing and consistent in use of punishments*
- *analyse your own behaviour and responses*, learning from your own classroom performance. This, as the Elton Report says, is the most important principle of all.

## Task 18 Observing teaching strategies

It can help reflection on one's own practice to observe a lesson in a colleague's classroom. The following is a suggested framework for observation:

| | Pupil behaviour | Action taken by teacher |
|---|---|---|
| 1 | | |
| 2 | | |
| 3 | | |

After the lesson discuss with your colleague her reasons for action or non-intervention, and reflect on possible alternative strategies.

Classroom control and discipline have for long been neglected areas in teacher training, both at college and in-service levels. Beginners have been told that if they have problems it is because their lessons are not interesting or sufficiently well planned. But a well-prepared curriculum, though necessary, is not by itself sufficient to command a class's undivided attention. In the best planned lessons children may talk out of turn or distract others from their work. Research findings suggest that certain simple techniques can help in maintaining desired levels of discipline and control. These strategies aim to encourage desirable behaviour and create a positive environment for learning.

# Encouraging good behaviour

So what should teachers do if they are having discipline problems? Research into effective ways of modifying children's behaviour suggests three key steps – rules, ignoring, praise.

## Rules

Negotiate with your class a few simple rules (no more than five) for appropriate classroom behaviour. They should be practical and positive, for example 'We try to work quietly'. Rules need to define behaviour in clear and specific ways; they should not be vague generalisations like 'You must behave' but for example 'Stop and listen when someone speaks'. It is more effective to tell children what to do than what not to do – for example 'Try to take turns' rather than 'Don't interrupt'. To be memorable, rules need to be kept short and they need to be repeated. Rules need to be clearly communicated. One strategy that helps is to write them up for all to see. Another is to ask the children from time to time what they are and what they mean. Discuss whether they should be modified or updated. Do the children think the rules are fair and reasonable?

## Ignoring

Undesirable behaviour is best extinguished by being ignored. Take no notice of minor infringements to classroom rules but intervene if something serious happens. For serious infringements of rules one way to implement the 'ignore' strategy is to enforce a period of 'time out' for the child in a quiet corner or chair. Sitting and watching on the periphery of an activity may enable the child to observe the appropriate behaviour of others. Research shows that chiding children and constantly telling them off pays diminishing dividends in terms of modifying their behaviour, and may in fact make matters worse. Avoid fussing and grumbling over trivial matters. Convert this energy into positive directions, try to 'catch them being good', and praise them in a way which tells them exactly what you approve of.

*Praise*

Good teachers praise children more than they reprimand them. Mostly praise is used for good work, and reprimands for bad behaviour. Children are rarely praised for good behaviour. So look for instances when children keep the rules, and let them see you have noticed their efforts. Public praise works well, especially with younger children. Reinforce good behaviour with your attention and approval. Be behaviour-specific, for example 'I like the way John is sitting and listening', rather than something vague and general like 'John is being good'. Take advantage of the 'ripple effect' that praise has in conveying your expectations to others in the class. Offer models and positive examples for others to follow.

Praise is the easiest strategy to implement and the one most likely to achieve lasting change in a child's behaviour. Some teachers like to augment verbal recognition with token rewards such as stars, credits or house points. Such tokens can provide useful initial reinforcement, especially with children who feel otherwise unrewarded, but this impact is lost over a period of time. Rewards need to be varied, appropriate and immediate for their most positive effects. Reducing bad behaviour through positive approaches is a realistic aim. Eliminating it is not. Children will always want to test the boundaries, and teachers will need to confirm the existence of boundaries firmly, unequivocally and at once. Uncertain or delayed response will invite new challenges.

Table 14 presents some questions to help you reflect on your approach to classroom discipline.

---

## TABLE 14 Discipline: a checklist of questions

- What behaviour interferes with learning?
- What annoys you but is essentially harmless to learners and peers?
- How much freedom can be allowed without interfering with the rights of other children?
- What are your responsibilities for good behaviour in the class?
- What are the children's responsibilities?
- Should silence be maintained, or reasonable communication? When?
- Are your classroom rules for the benefit of the children, or for your own comfort and convenience?
- Are you thinking how a disruptive child can be helped to learn better, or just how disruptive behaviour can be decreased?
- Are you open to new ideas and approaches?
- Have you discussed rules of good behaviour with your class? With colleagues, parents or governors? Are your standards in conflict with any of these?

# Sanctions and punishments

Teachers need a variety of strategies involving both reward and punishment to deal with the wide range of children's behaviour. As the Elton enquiry found, there is no uniform agreement among teachers as to the most effective strategies, except for one. Reasoning with pupils outside the class setting was found to be the most common policy for dealing with difficult children. Verbal reprimands if used sparingly and decisively are more effective in the face of undesirable behaviour than vague appeals to the child. Much can also be communicated through body language such as the timely glare, gesture or shake of the head.

The following are some of the most widely used control strategies:

- stopping and waiting – use of eye contact or gesture to signal disapproval
- withholding praise – focusing on other children behaving or responding well
- verbal reprimand – picking out individuals, privately or publicly
- withdrawal of privileges
    - staying behind after the lesson to be spoken to or to complete a task
    - isolating the child, separation from peers, 'time out'
    - excluding the child from the activity, allowing back after a timed break
    - splitting up chatterers/disturbers, temporarily at first
- positive punishment
    - writing a letter of apology
    - completing a socially useful task
    - having a quiet 'cooling off' period
    - being reasoned with by a senior teacher
    - negotiating a contract for good behaviour

Clear distinctions should be made between minor and serious offences. Individuals rather than whole groups should be punished. Sanctions should as far as possible be positive, not damage relationships or a child's self-esteem, and they should not infringe the aims and principles of the school.

# School policies

The teacher is the primary influence on determining the behaviour of children in the classroom. But the climate in the classroom is also strongly affected by the policies and ethos of the school. A positive ethos and atmosphere in a school is hard to define, but can be almost tangibly felt by a visitor. It is characterised by a visible sense of commitment from staff and pupils, by high expectations of behaviour and high standards of work. Indications of a failure to achieve a sense of community include litter, graffiti, unpunctuality of pupils, poor playground and corridor behaviour, lack of display of children's work and frequent use of punishment.

Just as a class teacher can alter the climate in her classroom through her style of management, so the way a school is run can be changed. All teachers should be part of the school management team, under the leadership of the head and senior staff, and have a part to play in formulating school policy on good behaviour and discipline, and in fostering the ethos of the school.

The HMI publication *Education Observed 5* (DES, 1987) on behaviour and discipline in schools noted the following important factors associated with good behaviour in schools.

- *Leadership of head and senior staff* in fostering commitment to the school by staff, pupils and parents, encouraging all teachers to accept responsibility in maintaining good behaviour in classrooms and elsewhere, and supporting staff in their work.
- *Teacher's high expectations of pupils*, including their academic and social abilities.
- *Providing opportunities for achievement and success* for all children, with challenging teaching well matched to pupils' needs.
- *Active involvement of pupils* in their own learning and in the wider life of the school, encouraging pride in the school and care for others.
- *Agreement on essential values*, consistently applied rewards and sanctions. The best results, say HMI, are to be found in schools which emphasise rewards such as praise to individuals or groups, merit awards, profiles of achievement, letters or reports to parents, and opportunities for exercising responsibility.
- *Good relationships* fostered by mutual respect between teachers and pupils, and good communications, internal and external (with parents, governors etc).

What priorities for action should there be in policies to improve behaviour and discipline in schools? More than half the teachers surveyed in the Elton Report thought that *establishing smaller classes* should be the key priority. Research by Mortimore et al (ILEA Junior Project) showed some correlation between class size and pupil behaviour, but no clear link between the two. Many teachers wanted more *opportunities for discussion* of discipline among the staff as a whole, as well as guidance or support from colleagues about particular problems. Such discussions are often best undertaken at an informal level over coffee at breaktime, but time also needs to be allocated at staff meetings to discuss issues relevant to policy and practice.

How should a positive school discipline policy be developed? There are usually three stages in formulating school policy – consultation, development and evaluation. In the consultation stage the views of staff, pupils, parents and governors may be sought about discipline and behaviour in school. In developing a detailed policy statement reference should be made to:

- clearly stated expectations about pupil behaviour
- ways to encourage positive social behaviour
- ways to discourage antisocial behaviour, including clear guidelines on the use of sanctions and punishments
- ways to ensure clear communication of aims to all involved in the welfare of the school, including parents, governors and non-teaching staff

The policy should set out clearly the characteristics of the civilised community the school is aiming to become. Particular attention will need to be paid to critical times during the day such as the midday break, playtimes and routine movements around the school. A working party may need to be set up to evaluate the policy and its effects.

Staff discussion in one primary school produced a list of four simple but all-embracing rules 'for the safety and comfort of everybody', to be included in the school brochure. These were:

- always walk about the school
- talk quietly inside the school
- be kind to each other
- be careful with all equipment in the school

The school policy should also include rules for specific locations like the school field, and occasions like snowy weather. It should suggest that each class negotiates its own special rules with the children and that they are positive and start with 'try to' rather than 'don't'.

## Task 19  Reviewing school policies

Look at the discipline policy as stated in your own school brochure or staff handbook. See how it relates to the points of reference noted above, and to policies stated in other school brochures. Ask the children in your class how they would encourage good behaviour at school. Compare their views with the school policy.

A school policy on good behaviour should help to secure a continuity of approach, and a sharing of common values. Both children and colleagues tend to resent a weak link in the chain of good order in a school community.

# Our rules for the class

1. We listen when someone is talking.
2. We put our hands up when we want to speak.
3. We do not shout or run around.
4. We always do our best.

Research shows that children like teachers who are strict, fair and have a sense of humour. Such teachers make children feel good about themselves. They are fair in the positive sense ('every child is innocent until proved guilty'). They listen to and respect children ('every child has a chance of a fair hearing'). They use humour to defuse awkward situations, and are ready to help the individual child who has problems. Their authority comes not only from personal confidence but from the shared sense of common purpose with others in the school.

For self-evaluation on discipline and child management see Unit 19, pp 243–254.

# Unit 6

# PLANNING THE CURRICULUM

> The heart of the matter is what each child takes away from the school. For each of them what he or she takes away is the effective curriculum.     Schools Council *The Practical Curriculum* (1981)

A major focus in any junior class must be the curriculum, which is the planned course of study through which children learn. The curriculum includes both the process of learning and the products of learning. It is therefore just as important to look at the way curriculum areas are taught as to examine the subject matter itself. It is easy to define the content of teaching without reference to the learning processes involved. But as HMI argue, 'Teaching and learning styles strongly influence the curriculum and in practice cannot be separated from it' (HMI, 1985).

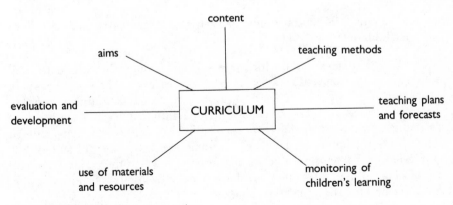

Figure 7 Planning the primary curriculum

Figure 7 shows some of the important aspects of the primary curriculum that need to be considered. Questions to ask during the planning stage include:

- What are the aims of the curriculum?
- What is the content of the curriculum?
- How is the curriculum to be taught?
- How is the teaching to be planned?
- How is the children's learning to be monitored?
- What materials and resources are to be used?
- How is the curriculum to be evaluated?

# 1 What are the aims of the curriculum?

The basic curriculum for state schools in England and Wales is prescribed by law. Aims for the National Curriculum were specified in the Education Reform Act (1988) as follows:

- to promote the spiritual, moral, cultural, mental and physical development of pupils
- to prepare the pupils for the opportunities, responsibilities and experiences of adult life

You may wish to take these aims into account when considering your own aims for teaching, and when you review with colleagues the stated aims for your school. Questions that relate to the aims of teaching include:

- What are we aiming to achieve for our children through the curriculum we offer them?
- Do we share our aims with parents, and others involved in the school community?
- Do we communicate our aims for each area of the curriculum clearly to our children?

In addition to general aims for the whole curriculum, the National Curriculum prescribes particular aims (targets) for each area of the curriculum. These are called Attainment Targets (ATs). Each attainment target consists of statements of attainment which are divided into ten levels. The aims or attainment targets are directions of travel, and the objectives or statements of attainment are points to be reached along the way. The content of the curriculum is the vehicle for achieving progress towards these aims. And you the teacher, although you may not have a vehicle entirely of your choosing, must decide how the vehicle is to be driven.

The ten levels of attainment relate to the primary years as follows. Levels 1 and 2 relate to Key Stage 1 (ages 5–7), levels 3 and 4 relate to Key Stage 2 (ages 7–11). The ages given for each stage correspond to the progress of the average child. Some children will be slower or quicker in particular subjects, eg at level 1 at age 7, or at level 5 or 6 at age 11. The levels achieved in different subject areas may also vary. Each child's levels of achievement will need to be regularly assessed.

## 2  What is the content of the curriculum?

The National Curriculum for juniors (KS2) comprises nine foundation subjects plus religious education. The foundation subjects are:

the core subjects:                English
                                          mathematics
                                          science
the other foundation subjects:  technology
                                          history
                                          geography
                                          music
                                          art
                                          physical education

The subjects are discussed individually in Units 7 to 14.

These prescribed subjects, each with their own attainment targets and programmes of study, are not intended to be the whole curriculum. Schools are free to add their own subject components, such as a foreign language (Welsh and English are taught compulsorily in Wales, with some difference of opinion as to which is the foreign language!). In addition there are other curricular elements that will need planning.

Cross-curricular elements enrich the educational experience of children and provide opportunities for links to be made between different areas of the curriculum. They can be taught through subject lessons as well as through topics or projects. There is a danger in either approach that children's learning will be piecemeal and unconnected. Teachers need to plan to give structure and coherence to the curriculum, so that it is not simply a set of random experiences for the child. Such planning will need to be at three levels:

- whole school (to guarantee continuity and consistency)
- class (to ensure coherence and progression)
- individual child (to match teaching to needs and abilities)

Teachers will need to collaborate in curriculum planning so that school policies can offer continuity and consistency of approach. The agreed curriculum

## TABLE 15 Cross-curricular aspects of planning

Cross-curricular aspects of planning include:

*Cross-curricular dimensions* such as:
- personal and social education (see Unit 14)
- multicultural education (see Unit 17)
- equal opportunities policies relating to culture, gender and disability (see Unit 17)

*Cross-curricular themes* such as:
- environmental education
- economic and industrial understanding
- health education
- citizenship (individual, family, community, national and international dimensions)
- careers education

*Cross-curricular skills* such as:
- communication (oral and written)
- problem solving
- numeracy
- study
- creative and imaginative
- personal and social
- information technology

provides the framework within which a teacher must work. It will be up to the teacher to make this framework achievable in the classroom, and to plan the teaching of it in a manageable and efficient way.

## Task 20  Reviewing curriculum content for your class

Questions to ask while reviewing the content of the curriculum for your class include:

- Do you know the content of the foundation subjects in the National Curriculum for the key stage you are teaching?
- Do you know the policy guidelines of your LEA, if any, on the curriculum for your school and for the age range of your class?
- Do you know the content of the curriculum guidelines or syllabus for your school?

Devise a short talk for parents giving them a description of the curriculum you intend to, or are, teaching for this term or school year.

# 3  How is the curriculum to be taught?

The National Curriculum is described in terms of subjects, and this may be a starting point for curriculum planning. Many primary teachers prefer to plan at least some of their work across subject boundaries through 'themes', 'topics' or 'projects'. Each teacher will need to decide what is to be taught through subject lessons and what through cross-curricular topics. The Junior Project researchers found only a small proportion of teachers who planned all their teaching as subject lessons, and likewise only a few who organised the whole curriculum around a particular project or theme. The great majority of junior teachers teach both separate subjects and integrated projects.

The term 'integrated work' can have different meanings. It can mean that several different subject-based tasks are being undertaken simultaneously in a single classroom or work area. Alternatively it can mean individuals or groups of children engaged in studying various aspects of a common theme. There can be many advantages from integrating several aspects of the curriculum into topics.

Unifying themes can:

● remove barriers between subjects, preventing a 'fragmented' curriculum
● stimulate varied approaches to investigation and study
● develop social skills through cooperative work
● foster individual interests and initiative
● allow a topic to be explored in depth
● reflect any or all subject areas of the curriculum
● provide opportunities for large groups to share their learning

There are also potential disadvantages in the topic-based approach. These were expressed in the HMI Report on Schools (1987/8) as follows: 'Although sometimes of high quality, topic work more often than not lacks continuity and progression, or any serious attempt to ensure that adequate time and attention are given to the elements said to comprise the topic.' Some of the dangers of the topic-based approach include:

● lack of breadth in topics, a 'bitty', haphazard approach
● lack of curriculum balance, ignoring certain key skills or concepts
● lack of progression within and between topics
● too strong a focus on art/display and end products
● thoughtless copying out and reproduction of unrelated facts

- stretching it out too long, making irrelevant links
- problems in group activity of monitoring/assessing individual progress

The worst topic work resembles a 'wet playtime' with children engaged in random and uncoordinated activities. The best of topic work creates the sort of teamwork and activity of successful industrial and college research projects.

One of the outcomes of the National Curriculum requirement that a specified range of attainment targets in each subject be studied, and that a 'reasonable' amount of time be allocated to each subject area, is that rigorous methods of curriculum planning and evaluation will be necessary. Part of this planning will involve identifying subject components in the topics undertaken, as well as the subjects to be taught separately. Traditionally the subjects taught separately in junior classes have included English, maths, music, PE and games. The major emphasis on English and maths (the '3 Rs') has been due to their central importance for all subsequent learning. Studies undertaken in the seventies and eighties have shown tremendous variations in the time spent on different aspects of the curriculum, for example the ORACLE researchers found time spent on maths varied between two and a half and seven hours a week (the average being four and a half hours). Some lessons such as music may need teachers with specialist training. Many schools look for specialist teachers to support other areas like science and technology, particularly for older and more able children. There is a need therefore for a junior teacher not only to plan a programme for her class covering all areas of the curriculum, but to ensure through the support of colleagues that she provides the best in teaching that is available at the school.

Given the need to ensure that every child experiences worthwhile study for a 'reasonable' time in every area of the National Curriculum, one of the most common questions that teachers ask is: 'How do we find time to teach it all?'. One way to begin seeking answers to this problem is to analyse the use of teaching time, and to see how much time is spent on work relating to the different subject areas.

 ## Task 21  Analysing time spent on curriculum subject areas

How is your teaching time allocated at present?
One way of analysing your teaching week is as follows:

1   Calculate the total time you spend on teaching the curriculum. (Deduct the time you spend on non-curriculum activities like assembly, registration, movement around school, changes between activities, unforeseen accidents/incidents etc from your total contact time.)

2   Assess the time you spend on different subject activities. Check that the total time matches the total time you calculated for curriculum teaching.

Note:   In analysing topic work, subject timings will only be approximate. Table 16 may be helpful in your analysis of the curriculum in terms of subject matter and of children's learning experience.

The whole curriculum includes cross-curricular elements as well as curriculum subjects. Task 22 may help in your planning.

## Task 22   Planning cross-curricular elements

Make a list of the cross-curricular elements you might wish to include in your teaching, such as those in Table 17 (page 64).
Analyse which elements are included in any particular topic, or in curriculum subject areas, over a period of time.

# 4   How is the teaching to be planned?

All teachers need to plan ahead in their teaching, and most are asked by their headteachers to produce some kind of written forecast of their work. The Junior Project found that in schools where teachers provided forecasts of work 'positive effects' were noted. Some teachers are asked to discuss their forecasts of work with the head or a senior teacher. They may also be asked to provide a written and/or verbal evaluation of their work at the end of a planned period of teaching.

From a given scheme of work each teacher needs to think out teaching plans. Within each teaching plan more precise intentions will emerge for daily or weekly lesson plans. These will have three components:

- plans for the class as a whole
- plans for children working in groups
- plans for individual pupils

To achieve a balance of work across the curriculum you will need to consider plans that cover varying periods of time, such as daily, weekly, monthly or half-termly, termly, yearly and across school years for each key stage of learning.

*Daily plans* might include opportunities during each day for children to:

- read something which increases knowledge, insight or enjoyment
- write something as a result of careful thought

## TABLE 16 A planning grid for the curriculum

| SUBJECTS | AREAS OF EXPERIENCE | | | | | | | |
|---|---|---|---|---|---|---|---|---|
| | Aesthetic & creative | Ethical & moral | Linguistic | Mathe-matical | Physical | Scientific | Social & political | Spiritual |
| English | | | | | | | | |
| Maths | | | | | | | | |
| Science | | | | | | | | |
| Technology | | | | | | | | |
| History | | | | | | | | |
| Geography | | | | | | | | |
| Music | | | | | | | | |
| Art | | | | | | | | |
| Physical education | | | | | | | | |
| Religious education | | | | | | | | |

Note: The subjects are those specified in the National Curriculum. The areas of experience are those identified by HMI (1985) as those which children should experience through the taught curriculum.

- investigate some aspect of mathematics
- ask a pertinent question and discuss ways of finding an answer
- feel challenged and yet meet with a measure of success
- express or interpret ideas, feelings or observations in a creative medium
- consider religious/moral/social issues

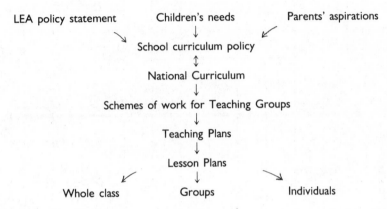

*Figure 8 The planning process*

*Weekly plans* might include opportunities during the week for children to:

- speak to others clearly and fluently in dialogue, discussion and/or drama
- listen to well read literature or poetry, and to music
- write in different styles for different purposes
- investigate, analyse and record mathematical information
- apply scientific methods to observations and experiences, and attempt to make logical deductions
- study some aspect of the environment, the world or the universe
- research into some aspect of the past and relate it to the present
- develop skills and self-expression through art or craft
- be involved in enjoyable physical activities which contain mental and physical challenges
- develop personal skills by having the time
  - for quiet thought and reflection
  - to initiate, lead, plan or organise
  - to take part in a cooperative venture

Such a programme broadly relates to subject areas, and encourages the development of personal qualities as well as skills and concepts.

*Longer-term planning* might involve a monthly, half-termly, termly or

# TABLE 17 A planning grid for cross-curricular elements

Topic:                     Class:                     Date:

|  | Maths | English | Science | Technology | History | Geography | Music | Art | PE | RE |
|---|---|---|---|---|---|---|---|---|---|---|
| DIMENSIONS: |  |  |  |  |  |  |  |  |  |  |
| Personal & social |  |  |  |  |  |  |  |  |  |  |
| Multicultural |  |  |  |  |  |  |  |  |  |  |
| Equal opportunities |  |  |  |  |  |  |  |  |  |  |
| THEMES: |  |  |  |  |  |  |  |  |  |  |
| Environmental education |  |  |  |  |  |  |  |  |  |  |
| Economic & industrial |  |  |  |  |  |  |  |  |  |  |
| Health education |  |  |  |  |  |  |  |  |  |  |
| Citizenship |  |  |  |  |  |  |  |  |  |  |
| Careers education |  |  |  |  |  |  |  |  |  |  |

|  | Maths | English | Science | Technology | History | Geography | Music | Art | PE | RE |
|---|---|---|---|---|---|---|---|---|---|---|
| SKILLS: |  |  |  |  |  |  |  |  |  |  |
| Communication<br>– oral<br>– written<br>– graphic |  |  |  |  |  |  |  |  |  |  |
| Problem solving |  |  |  |  |  |  |  |  |  |  |
| Numeracy |  |  |  |  |  |  |  |  |  |  |
| Physical |  |  |  |  |  |  |  |  |  |  |
| Study |  |  |  |  |  |  |  |  |  |  |
| Creative/imaginative |  |  |  |  |  |  |  |  |  |  |
| Personal/social |  |  |  |  |  |  |  |  |  |  |
| Information technology |  |  |  |  |  |  |  |  |  |  |

annual forecast aimed at ensuring there is appropriate breadth, balance and progression in the curriculum. Some integrated or thematic work may be helpful in developing in a purposeful way the skills and concepts of the main subject areas. Topic themes may be laid down in school guidelines for each class, or the choice of topic may be left open for the teacher. Topics can be undertaken by the whole school, department, year group, class, or by groups within a class, or done on an individual basis. Sources of topic themes could include current events such as the Olympic Games, seasonal events, environmental projects, subject-based themes, group experiences such as visits or TV/video programmes, or the individual interests of children in the class.

In planning a topic or research project with children the following are some aspects of learning activity that you may wish to consider:

- *what* – curricular areas of study and attainment targets
- *why* – knowledge, skills and attitudes you aim to develop, the purposes of the research
- *how* – teaching methods, activities and resources
- *when* – timetable time, length of study programme
- *where* – learning activity in class, school, outside visits
- *with whom* – other children, teachers, speakers to support learning
- *which outcome* – what is to be the end result; display, quiz, talk, books, exhibition of work, assembly, video etc.

Initial planning of this sort often takes the form of topic 'webs' to provide an outline or framework of the various elements to be included (see Figure 9).

One of the drawbacks of this traditional kind of topic web is that it tends to focus on content and pays little attention to the process of learning. Other factors that a teacher needs to consider are:

- *intentions* – how can I use and build on what children know?
    what do I want children to gain from the activities?
    what attitudes do I want to foster?
- *strategies* – what starting points will I use?
    what groupings of children?
    what ways of learning?
- *outcomes* – what outcomes?
    what audience for outcomes?
    what opportunities for evaluation?

After the initial planning the next stage may be to consider how the outline plans will be translated into lesson plans that take account of differing levels of ability. Another element in planning will be to consider ways in which the children's learning is to be monitored and assessed.

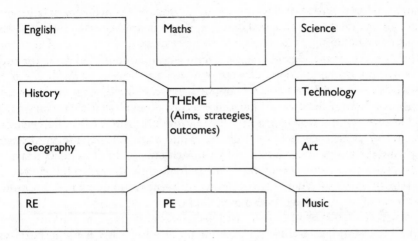

*Figure 9 Outline topic plan*

Note: Curriculum areas could contain reference to attainment targets (ATs), study skills/
activities and resources to be used. See also the planning grid for cross-curricular
elements (pp 64–65) and an example of a topic plan on p 205 (Figure 23).

## 5  How is the children's learning to be monitored?

The work of children in the classroom needs to be monitored. How is it to be
done? Probably not by staying at your desk, but by being active, by moving
around the class observing and checking, and offering help where it is
needed. The word *supervision* is an apt one in this context. When children
are working the teacher needs to be on hand to offer the following kinds of
support:

- communication of factual information (extending knowledge)
- higher-order questioning (encouraging problem solving)
- task supervision (keeping children on task)
- feedback on work (supporting, assessing, praising/criticising)

The Junior Project showed there was much variation in the teachers' use
of these different forms of monitoring. On average only one per cent of
classroom time was spent by teachers in asking higher-order questions that
encouraged children to make a reasoned or imaginative response to their
work, for example by asking 'How do you think this story will end?' or
'What different ways are there of measuring the classroom?'. Much more of
teacher–pupil interaction (about 11 per cent) was seen to be concerned with

telling children what to do, how to do it, and asking whether instructions were understood, for example 'Draw a picture like this' or 'Do you remember what to do?'.

Feedback on work includes verbal comment and non-verbal feedback such as marking. A large proportion of any teacher's time is taken up with communicating with the children about work they are doing, are intending to do, or should be doing. The Junior Project found that there was much variation between teachers as to the nature of their feedback – neutral, positive or critical. Positive feedback on children's work in the form of praise was observed very infrequently. But positive effects on effort and progress was observed in classes where the teacher frequently offered children specific and justified praise. Many teachers however seemed to be missing opportunities to reinforce good work habits in this way.

Teachers often spend a considerable amount of time in marking work. Indeed the marking of work can become the bane of a teacher's life, particularly as children get older and the volume of their work increases. There are various forms that the marking and assessment of children's work can take, for example:

- detailed marking of child's work by the teacher
- mark by teacher to show she has seen/checked child's work
- assessment of child's work discussed with child
- child's work assessed by other adult, eg parent or colleague
- child corrects and assesses own work
- other child or children correct or assess child's work
- child's work is left unseen, unchecked or unmarked

When checking a child's work the ideal situation is for the child to be with you. To do this all the time would leave you with little time for anything else. You will need to look for other ways of monitoring their work. In practice it should prove impossible to mark everything produced by a large class of fluent and hard-working children. You will need to devise a systematic policy to see and check the work of every child in your class over a period of time. Share your policy with the children so that they can support you in keeping up to date with their work.

Many teachers like to offer children opportunities to assess their own work, and the work of others. This encourages children to exercise their judgement, and to feel a sense of responsibility about their own work and the efforts of others. They will need to discuss and be aware of what to look for, good points as well as mistakes, in checking their class work. Parents too can be involved in assessing and supporting their child's work, for example in recording reading done at home. Teachers sometimes share marking between classes. This can be particularly useful in reviewing or formulating a marking/ assessment policy for the school to ensure some conformity of approach and sharing of standards.

Questions to consider in providing feedback on children's work include:

- What is the *purpose* of the marking or assessment?
- What *criteria* are you using to judge the work?
- What good things are you looking to *praise*, what errors to *correct*?
- What are you wishing to show or teach the child?
- How do you wish the child to *respond*?

## Task 23  Reviewing your response to children's work

Questions to discuss with colleagues, or with children in your class, might include:

- What makes a particular piece of work good or bad?
- Do I pick out the good things as well as the errors in children's work?
- What am I looking for in their work?
- Am I fair in what I say, and in my marking?
- Are there any better ways of organising the marking in our class?

# 6  What materials and resources are to be used?

Teachers draw upon a variety of resources for their lessons. These include:

- ideas and experiences of children, teachers and others
- textbooks, reference or library books
- duplicated worksheets, workcards or workbooks
- blackboard, whiteboard and display board
- pictures, posters, photographs, wallcharts
- objects, models, found materials
- instruments for observing, measuring, recording
- TV/video, sound tape and computer
- materials for artwork, craftwork and creative expression
- visits to local and distant environment

The key resource in any classroom is the teacher and the best learning often comes through the interaction of children and teacher. There is nothing wrong with the traditional approach of 'chalk and talk' provided it is not the teacher who does all the talking, and children receive other forms of stimulus.

Children need to experience a stimulating range of resources. In planning the resources for your teaching programme, questions to ask include:

- What resources could enrich the children's learning?
- Where are resources available (in class, the school, homes, locally, in libraries, teachers' centres etc)?
- Which of these resources would best support my teaching?
- How can I present/use these resources in a clear and meaningful way?
- When should the resources be used?
- Who should use and be responsible for them?

## Task 24  Reviewing materials and resources

Plan the resources to be used for a particular topic or curriculum theme. The questions above may help in your review of resources. This chart offers one way of organising the information.

| Topic: | | |
| --- | --- | --- |
| Resource | Where available | How used (possible teaching/learning activities) |
| | | |

Note: Think of the best ways to store this information, and to communicate or make it available to others, for example in a topic box or file or on a computer.

Schools store resources in differing ways, for example in resource areas, resource boxes or in separate locations. Teachers also build up their own personal collection of resource materials. Useful resources may be kept by colleagues or stored in odd cupboards unknown to other teachers. Parents and children can be a rich store of hidden resources. It is not unknown for teachers to order interesting-sounding resources, and then wonder later what on earth to do with them, or for a teacher to depart leaving their bright idea gathering dust on a shelf. A more efficient approach is curriculum-led resourcing, where forward planning by the staff identifies resource needs, evaluates what they have, and orders new materials for particular curriculum purposes. We may never have sufficient resources for all our teaching needs, but we can utilise what we have to the best advantage, and find out what colleagues, children and the local community may have to offer.

# 7 How is the curriculum to be evaluated?

How are we to judge how successful our planning and teaching have been? There are various ways in which the curriculum can be evaluated, for example through:

- teacher assessment
- the testing of children
- assessment by children, for example through learning logs or diaries
- parent assessment, for example by commenting on how they see their child's progress
- assessment by outside agencies such as inspectors, governors or the local community

As teachers we need to reflect on, assess and evaluate our professional practice. The classic process for teachers (and for children in their work) is to plan – do – review. Without a review or evaluation stage there can be no curriculum or professional development. We need to look at what we offer (the curriculum) and how it is taught (our teaching strategies) as well as the outcomes (achievements in learning).

Questions to ask at the end of a lesson, topic or period of teaching might include:

- What worked, and why?
- What didn't work and why?
- What could be changed/improved? How and why?
- Were my original intentions (aims) fulfilled?
- What did the children learn?
- What did I learn?
- What next?

Not all the factors that affect the curriculum are of course under our control; some are determined by the school and its teachers, others are determined by outside agencies.

These areas are not separated very clearly, particularly in terms of the school governors, who have a responsibility to 'overview' and monitor the curriculum, and on which parents, teachers and community interests are represented. As teachers we need to inform governors and parents not only about the general direction of the curriculum, which is usually set out in the school prospectus, but also about the details of the teaching provided in each subject area. We need therefore to plan carefully and to communicate these plans clearly to those involved in the education of the children in our class –

## TABLE 18 Factors that affect the curriculum

| Factors outside direct school/teacher control | Factors within school/teacher influence or control |
| --- | --- |
| Government policy and legislation | Curriculum materials and policies |
| National Curriculum framework | Teaching styles and methods |
| Local education authority policy | Use of time and resources |
| Location of school | Children's learning |
| School building and facilities | Behaviour of children |
| Children and their parents | School organisation |
| Head and staff of school | Parental support and attitudes |
| | Use of money, building, facilities |

———————————— School governors ————————————

to those who are our partners in the process of evaluating what we do. The following units (7 to 14) look in more detail at the planning needed for each area of the curriculum. The final units (15 to 19) then deal with aspects of assessment and evaluation.

# Unit 7

# ENGLISH

> To know what children mean you need to listen to, or see, what
> they say ...                    English advisory teacher

The ways in which children use language, and respond to the language use of others, lies at the heart of their success as learners. Language is the child's primary vehicle for learning and is involved in all curriculum areas. The major modes for learning through language are shown in Figure 10.

If what the child learns through the use of language is to be useful, meaningful and lasting then the child must make it his or her own. This means the child must do something with it, take it further in some way, through thinking about it and expressing it – for example by talking, reading, writing, investigating and planning ways to solve problems – sometimes as individuals and sometimes in cooperation with others through group and classwork. The teacher will need to plan programmes of study, with attainment targets in mind, that will support each child's language and learning in the key areas of:

1 speaking and listening
2 reading
3 writing

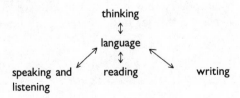

Figure 10 Learning through language

# 1 Speaking and listening

Talk as a process of learning is very good for:

- recounting news and events
- telling stories
- communicating instructions and directions
- exchanging ideas
- forming views and opinions
- solving problems
- investigating and exploring issues

Children should be given opportunities to develop these abilities through all aspects of the curriculum. Some of the activities that appear in the National Curriculum programme of study for developing speaking and listening skills are described below.

## Recounting news and events

Children can talk about experiences in and out of school, and gain much from listening to the experiences of others, talking for example about school trips, sporting activities, family events, books read or television programmes seen. Children should be given opportunities to talk individually and to wider audiences, for example to a group, a class or school assembly.

## Telling stories, reciting and reading aloud

Children need to listen and respond to stories, poems and songs at all ages and stages in their school lives. Sources should include the familiar and unfamiliar, examples from different cultures, varied authors and from children's own work. Children should retell stories in their own words, narrate their own stories, recite poetry they have learnt, and read aloud in a variety of contexts, with increasing fluency and awareness of audiences.

## Communicating instructions and directions

Opportunities to communicate should include the giving and receiving of information, instructions and explanations. Through questioning children should become increasingly precise in their verbal messages. They should be encouraged to present factual information in a clear, logical and structured manner, learning to discriminate between what is relevant and irrelevant.

## Exchanging ideas

Planned activities could include discussion with others, learning how to listen to and give weight to the opinions of others. This will involve understanding the need for turntaking and practising gaining and holding the attention of listeners. Children should present their ideas, experiences and understanding in a widening range of contexts across the curriculum, for example in predicting the outcomes of science experiments.

## Forming views and opinions

In discussing issues in small and large groups children need to take account of the views of others and to negotiate a consensus. They should be encouraged to express and justify their own feelings, opinions and viewpoints in all areas of their learning. They will need to practise reporting and summarising their own thoughts as well as surveying the ideas of others.

## Solving problems

Children need experience in responding to problems, and being involved in problem-solving activities across the curriculum. This should involve the collaborative planning of activities in ways which require them to speak and listen, as well as explain their attempted solutions to particular problems, such as a technological challenge.

## Investigating and exploring issues

Children should be given opportunities to engage in prediction, speculation and hypothesis. Their investigations should include the use where appropriate of audio and visual resources and the computer. Ways of exploring issues should include the use of role play, simulation and improvised drama.

While developing proficiency in spoken Standard English, children should be encouraged to value regional and social variations in English accents and dialects. In particular they should be encouraged to respect their own mother tongue, if it is not English, and to respect the languages of others.

## Task 25 Analysing opportunities for speaking and listening

Analyse the opportunities you plan to offer children over a period of time, or for a given topic/theme, to engage in different aspects of speaking and listening.
The categories given above may help in providing headings for planning and analysis.

Table 19 shows the National Curriculum Attainment Targets for speaking and listening.

---

### TABLE 19 English AT1: Speaking and listening

| Level | Statements of attainment | Example |
|---|---|---|
| | Pupils should be able to: | |
| 1 | a) participate as speakers and listeners in group activities, including imaginative play. | *Suggest what to do next in a practical activity; tell stories; play the role of shopkeeper or customer in the class shop.* |
| | b) listen attentively, and respond, to stories and poems. | *Ask questions about a story or poem; re-tell a story; enact a poem; draw a picture to illustrate a story or poems.* |
| | c) respond appropriately to simple instructions given by a teacher. | *Follow two consecutive instructions such as 'Choose some shells from the box and draw pictures of them'.* |
| 2 | a) participate as speakers and listeners in a group engaged in a given task. | *Compose a story together; design and make a model; assume a role in play activity.* |
| | b) describe an event, real or imagined, to the teacher or another pupil. | *Tell the listener about something which happened at home, on the television or in a book.* |
| | c) listen attentively to stories and poems, and talk about them. | *Talk about the characters; say what they like or dislike about a story or poem.* |
| | d) talk with the teacher, listen, and ask and answer questions. | *Talk about events or activities in or out of school — such as a school trip, a family outing or a television programme.* |
| | e) respond appropriately to a range of more complex instructions given by a teacher, and give simple instructions. | *Follow three consecutive actions such as 'Write down the place in the classroom where you think your plant will grow best, find out what the* |

| Level | Statements of attainment | Example |
|---|---|---|
| | | *others on your table think and try to agree on which is likely to be the best place'.* |
| 3 | a) relate real or imaginary events in a connected narrative which conveys meaning to a group of pupils, the teacher or another known adult. | *Tell a story with a beginning, middle and end; recount a series of related incidents that happened at home or in a science activity.* |
| | b) convey accurately a simple message. | *Relay a simple telephone message in role-play or real life; take an oral message to another teacher.* |
| | c) listen with an increased span of concentration to other children and adults, asking and responding to questions and commenting on what has been said. | *Listen to the teacher or to a radio programme on a new topic, then discuss what has been said.* |
| | d) give, and receive and follow accurately, precise instructions when pursuing a task individually or as a member of a group. | *Plan a wall display or arrange an outing together.* |
| 4 | a) give a detailed oral account of an event, or something that has been learned in the classroom, or explain with reasons why a particular course of action has been taken, or express a personal view. | *Report on a scientific investigation, or the progress of a planned group activity, to another group or the class.* |
| | b) ask and respond to questions in a range of situations with increased confidence. | *Guide other pupils in designing something; conduct an interview on a radio programme devised with other pupils.* |
| | c) take part as a speaker and listener in a group discussion or activity, commenting constructively on what is being discussed or experienced. | *Draft a piece of writing, with others, on a word processor; contribute to the planning and implementation of a group activity.* |
| | d) participate in a presentation. | *Describe the outcome of a group activity; improvise a scene from a story or poem.* |

| Level | Statements of attainment | Example |
|---|---|---|
| **5** | a) give a well organised and sustained account of an event, a personal experience or an activity. | *Describe a model which has been made, indicating the reasons for the design and the choice of materials.* |
| | b) contribute to and respond constructively in discussion, including the development of ideas; in debate, advocate and justify a point of view. | *Explain the actions taken by a character in a novel; work in a group to develop a detailed plan of action; provide arguments in favour of an approach to a problem.* |
| | c) use language to convey information and ideas effectively in a straightforward situation. | *Provide an eye witness account of an event or incident; explain the effects of the loss of a personal possession.* |
| | d) plan and participate in a group presentation. | *Compile a news report or a news programme for younger children; perform a story or poem after improvisation, making use of video, or audio recorders where appropriate.* |
| | e) recognise variations in vocabulary between different regional or social groups, and relate this knowledge where appropriate to personal experience. | *Talk about dialect vocabulary and specialist terms; discuss the vocabulary used by characters in books or on television.* |

# 2 Reading

Progress in learning to read is closely related to the development of oral language and also of writing. The stages in a child's reading development may be summarised as in Table 20.

*Teachers* need to provide a wide range and variety of texts to encourage children in developing their personal taste in reading, helping them to become more independent and selective. The reading material provided should include fiction, non-fiction and poetry that will offer challenge and variety in reading experience. The teacher should read stories, poems and non-fiction to them and provide an audience for the child.

## TABLE 20 Stages of reading development

| | | |
|---|---|---|
| 0–5+ years | Pre-reading | (Level 1) |
| | Learning language, becoming aware of literacy | |
| 5–7+ years | Learning to read/emergent reading | (Level 2) |
| | Constructing meaning, learning letter/sound association | |
| 7–9+ years | Extending early reading | (Level 3) |
| | Reading familiar books, increasing reading skills | |
| 9–11+ years | Reading to learn the new | (Levels 4/5) |
| | Using reading to gain knowledge and new experience | |

*Children* should be given opportunities to discuss with others and with the teacher what they read. In doing so they should be encouraged to respond to plot, character or ideas in the stories or poems, and to refer to relevant passages or episodes to support their opinions. They should be helped to look in a text for clues about characters or actions, and be encouraged to evaluate and predict what may happen.

The teacher's role in supporting reading in the classroom is summarised in Table 21.

Provision needs to be made for children to read for pleasure, and also to read for the purpose of gaining information.

## TABLE 21 Reading in the classroom: the teacher's role

In planning for the implementation of the programme of study for Reading the teacher should be:

- a responsive and interested listener to children's reading of their own writing and chosen texts
- an organiser of opportunities to read with other adults and children
- a partner/guide in discussion of reading experience
- a reader of books and children's own stories, in order to provide an example and encourage interest
- a support, helping children to use all the available cues to making sense of their reading
- a monitor of reading development
- a recorder of progress

From *English Non-Statutory Guidance* (NCC, 1990)

# TABLE 22  Extract from programme of study for key stage 2: reading

Pupils should:

- hear stories, poems and non-fiction read aloud;
- have opportunities to participate in all reading activities, *eg preparing and reading a selection of poems, reciting some from memory, or taking part in storytelling sessions or dramatic activities*;
- select books for their own reading and for use in their work;
- keep records of their own reading and comment, in writing or in discussion, on the books which they have read;
- read aloud to the class or teacher and talk about the books they have been reading;
- be encouraged to respond to the plot, character or ideas in stories or poems, and to refer to relevant passages or episodes to support their opinions;
- be encouraged to think about the accuracy of their own reading and to check for errors that distort meaning;
- be shown how to read different kinds of materials in different ways, *eg 'search' reading to find a scientific or geographical fact*;
- learn how to find information in books and databases, sometimes drawing on more than one source, and how to pursue an independent line of inquiry.

# TABLE 23  English AT2: Reading

| Level | Statements of attainment | Example |
|---|---|---|
| | Pupils should be able to: | |
| 1 | a) recognise that print is used to carry meaning, in books and in other forms in the everyday world. | *Point to and recognise own name; tell the teacher that a label on a container says what is inside or that the words in a book tell a story.* |
| | b) begin to recognise individual words or letters in familiar contexts. | *In role-play, read simple signs such as shop names or brand names; recognise 'bus-stop', 'exit', 'danger'.* |
| | c) show signs of a developing interest in reading. | *Pick up books and look at the pictures; choose books to hear or read.* |
| | d) talk in simple terms about the content of stories, or information in non-fiction books. | *Talk about characters and pictures, including likes and dislikes.* |
| 2 | a) read accurately and understand straightforward signs, labels and notices. | *Read labels on drawers in the classroom; read simple menus.* |

| Level | Statements of attainment | Example |
|---|---|---|
| | b) demonstrate knowledge of the alphabet in using word books and simple dictionaries. | *Turn towards the end to find words beginning with 's', rather than always starting from the beginning.* |
| | c) use picture and context cues, words recognised on sight and phonic cues in reading. | *Use a picture to help make sense of a text; recognise that 'Once' is often followed by 'upon a time'; use initial letters to help with recognising words.* |
| | d) describe what has happened in a story and predict what may happen next. | *Talk about how and why Jack climbs the beanstalk and suggest what may be at the top.* |
| | e) listen and respond to stories, poems and other material read aloud, expressing opinions informed by what has been read. | *Talk about characters, their actions and appearance; discuss the behaviour of different animals described in a radio programme.* |
| | f) read a range of material with some independence, fluency, accuracy and understanding. | *Read something unprompted; talk with some confidence about what has been read; produce craftwork related to reading work.* |
| 3 | a) read aloud from familiar stories and poems fluently and with appropriate expression. | *Raise or lower voice to indicate different characters.* |
| | b) read silently and with sustained concentration. | |
| | c) listen attentively to stories, talk about setting, story-line and characters and recall significant details. | *Talk about a story, saying what happened to change the fortunes of the leading characters.* |
| | d) demonstrate, in talking about stories and poems, that they are beginning to use inference, deduction and previous reading experience to find and appreciate meanings beyond the literal. | *Discuss what might happen to characters in a story, based on the outcome of adventures in other stories.* |
| | e) bring to their writing and discussion about stories some understanding of the way stories are structured. | *Refer to different parts of the story such as 'at the beginning' or 'the story ends with'; notice that some stories build up in a predictable way, eg 'The Three Little Pigs', 'Goldilocks and the Three Bears'.* |
| | f) devise a clear set of questions that will enable them to select and use appropriate information sources and reference books from the class and school library. | *Decide that the wildlife project needs information about the size and colour of birds, their food and habitat, and look it up.* |

| Level | Statements of attainment | Example |
|---|---|---|
| 4 | a) read aloud expressively, fluently and with increased confidence from a range of familiar literature. | *Vary the pace and tone of the voice to express feelings, or to represent character or mood.* |
| | b) demonstrate in talking about a range of fiction and poetry which they have read, an ability to explore preferences. | *Describe those qualities of the poem or story which appeal and give an indication of personal response to such matters as mood or character.* |
| | c) demonstrate, in talking about stories and poems, that they are developing their abilities to use inference, deduction and previous reading experience. | *Recognise and use those clues in a text which help the reader predict events.* |
| | d) find books or magazines in the class or school library by using the classification system, catalogue or data base and use appropriate methods of finding information, when pursuing a line of enquiry. | *Use search reading techniques, contents lists and indexes.* |
| 5 | a) demonstrate, in talking and writing about a range of stories and poems which they have read, an ability to explain preferences. | *Make simple comparisons between stories or poems; offer justification for personal preference.* |
| | b) demonstrate, in talking about fiction, non-fiction, poetry, and other texts that they are developing their own views and can support them by reference to some details in the text. | *Discuss character, action, fact and opinion relating them to personal experience.* |
| | c) show in discussion that they can recognise whether subject matter in non-literary and media texts is presented as fact or opinion. | *Look for evidence in a film which will help determine what is fact and what is opinion.* |
| | d) select reference books and other information materials and use organisational devices to find answers to their own questions. | *Use chapter titles, sub-headings, typefaces, symbol keys and the selective framing of illustrations.* |
| | e) show through discussion an awareness of a writer's choice of particular words and phrases and the effect on the reader. | *Recognise puns, word play, unconventional spellings and the placing together of pictures and text.* |

## Reading for pleasure

Children need opportunities to develop the habit of silent reading, both at school and at home. The link between home and school is an important one, particularly for the development of reading. Teachers need actively to encourage parents to participate and share in the child's reading. Children can be encouraged to keep a reading diary or record sheet and to comment in writing or in discussion on books they have read. They should select their own books for reading, with guidance from the teacher where necessary. The influential report *Extending Beginning Reading* (Southgate et al, 1981) suggested that more opportunities be found for personal reading and for discussion of books in the junior school. One approach is to timetable a period of Uninterrupted Sustained Silent Reading where the children, and teacher, are expected to read their own chosen reading material, for pleasure, for a quiet regular period of time (see R Campbell in *Education 3–13*, June 1988).

## Reading for information

Children should be shown how to read different kinds of materials in different ways, for example how to search to find a historical or scientific fact. They will need access to a variety of resources for this, including information books, encyclopedias, dictionaries, thesauruses, computer databases, guide books, text books, newspapers and magazines. They will need training in how to study from books using contents tables, indexes and cross references, how to draw on different sources and use the library system. They need opportunities to make notes, collate information, assess reliability and suitability, and produce a bibliography, as well as to develop the study skills of skimming, scanning and rapid reading.

The list in Table 24 of higher-order reading or study skills may help in planning the reading programme or provide a basis for an assessment or profile for each child.

## Task 26  Surveying children's attitudes to reading

Research into the attitudes your children have towards reading through, for example:

- devising a questionnaire on reading preferences
- children keeping a weekly log of reading habits
- children writing/brainstorming 'Reasons for Reading'

Discuss and record results of the survey.
Did the results of the survey match your predictions?
Have the children's attitudes to reading changed over time, or do you think they will?
What do the children think of themselves as readers?
What do they think will help them in their reading?
Do you agree?

---

### TABLE 24 Study skills: a checklist

- uses contents table
- uses index
- uses dictionary
- uses encyclopedia
- uses library system
- defines purpose for reading
- surveys – can locate information in a text
- skims – can gain quick impression of a text
- scans – can locate specific parts of a text
- reads rapidly
- reads intensively
- forms questions about reading
- summarises – main features of a text
- assesses reliability of information in texts
- assesses quality and suitability of texts
- makes notes
- collates information
- constructs flow diagrams
- produces indexes and cross references
- produces bibliography

---

# 3 Writing

Children should have frequent opportunities to write, using writing to learn and record their experiences in a wide range of activities across the curriculum. They should be helped to recognise that writing involves:

- *audience* – who the writing is for, for example themselves, their classmates, their teacher, younger children, their parents or other adults

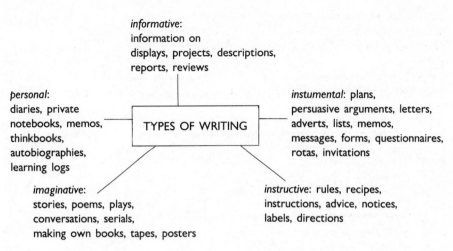

*informative*:
information on
displays, projects, descriptions,
reports, reviews

*personal*:
diaries, private
notebooks, memos,
thinkbooks,
autobiographies,
learning logs

TYPES OF WRITING

*instumental*: plans,
persuasive arguments, letters,
adverts, lists, memos,
messages, forms, questionnaires,
rotas, invitations

*imaginative*:
stories, poems, plays,
conversations, serials,
making own books, tapes, posters

*instructive*: rules, recipes,
instructions, advice, notices,
labels, directions

*Figure 11 Types of writing*

- *purpose* – why they are writing, for example to create pleasure, help thinking, plan an activity, describe, explain, argue
- *decision making* – what kind of writing, for example story form, poem (rhyming or free verse), play, letter, serial, novel, notes
- *plan or method* – how it is to be written, initial thoughts and framework of writing
- *drafting* – when thoughts are to be developed, evaluated and reshaped by extending, adding to or amending the text
- *proofreading* – where work is checked for errors, reread and revised, so as to improve meaning
- *presentation* – with whom to share the writing, and in which form, for example to be read aloud, displayed, word processed, illustrated or anthologised.

The development of writing skills is closely linked to the development of oral and reading skills. Children should read and talk about good examples of writing (descriptions, explanations, stories etc) and be helped to plan and produce these types of writing for themselves. The types of writing task they should experience include those in Figure 11. The teacher's role in supporting writing in the classroom is summarised in Table 25.

Teachers and children often have different views about the writing they do, what writing is and what constitutes a good piece of writing. Children can discuss or jot down their responses to questions such as these in small groups, and then report back to the class to compare ideas and responses.

The writing tasks that children are given should be purposeful, for example

---

**TABLE 25** Writing in the classroom: the teacher's role

In planning for the implementation of the programme of study for Writing the teacher should be:

- an organiser of adults other than teachers who can work alongside children, 'scribing' for them, or using a keyboard, and enabling them to compose at greater length than they could on their own
- an editorial consultant
- a praiser of achievement
- an example of adult writing behaviour
- a setter of procedures
- a setter of standards
- a recorder of progress
- a monitor of learning development

---

From English Non-Statutory Guidance (NCC, 1990)

in writing personal letters to known recipients, children should be helped to increase their control over different forms of writing, for example by being shown how to set a letter out. Through the experience of hearing and reading stories they should be helped to realise that the setting and outcome need to be made explicit to the reader. In writing poetry either individually, in groups or as a class they should be encouraged to experiment with different layouts, rhymes, verse structures and word plays.

## Grammar – knowing about language

As children become more fluent and competent writers, they should become more aware of the value of punctuation and gain some knowledge of the grammatical structure of language. This should be taught in the context of the children's own writing, aiming to give them more knowledge and control over the writing process. Children's vocabulary should be enriched and extended, for example through the use of a thesaurus and dictionary. Attention should be drawn through their reading and writing to the use of capital letters, full stops, question and exclamation marks, the use of paragraphs, commas and apostrophes. The aim should be to help them think about ways of making their meaning clear, by redrafting, proofreading and considering features of layout – finding ways to reduce repetition and to bring life and colour to the use of words.

## Task 27  Investigating the child's view of writing

The following are some questions that may help you to investigate your children's views on writing:

- Of all the things you have written at school/home, which one did you enjoy most?
- What types of writing, if any, do you dislike?
- What do you think the most important thing about writing is?
- Apart from your school work, what other writing do you do?
- Are you good at writing?

---

## TABLE 26  Extract from programme of study for key stage 2: writing

Pupils should:

- use writing to learn, and to record their experiences in a wide range of classroom activities across the curriculum;
- undertake chronological writing, eg *reports of work in science and mathematics, instructions for carrying out a task, and accounts of personal experiences, as well as imaginative stories;*
- be helped to understand that non-chronological types of writing can be organised in a variety of ways and so, generally, require careful planning; this might include the presentation of information or imaginative prose;
- read good examples of descriptions, explanations, opinions, etc, and be helped to plan and produce these types of writing by being given purposeful opportunities to write their own;
- write personal letters to known recipients and be shown how to set them out;
- be helped to increase their control of story form, through their experience of the stories they have read and heard, recognising, for example, that the setting and the outcome need to be made explicit to the reader;
- have opportunities to write poetry (individually, in small groups or as a class) and to experiment with different layouts, rhymes, rhythms, verse structures, and with all kinds of sound effects and verbal play;
- have opportunities to create, polish and produce individually or together, by hand or on a word processor, extended written texts, appropriately laid out and illustrated, eg *class newspapers, anthologies of stories or poems, guidebooks, etc;*
- write in response to a wide range of stimuli, including stories, plays and poems they have read and heard, television programmes they have seen, their own interests and experiences, and the unfolding activities of the classroom;

---

- be encouraged to be adventurous with vocabulary choices;
- be taught how to use a thesaurus;
- be introduced to the idea of the paragraph and encouraged to notice paragraph divisions in their reading;
- be shown how to set out and punctuate direct speech;
- be introduced to some of the uses of the comma and the apostrophe;
- be taught the meaning, use and spelling of some common prefixes and suffixes, eg *un-, in- (and im-, il-, ir-), -able, -ness, -ful*, etc, in the context of their own writing and reading;
- think about ways of making their meaning clear to their intended reader in redrafting their writing;
- be encouraged and shown how to check spellings in a dictionary or on a computer spelling checker when revising and proof-reading;
- have opportunities to develop a comfortable, flowing and legible joined-up style of handwriting;
- consider features of layout, eg *headings, side headings, the use of columns or indentation*, in the materials they read, so that they can use some of these features to clarify structures and meaning in their own writing;
- be encouraged to find ways to reduce repetition in their own writing;
- be introduced to the complex regularity that underlies the spelling of words with inflectional endings, eg *bead-ing, bead-ed, bed-d-ing, bed-d-ed*, in the context of their own writing and reading.

## TABLE 27  English AT3: Writing

| Level | Statements of attainment | Example |
|---|---|---|
| | Pupils should be able to: | |
| 1 | a) use pictures, symbols or isolated letters, words or phrases to communicate meaning. | *Show work to others, saying what writing and drawings mean.* |
| 2 | a) produce, independently, pieces of writing using complete sentences, some of them demarcated with capital letters and full stops or question marks. | |
| | b) structure sequences of real or imagined events coherently in chronological accounts. | *An account of a family occasion, a practical task in mathematics or an adventure story.* |
| | c) write stories showing an understanding of the rudiments | *A story with an opening which suggests when or where the action* |

| Level | Statements of attainment | Example |
|---|---|---|

|  | of story structure by establishing an opening, characters, and one or more events. | takes place and which involves more than one character. |
|  | d) produce simple, coherent non-chronological writing. | Lists, captions, invitations, greetings cards, notices, posters etc. |
| 3 | a) produce, independently, pieces of writing using complete sentences, mainly demarcated with capital letters and full stops or question marks. |  |
|  | b) shape chronological writing, beginning to use a wider range of sentence connectives than 'and' and 'then'. | but when after so because |
|  | c) write more complex stories with detail beyond simple events and with a defined ending. | Stories which include a description of setting and the feelings of characters. |
|  | d) produce a range of types of non-chronological writing. | Plans and diagrams, descriptions of a person or place, or notes for an activity in science or design. |
|  | e) begin to revise and redraft in discussion with the teacher, other adults, or other children in the class, paying attention to meaning and clarity as well as checking for matters such as correct and consistent use of tenses and pronouns. |  |
| 4 | a) produce, independently, pieces of writing showing evidence of a developing ability to structure what is written in ways that make the meaning clear to the reader; demonstrate in their writing that they have understood the use of sentence punctuation. | Make use of titles, paragraphs or verses, capital letters, full stops, question marks and exclamation marks; setting out and punctuating direct speech. |
|  | b) write stories which have an opening, a setting, characters, a series of events and a resolution and which engage the sympathy and interest of the reader; produce other kinds of chronologically organised writing. | Write, in addition to stories, instructions, accounts or explanations, perhaps of a scientific investigation. |

| Level | Statements of attainment | Example |
|---|---|---|

    c) organise non-chronological writing for different purposes in orderly ways.

*Record in writing an aspect of learning; present information and express feelings in forms such as letters, poems, invitations, etc.*

    d) begin to use the structures of written Standard English and begin to use some sentence structures different from those of speech.

*Make use of a wider range of subordinate clauses and expanded noun phrases.*

    e) discuss the organisation of their own writing; revise and redraft the writing independently in the light of that discussion.

*Talk about content and those features which ensure clarity for the reader.*

**5**

    a) write in a variety of forms for a range of purposes and audiences, in ways which engage the interest of the reader.

*Write notes, letters, instructions, stories and poems in order to plan, inform, explain, entertain and express attitudes or emotions.*

    b) produce, independently, pieces of writing showing evidence of the use of organisational devices, accuracy in sentence punctuation, including commas, and the setting out of direct speech, so as to clarify the meaning for the reader.

*Make use of layout, headings, paragraphs, and verse structure; make use of the comma.*

    c) write in Standard English (except in contexts where non-standard forms are needed for literary purposes) and show an increasing differentiation between speech and writing.

*Understand that non-standard forms for literary purposes might be required in dialogue, in a story or playscript; use constructions which reduce repetition.*

    d) assemble ideas on paper, or on a computer screen, or in discussion with others and show evidence of an ability to produce a draft from them and then to revise and redraft as necessary.

*Draft a story, a script, a poem, a description or a report.*

    e) show in discussion the ability to recognise and choose variations in vocabulary appropriate to purpose, topic and audience and according to whether language is spoken or written.

*Understand the place of slang, formal vocabulary and technical vocabulary.*

# 4 Spelling

There has been some detailed research into what distinguishes good spellers from weak ones. The factors that emerge from this research (see Table 28) will suggest ways in which children can be helped to attain mastery in spelling.

---

**TABLE 28 Factors associated with good spelling**

The following attitudes and skills are crucial to good spelling:

ATTITUDES    *1 A wish to be accurate*, in seeing the extra effort as worthwhile, supported by success, praise and encouragement.
*2 A willingness to check* to see if it 'looks' right, helps overcome slapdash mistakes.
*3 An interest in words* associated with enjoying word games, and a rich variety of language experience.

SKILLS    *1 Visual memory*, being able to visualise word shapes and letter sequences, helps memory for spelling.
*2 Knowledge of common letter sequences* and their phonic sounds helps especially in spelling unfamiliar words.
*3 Fluent joined handwriting* helps children in storing the 'feel' of many words.
*4 Reference techniques and* use of dictionaries are helped by knowing letter sequences and alphabetical order.

---

Various strategies can help support children in their spelling. These include:

- The Look/Think/Cover/Write/Check strategy for learning new words and revising 'problem' words
- encouraging children to 'sound out' words, such as 'sci*ssors*', Wed-nes-day' etc
- training children to use class dictionaries, alphabetical indexes or word banks
- displaying charts of common, topic or irregular words
- learning groups or families of words with common letter strings
- discussing words, their origins and patterns
- encouraging children to invent and check later words they are unsure of
- encouraging children to proofread and to identify some words they may have spelled wrong

- learning common spelling rules such as 'u after q', 'i before e', 'ie = y' at ends of words, the magic 'e'
- offer some memory tricks, mnemonics such as 'b*eau*tiful = beautiful elephants aren't ugly'

In correcting children's work there is less emphasis nowadays on correcting all mistakes, than on encouraging children to check their own spellings or those of their peers, and on using *selective correction* to allow each child to work on a manageable number of key mistakes, such as three or four. Using a spell checker computer program can help draw children's attention to the need for accuracy. The close link with fluency in handwriting is recognised in levels 4 and 5 of the National Curriculum attainment targets for spelling and handwriting, which appear under the heading of *presentation*, and this has much to do with giving children a pride in and control over their work.

## Task 28  Looking for reasons to write

All aspects of children's writing will improve with practice. Development in writing is a matter not only of skill but of attitude. Willing writers, who have a reason to write, will tend to practise more at their writing. It is important therefore to *look for reasons to write* in encouraging children's writing. Try to:

- Identify the *reasons for writing* in the tasks you give to children.
- Discuss with children possible reasons for their writing.
- Think of ways of sharing the writing of all children with a wider audience, such as other children, parents, colleagues and the local community.


## 5  Handwriting

Children need opportunities to develop a comfortable, flowing and legible joined-up style of handwriting. They are more likely to achieve a style which pleases them and those that read their words (especially their peers and parents) if children are supported by clear aims and a consistent handwriting policy in school. The following are some of the aims which might relate to the handwriting policy of a class or school:

- legibility, including the ability to write at different speeds for different purposes
- individual style (or set style of the school/class?)
- correct letter formation
- sensible posture and pen/pencil grip

# TABLE 29  English AT4: Spelling

| Level | Statements of attainment | Example |
|-------|--------------------------|---------|
| | Pupils should be able to: | |
| I | a) begin to show an understanding of the difference between drawing and writing, and between numbers and letters. | |
| | b) write some letter shapes in response to speech sounds and letter names. | *Initial letter of own name.* |
| | c) use at least single letters or groups of letters to represent whole words or parts of words. | |
| 2 | a) produce recognisable (though not necessarily always correct) spelling of a range of common words. | |
| | b) spell correctly, in the course of their own writing, simple monosyllabic words they use regularly which observe common patterns. | *see car man sun hot cold thank* |
| | c) recognise that spelling has patterns, and begin to apply their knowledge of those patterns in their attempts to spell a wider range of words. | *coat goat    feet street* |
| | d) show knowledge of the names and order of the letters of the alphabet. | *Name the letters when spelling out loud from a simple dictionary or word book.* |
| 3 | a) spell correctly, in the course of their own writing, simple polysyllabic words they use regularly which observe common patterns. | *because after open teacher animal together* |
| | b) recognise and use correctly regular patterns for vowel sounds and common letter strings. | *-ing -ion -ous* |

| Level | Statements of attainment | Example |
|---|---|---|
| | c) show a growing awareness of word families and their relationships. | *grow growth growing grown grew* |
| | d) in revising and redrafting their writing, begin to check the accuracy of their spelling. | *Use a simple dictionary, word book, spell checker, or other classroom resources; make spelling books or picture books.* |
| 4 | a) spell correctly, in the course of their own writing, words which display other main patterns of English spelling. | *Words using the main prefixes and suffixes.* |

- appropriate size and proportion of writing, including the ability to write different sizes for different purposes
- constant slant strokes
- constant spacing of words and letters

Planning a policy for handwriting will require answers to various much-debated questions, including:

1   *When to begin joined-up writing (running hand)?* Some schools begin teaching this from the very beginning – reception or year 1 – some begin at the beginning of junior years – year 3 – others begin at variable times according to the 'readiness' of children.
2   *When to use lined or plain paper?* Many teachers encourage children to use ready-ruled guidelines under plain paper for 'best' writing. (They can then decorate the borders for their 'best work'.) It is generally agreed that children need practice in writing on both lined and plain paper.
3   *When to use pen, and which types of pen?* Year 3 is often a time when children are introduced to writing in pen, but again practice varies between schools. Some teachers forbid the use of ball points, others argue that children need practice in writing well with all kinds of pen. Some provide handwriting pens for children, others allow children to use whatever pens are provided from home.

Activities that can form part of a programme which encourages children to practise and develop their presentational skills include:

- illuminating capital letters, and other calligraphic flourishes
- shaping writing in different layouts, curves, patterns, pictures, and to fit illustrations
- writing words as they sound, eg

    *Ghostly writing*

- writing words to look like their meaning, eg calligrams    'LO**O**K'
- studying print types, eg using letters cut from newspapers, magazines etc
- using letters, words in art activities, eg name designs
- speedwriting – how many words per minute? inventing contractions for note-taking
- studying the history of English, the development of writing
- studying other languages – encouraging the sharing of mother tongues

## TABLE 30 English AT5: Handwriting

| Level | | Statements of attainment | Example |
|---|---|---|---|
| | | Pupils should be able to: | |
| 1 | a) | begin to form letters with some control over the size, shape and orientation of letters or lines of writing. | |
| 2 | a) | produce legible upper and lower case letters in one style and use them consistently (ie not randomly mixed within words). | *Produce capital letters and lower case letters which are easily distinguishable.* |
| 3 | a) | begin to produce clear and legible joined-up writing. | |
| | b) | produce letters that are recognisably formed and properly oriented and that have clear ascenders and descenders where necessary. | *b and d,*<br><br>*p and b.* |
| 4 | a) | produce more fluent joined-up writing in independent work. | |

### ATTAINMENT TARGET 4/5: PRESENTATION

| Level | | Statements of attainment | Example |
|---|---|---|---|
| 5 | a) | spell correctly in the course of their own writing, words of increasing complexity. | *Words with inflectional suffixes, such as '-ed' and '-ing,' where consonent doubling (running) or '-e' deletion (coming) are required.* |
| | b) | check final drafts of writing for misspellings. | *Using a dictionary and spell checker when appropriate.* |
| | c) | Produce clear and legible handwriting in printed and cursive styles. | |

# Task 29 Setting the scene for language learning

Consider how best to prepare your classroom environment for language learning. Think how best to stimulate *interest* and encourage *independent learning* in:

- *Writing*

  Is there stimulus for children's writing, for example a writing corner for them to use?

  Is there a selection of suitable materials such as papers, pens, typewriters or a computer available for use?

  Are there examples of various forms of writing and collections of children's work for them to share and respond to?

- *Reading*

  Are book resources well organised and attractively displayed?

  Is there a suitable selection of fiction, non-fiction and reference books?

  Can the children choose books appropriate to their needs?

- *Talking/Listening*

  Are there resources available for children's use that encourage development in talking and listening, for example tape recorders, taped stories/recordings, take-part drama books.

# Unit 8

# MATHEMATICS

> The maths I was taught was boring. I hated it, and couldn't do it.
> I am determined to make it better for the children I teach.
>
> Student teacher

Student teachers, like many adults, often have a fear of teaching mathematics born of fear of the subject itself, or of frustration or a past boredom with the way it was taught. It need not be so. Like all teaching it is hard work, and there are no easy answers, but maths can be made interesting, exciting and even beautiful to teach.

According to HMI reports, most primary schools give high priority to maths and teach it for the equivalent of one day a week (20 per cent of timetable time). The most successful teachers often relate the study of maths to other subjects, especially to science and technology. Maths does not have to be taught in isolation, it can enrich and be enriched by topic work and by other subjects. HMI have found that many children cannot apply their computational skills in practical situations and are 'barely adequate' at estimating. More attention, say HMI, should be given to planning schemes of work, and here the National Curriculum guidelines can offer the teacher much support.

Planning for maths will need to take account of not only the content, but also the organisation of learning. Setting or grouping the children by ability is more common in maths than in any other subject, and it occurs in most classes. Many teachers plan to give extra support and practice to slow learners, and more advanced extension work to the 'high fliers'. HMI found 'there was no evidence that any particular form of organising teaching groups had a direct relationship with the pupils' standard of achievement.' The factors most closely associated with children's confidence and competence in learning was the confidence and competence of their teachers. How does one develop justifiable confidence and competence in maths teaching?

Several important elements can help support confidence in maths teaching. These include:

1   being clear about one's aims and expectations
2   establishing an agreed school policy and scheme of work
3   building up and having access to suitable resources
4   preparing the classroom environment for maths learning
5   selecting appropriate mathematical activities for children
6   developing your teaching role
7   maintaining an effective system of record keeping and assessment

Let us look at these factors in more detail, and review what we should be helping children to learn.

# Building confidence in maths teaching

## 1 Aims and expectations

As in all teaching, the clearer your communication of aims and expectations in maths the more likely it is that children will rise to the challenge of your teaching. The attitudes and qualities you wish to communicate and develop might include:

- an interest in and fascination with the subject
- pleasure and enjoyment from maths activities
- an appreciation of the usefulness of maths
- a sense of achievement from success in maths
- a confidence and willingness to 'have a go' at maths
- a flexibility of approach and creative thinking in maths
- a willingness to persevere with a problem
- a willingness to check for accuracy
- an ability to think for oneself and to work with others
- a systematic approach to work

## Task 30  Assessing aims and expectations in maths

List the aims and expectations you have for your children in maths. Select what you consider to be your three or four most important aims or expectations. Consider how to communicate these to the children in your class.

## 2 Formulating a policy

The formulation of clear plans and policies for maths teaching can help foster confidence in the classroom. The elements of such a policy are outlined in Table 31.

The National Curriculum Attainment targets (pp 109–135) provide a framework for planning but they leave important decisions for the school and teacher to take. These include:

- specifying the amount of time to be spent on maths
- deciding how maths teaching is to be organised
- selecting books and materials to be used in the classroom
- defining a sequence of maths themes, topics or activities
- identifying ways to assess and record pupil progress

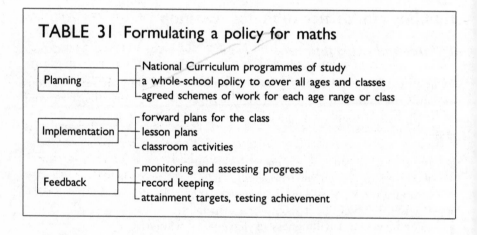

**TABLE 31 Formulating a policy for maths**

Planning
- National Curriculum programmes of study
- a whole-school policy to cover all ages and classes
- agreed schemes of work for each age range or class

Implementation
- forward plans for the class
- lesson plans
- classroom activities

Feedback
- monitoring and assessing progress
- record keeping
- attainment targets, testing achievement

## 3 Resources for teaching

In maths as in other subjects the most important resources are the human ones. Many reports have stressed the value for teachers of utilising the expertise of subject specialists in schools. The motto for the new class teacher is 'You are not alone'; there are usually colleagues at hand able and willing to help and advise when needed. Figure 12 shows some of the sources of support for your maths teaching.

Published schemes of textbooks or workcards may provide an overall structure which ensures continuity and progression. They can also provide a

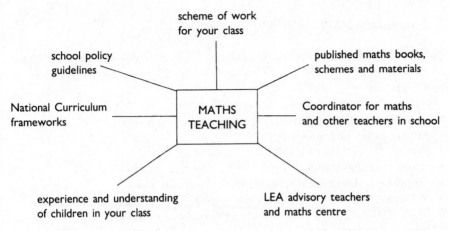

Figure 12 Resources for maths teaching

source of ideas for the teacher to use and develop in her own way. The teachers' manuals of these schemes are often more valuable than the text-books, since they suggest a range of investigations and activities from which teachers can choose and which they can adapt for their own purposes. Up-to-date schemes also relate suggested maths activities to National Curriculum attainment targets and provide a clear guide as to the equipment and materials that need to be available in the classroom.

Maths schemes need to be used with care. Sometimes the maths content is limited in scope, perhaps in presenting too many closed tasks ('not sums again!') and providing little that appeals to children's interests and experiences. One scheme is unlikely to satisfy the mathematical needs of all children. It will need to be extended and supplemented by other activities, games, puzzles and investigations.

## 4 Preparing the environment

The classroom that encourages mathematics needs careful preparation. Children need access to a variety of resources, such as measuring equipment, calculators, counters, puzzles, computer software, different kinds of graph paper. A planned environment should offer stimulus and interest for mathematical thinking, for example displays of interesting objects, puzzles, posters, brainteasers, graphs and diagrams. Sometimes this can be achieved through setting up a maths display area, corner or table which can help to inform, motivate and communicate a sense of what is valued in the classroom.

## 5 Selecting appropriate maths activities

Figure 13 shows some of the modes of learning that can be related to a particular topic in maths. In planning a sheme of work, the teacher should aim for a balance between

- different modes of learning (Figure 13)
- independent and cooperative work
- the use of mental arithmetic and the use of tools such as calculators
- short activities and extended tasks
- applied mathematics and purely mathematical ideas
- subject-based and cross-curricular topics
- activities which have an exact result or answer and those with many possible outcomes
- activities inspired by the teacher and those stimulated by the children's interests and questions

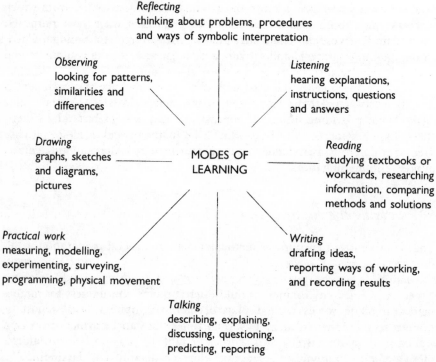

*Reflecting*
thinking about problems, procedures and ways of symbolic interpretation

*Observing*
looking for patterns, similarities and differences

*Listening*
hearing explanations, instructions, questions and answers

*Drawing*
graphs, sketches and diagrams, pictures

MODES OF LEARNING

*Reading*
studying textbooks or workcards, researching information, comparing methods and solutions

*Practical work*
measuring, modelling, experimenting, surveying, programming, physical movement

*Writing*
drafting ideas, reporting ways of working, and recording results

*Talking*
describing, explaining, discussing, questioning, predicting, reporting

Figure 13 Modes of learning

## 6 Developing your teaching role

Part of the fascination of teaching maths is that there is always something new to learn about children's learning and about maths itself, such as a new pattern, puzzle, problem or topic of investigation. Children, like adults, learn maths best when they learn it with and from each other. It is important to give children opportunities to work together, and to show by your example how to value each child's ideas. The teacher is very much a model for her children, and just as you might read with the child, so you might also involve yourself in doing maths in a variety of contexts, for example sharing real-life or school-based applications.

As a teacher you can learn a great deal about children by watching and listening and by asking open-ended questions that stimulate and extend children's thinking – 'What do you think?', 'What are you doing?', 'Can you show me another way?', 'How can you change the problem?', 'What would happen if ...?', 'How can you be sure ...?', 'Is there anything missing?', 'Can you show me how ...?', 'That's interesting, can you explain?'.

Children need time to reflect on what they have done, and help in focusing on what was important about it. Feedback sessions need to be built regularly into the daily routine, so that children can share their ways of working. This will also give you the chance to praise good effort, reinforce good work habits and monitor what the children have learnt.

## 7 Assessing outcomes and keeping records

In assessing the progress of children, it will be important to focus on what they can do, their achievements in mathematics. You will need to take time to observe children at work, and to listen to what they say. Questions to help in your assessment include:

- What areas of maths is the child confident about? How can I develop these further?
- What is the child not confident about? How can I provide a foundation to build on?

There are two fundamental strategies that can be applied to planning and assessment. These are identified in National Curriculum guidelines as *differentiation by task* (strategy 1) and *differentiation by outcome* (strategy 2).

*Strategy 1:* Start with a particular element of study or attainment and design tasks that relate to that element. This is the step-by-step approach common to many published maths schemes, allowing for a systematic approach to covering a programme of study, and providing a narrow focus for teaching and assessment.

*Strategy 2*:  Start with an activity, topic or task which allows for a wide range of possible outcomes, and covers a range of possible attainment targets. A more open-ended and investigative approach should allow different levels to be reached through a single activity, but will present problems in assessing different levels of outcome and achievement.

Both approaches should have a place in a balanced programme of study and assessment. Task 31 illustrates open-ended activities which allow for a range of outcomes and levels of ability.

## Task 31  Planning/assessing a maths investigation

Present an open-ended investigation to a group of children, allowing them to demonstrate their full ability and offering challenges both to bright children and to slow learners. Focus in your assessment of the outcomes on the range of responses, the levels of attainment, and any possibly unexpected abilities shown by your pupils. The following are examples of such open-ended investigations:

- How many different shapes can you make using six squares?
- Make as many numbers as you can up to 20 (or beyond) using only 1, 2, 3, 4 and the signs $+ - \times \div$ (use a calculator to help).
- If five people each shook each other's hands, how many handshakes would there be?

Reflect on what teaching strategies would support children in this kind of problem-solving work.

Good mathematics teaching involves providing a purpose for children's learning, putting the mathematics wherever possible into a meaningful context – showing its links with other areas of learning, and its relevance to real-life situations. Questions to consider include:

- Do your children know why mathematics is important in the world? Who needs maths?
- Do they think that learning maths is important for their own lives? Do they need maths?
- Can they find maths around them in the world, eg in a newspaper?
- Can they pose mathematical questions, eg can they think of ten maths questions to ask about an empty box?

- Can they estimate answers, eg how tall is the door, how many beans are in a can?
- Can they use different ways to work out and check answers, eg mental estimation/calculation, pencil and paper methods, calculator?
- Can they record maths in different ways – in words, pictures, diagrams, tables and symbols?
- Can they create their own mathematical problems, puzzles and challenges, for themselves or others to solve?
- Can they think of ways of helping others such as younger children to learn maths, eg inventing maths games?
- Can they think of ways to help themselves/each other to learn maths?

Children can also be encouraged to monitor their own maths, for example by selecting samples of work to keep as a record of their progress, or keeping a maths diary to record their activities and responses. Record keeping is important to keep a track of development and provide a basis for assessment reports for parents and colleagues. These will include checklists, samples of work and notes on your observations. They will also provide a basis for future planning. (See Unit 15 for more on assessment.)

## Task 32  Assessing your own teaching

In assessing your own teaching, consider the balance of:

- individual, group and classwork
- time children spend practising old, and learning new, skills and knowledge
- use of practical, oral and written investigation and problem-solving activities
- use of range of books, maths instruments, calculators, computers
- your use of the interests of individual children, eg topic work

# The maths curriculum

The National Curriculum provides a framework for planning. It divides the mathematics curriculum into five broad areas – number, algebra, measurement, shape and space, and data handling, and identifies within these areas 14 attainment targets, listed in Table 32.

## Number

Number is the most important aspect of the maths curriculum. Learning about number involves understanding the number system and how it works,

---

## TABLE 32 Attainment targets in maths and associated statements of attainment

Knowledge, skills, understanding and use of number, algebra and measures

| | | |
|---|---|---|
| **AT1** | Using and applying mathematics | Use number, algebra and measures in practical tasks, in real-life problems, and to investigate within mathematics itself. |
| **AT2** | Number | Understand number and number notation. |
| **AT3** | Number | Understand number operations (addition, subtraction, multiplication and division) and make use of appropriate methods of calculation. |
| **AT4** | Number | Estimate and approximate in number. |
| **AT5** | Number/Algebra | Recognise and use patterns, relationships and sequences, and make generalisations. |
| **AT6** | Algebra | Recognise and use functions, formulae, equations and inequalities. |
| **AT7** | Algebra | Use graphical representation of algebraic functions. |
| **AT8** | Measures | Estimate and measure quantities, and appreciate the approximate nature of measurement. |

Knowledge, skills, understanding and use of shape and space and data handling

| | | |
|---|---|---|
| **AT9** | Using and applying mathematics | Use shape and space and handle data in practical tasks, in real-life problems, and to investigate within mathematics itself. |
| **AT10** | Shape and space | Recognise and use the properties of two-dimensional and three-dimensional shapes. |
| **AT11** | Shape and space | Recognise location and use transformations in the study of space. |
| **AT12** | Handling data | Collect, record and process data. |
| **AT13** | Handling data | Represent and interpret data. |
| **AT14** | Handling data | Understand, estimate and calculate probabilities. |

*Note:* Statements of attainment are given below for levels 1–5 in the National Curriculum. Some juniors may of course reach levels 6 or above.

knowing about the relative sizes of numbers, having the ability to estimate the approximate outcome of a calculation, and using number in practical tasks (see Figure 14).

One of the most important ways of calculating is 'in your head' – mental arithmetic. The Cockroft Report (1982) stated 'that the decline of mental and oral work within mathematics classrooms represents a failure to recognise the central place which "working in the head" occupies throughout mathema-

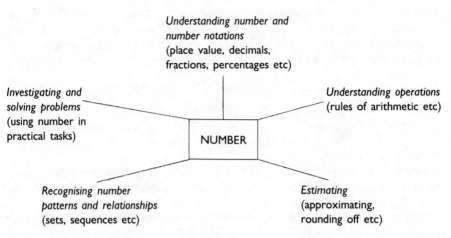

Understanding number and
number notations
(place value, decimals,
fractions, percentages etc)

Investigating and
solving problems
(using number in
practical tasks)

Understanding operations
(rules of arithmetic etc)

NUMBER

Recognising number
patterns and relationships
(sets, sequences etc)

Estimating
(approximating,
rounding off etc)

*Figure 14 Number*

tics.' Time needs to be set aside, on a regular basis, to talk about numbers, to develop and use mental strategies for adding, subtracting, multiplying and dividing. Work with real objects such as money can provide valuable opportunities for mental calculation, as can number games, puzzles, problems and investigations.

Calculators can be used for operations which are too difficult to carry out in the head, and to check the accuracy of pencil-and-paper methods. Both the calculator and computer can be used to investigate number patterns and relationships. Children need opportunities to work on practical, real-life problems such as shopping and cooking. They also need encouragement to explore numbers in their own right, for example looking for and creating number patterns or numbers with special properties like even, square or prime.

Pencil and paper are useful for jotting down the stages of a calculation, for representing number problems in words or diagrams, or for recording and displaying results. The following is an example of an investigation which can be tackled in different ways – mentally, using pencil and paper, or with a calculator:

Using the numbers and symbols ☐1 ☐2 ☐3 ☐4 ☐5 ☐× ☐= once only, what is the largest product that can be made?
Can you make it in different ways?

Often in the past maths work was presented only as a series of 'closed' tasks – of sums with right answers. There is certainly value in practising recently learned skills in a purposeful way. But sometimes the 'closed' tasks presented in textbooks and workcards can be modified to present more challenging 'open' activities. For example:

| Closed task | Modified 'open' task |
|---|---|
| 2 + 5 − 3 | What numbers can you make from 2, 5 and 3 |
| 5 × 3 = | Make up some questions whose answer is 15 |
| Continue this sequence 1, 2, 4 ... | How might this sequence continue? 1, 2, 4 ... |

What is important at all levels is for children to be encouraged to develop *their own methods* (or algorithms) for doing calculations, and to try a range of ways of tackling problems.

The National Curriculum attainment targets for number work are shown in Tables 33–36.

## Algebra

The foundations of algebra are laid through the use of number patterns, relationships and sequences (see attainment target 5). The child who says 'It doesn't matter which you multiply first, the answer is the same,' has generalised a law of arithmetic which applies to symbols (algebra) as well as numbers. Children need to explore and generalise number patterns, for example triangular numbers etc, and be helped to see the relationship between them. They need to describe them verbally, pictorially or with the use of symbols. They need also to recognise and use functions and equations (attainment target 6), for example inputs and outputs from a simple function machine such as:

(Input) 3 → 5 (Output)
7 → 9
4 → 6 etc

What is happening to the numbers, what is the function of →?
Invent your own input/output machine.

This can lead on to the third area of algebra – representing results of number patterns and functions in graphical form (attainment target 7).

---

## TABLE 33  Maths AT1: Using and applying mathematics

Pupils should use number, algebra and measures in practical tasks, in real-life problems, and to investigate within mathematics itself.

| Level | Statements of attainment | Example |
|---|---|---|
| | Pupils should: | |
| 1 | ● use materials provided for a task. | Compare objects to find which is the longest, tallest, etc. |
| | ● talk about own work and ask questions. | Talk about a set of objects being compared; ask questions such as: 'Which is the longest pencil?' |
| | ● make predictions based on experience. | Use a balance to compare objects; predict which of two objects will be the heavier. |
| 2 | ● select the materials and the mathematics to use for a task. | Use handspans to measure the length of a table. |
| | ● describe current work, record findings and check results. | Devise stories for adding and subtracting numbers up to 10 and check with a calculator or apparatus. |
| | ● ask and respond to the question: 'What would happen if . . .?' | Predict whether the contents of a cylinder will fill a cylinder of different dimensions. |
| 3 | ● select the materials and the mathematics to use for a task; | Estimate the distance around the school hall; select appropriate method |

| Level | Statements of attainment | Example |
|---|---|---|

check results and consider whether they are sensible.
- explain work being done and record findings systematically.
- make and test predictions.

*for measuring and units to be used; measure and compare the results. Sketch a plan of the school hall and enter measurements made.*

*Predict the number of cubes needed to construct this figure and test the prediction.*

**4**
- select the materials and the mathematics to use for a task; plan work methodically.
- record findings and present them in oral, written or visual form as appropriate.

- use examples to test statements or definitions.

*Devise a seating plan for a school concert using a system of coordinates for numbering tickets.*
*Explore the last digits of the multiples of various numbers: 8, 16, 24, 32, 40, 48, . . .; record and present the results.*
*Test the statement: 'If you add the house numbers of three houses next to one another you always get a multiple of 3', for various examples.*
$$34 + 36 + 38 = 108 = 3 \times 36$$
$$81 + 83 + 85 = 249 = 3 \times 83$$

**5**
- select the materials and the mathematics to use for a task; check there is sufficient information; work methodically and review progress.
- interpret mathematical information presented in oral, written or visual form.
- make and test simple statements.

*Design a board game that makes use of coordinates in all four quadrants.*

*Use bus and train timetables to plan a journey.*

*Explore the results of multiplying together the house numbers of adjacent houses*
*(eg 6 × 4 = 24   7 × 9 = 63*
*8 × 10 = 80   5 × 7 = 35);*
*make a statement about the results and check using a calculator.*

# TABLE 34  Maths AT2: Number

Pupils should understand number and number notation.

| Level | Statements of attainment | Example |
|---|---|---|
| | Pupils should: | |
| 1 | • count, read, write and order numbers to at least 10; know that the size of a set is given by the last number in the count. | |
| | • understand the conservation of number. | Know that if a set of 8 pencils is counted, the answer is always the same however they are arranged. |
| 2 | • read, write and order numbers to at least 100; use the knowledge that the tens-digit indicates the number of tens. | Know that 37 means 3 tens and 7 units; know that three 10p coins and four 1p coins give 34p. |
| | • understand the meaning of 'a half' and 'a quarter'. | Find a quarter of a piece of string; know that half of 8 is 4. |
| 3 | • read, write and order numbers to at least 1000; use the knowledge that the position of a digit indicates its value. | Know that 'four hundred and two' is written 402 and why neither 42 nor 4002 is correct. |
| | • use decimal notation as the conventional way of recording in money. | Know that three £1 coins plus six 1p coins is written as £3.06, and that 3.6 on a calculator means £3.60 in the context of money. |
| | • appreciate the meaning of negative whole numbers in familiar contexts. | Read a temperature scale; understand a negative output on a calculator. |
| 4 | • read, write and order whole numbers. | |
| | • understand the effect of multiplying a whole number by 10 or 100. | Explain why the cost of 10 objects costing £23 each is £230. |
| | • use, with understanding, decimal notation to two decimal places in the context of measurement. | Read scales marked in hundredths and numbered in tenths (1.89 m). |
| | • recognise and understand simple everyday fractions. | Estimate $\frac{1}{3}$ of a pint of milk or $\frac{3}{4}$ of the length of a piece of wood. |
| | • recognise and understand simple percentages. | Know that 7 books out of a total of 100 books represents 7%. |

| Level | Statements of attainment | Example |
|---|---|---|
| | • understand and use the relationship between place values in whole numbers. | Know that 5000 is 5 thousands or 50 hundreds or 500 tens or 5000 ones. |
| 5 | • use index notation to express powers of whole numbers. | Know that $2^5 = 2 \times 2 \times 2 \times 2 \times 2$. |
| | • use unitary ratios. | Use a ratio of 1:50 for drawing a plan of the classroom. |

## TABLE 35  Maths AT3: Number

Pupils should understand number operations (addition, subtraction, multiplication and division) and make use of appropriate methods of calculation.

| Level | Statements of attainment | Example |
|---|---|---|
| | Pupils should: | |
| 1 | • add or subtract, using objects where the numbers involved are no greater than 10. | Add to or remove from a set of everyday objects. |
| 2 | • know and use addition and subtraction facts up to 10. | Know that if 6 pencils are taken from a box of 10, there will be 4 left. |
| | • compare two numbers to find the difference. | Find the difference between 7 and 3. |
| | • solve whole number problems involving addition and subtraction, including money. | Work out the change from 20p when two biscuits costing 5p and 7p are purchased. |
| 3 | • know and use addition and subtraction number facts to 20 (including zero). | State that the date of the next Friday after Friday 8 May must be 15 May. |
| | • solve problems involving multiplication or division of whole numbers or money, using a calculator where necessary. | Find the cost of four calculators at £2.45 each. |
| | • know and use multiplication facts up to 5 × 5, and all those in 2, 5 and 10 multiplication tables. | Know that if tickets cost £4 each, only 4 can be bought with £18. |

| Level | Statements of attainment | Example |
|---|---|---|
| 4 | ● know multiplication facts up to 10 × 10 and use them in multiplication and division problems. | *Calculate mentally that there are 63 days in 9 full weeks.* |
| | ● (using whole numbers) add or subtract mentally two 2-digit numbers; add mentally several single-digit numbers; without a calculator add and subtract two 3-digit numbers, multiply a 2-digit number by a single-digit number and divide a 2-digit number by a single-digit number. | *Work out without a calculator how much longer 834 mm is than 688 mm. Work out mentally how much heavier an object weighing 75 kg is than one weighing 48 kg.* |
| | ● solve addition or subtraction problems using numbers with no more than two decimal places; solve multiplication or division problems starting with whole numbers. | *Work out how many chocolate bars can be bought for £5 if each costs 19p, and how much change there will be.* |
| 5 | ● (using whole numbers) understand and use non-calculator methods by which a 3-digit number is multiplied by a 2-digit number and a 3-digit number is divided by a 2-digit number. | |
| | ● calculate fractions and percentages of quantities using a calculator where necessary. | *Calculate 15% of £320; ³/₅ of 170 m; 37% of £234; ¹/₁₀ of 2m.* |
| | ● multiply and divide mentally single-digit multiples of powers of 10 with whole number answers. | *Calculate 70 × 100 leading to 70 × 500 = 35000; 800 ÷ 10 leading to 800 ÷ 20 = 40.* |
| | ● use negative numbers in context. | *Calculate the increase in temperature from −4°C (4 degrees of frost) to +10°C.* |

# TABLE 36  Maths AT4: Number

Pupils should estimate and approximate in number.

| Level | Statements of attainment | Example |
|---|---|---|
| | Pupils should: | |
| 1 | • give a sensible estimate of a small number of objects (up to 10). | *Estimate the number of apples in a bag.* |
| 2 | • make a sensible estimate of a number of objects up to 20. | *Estimate the number of coats on the coat pegs.* |
| 3 | • recognise that the first digit is the most important in indicating the size of a number, and approximate to the nearest 10 or 100. | *Know that 37 is roughly 40.* |
| | • understand 'remainders' given the context of calculation, and know whether to round up or down. | *Know that if egg boxes each hold 6 eggs, 4 boxes will be needed for 20 eggs, and if 3 boxes are filled the fourth box will have 2 eggs.* |
| 4 | • make use of estimation and approximation to check the validity of addition and subtraction calculations. | *Estimate that 1472 – 383 is about 1100.* |
| | • read a calculator display to the nearest whole number. | |
| | • know how to interpret results on a calculator which have rounding errors. | *Interpret $7 \div 3 \times 3 = 6.9999999$ if it occurs on a calculator.* |
| 5 | • use and refine 'trial and improvement' methods. | *Find the edge of a cube whose volume is $100 \text{ cm}^3$ in the following way: $4^3 = 64$; $5^3 = 125$ so the side is more than 4 cm, but less than 5 cm. As $4.5^3 = 91.125$, the side is greater than 4.5 cm etc.* |
| | • approximate using a specified number of significant figures or decimal places. | *Read a calculator display, approximating to 3 significant figures.* |

# TABLE 37  Maths AT5: Number/Algebra

Pupils should recognise and use patterns, relationships and sequences and make generalisations.

| Level | Statements of attainment | Example |
|---|---|---|
| | Pupils should: | |
| 1 | ● copy, continue and devise repeating patterns represented by objects/apparatus or one-digit numbers. | *Continue a threading bead pattern: red, red, blue, red, red, blue, . . . Continue the pattern 2, 1, 2, 1, 2, 1, 2, 1, . . .* |
| 2 | ● explore and use the patterns in addition and subtraction facts to 10. | *Use counters to make various combinations to given totals.* $5 + 0 = 5$   $5 = 4 + 1$ $4 + 1 = 5$   $= 3 + 2$ $3 + 2 = 5$   $= 3 + 1 + 1$ $2 + 3 = 5$   $= 2 + 2 + 1$ *etc.* $1 + 4 = 5$ $0 + 5 = 5$ |
| | ● distinguish between odd and even numbers. | |
| 3 | ● explain number patterns and predict subsequent numbers where appropriate. | *Continue:*   5, 10, 15, 20, . . . *Continue:*   $4 + 10 = 14,$ $14 + 10 = 24,$ $24 + 10 = 34, . . .$ |
| | ● find number patterns and equivalent forms of 2-digit numbers and use these to perform mental calculations. | $27 + 31 = 20 + 7 + 30 + 1$ $= 50 + 8$ $= 58.$ $35 + 29 = 35 + 30 - 1$ $= 65 - 1$ $= 64$ |
| | ● recognise whole numbers which are exactly divisible by 2, 5 and 10. | |
| 4 | ● apply strategies, such as doubling and halving, to explore properties of numbers, including equivalence of fractions. | *Recognise that* $23 \times 8 = 46 \times 4 = 92 \times 2 = 184 \times 1$ *and* $\frac{2}{3} = \frac{4}{6} = \frac{6}{9} = \frac{8}{12} = . . .$ . . . |
| | ● generalise, mainly in words, patterns which arise in various situations. | *Understand the patterns in addition and multiplication tables, including symmetry of results and relationships* |

| Level | Statements of attainment | Example |
|---|---|---|
| | | between multiplication by 2, 4 and 8 etc. |
| | | Construct matchstick squares, using an appropriate number of matchsticks to make 1, 2, 3, 4, . . . squares. |
| 5 | • understand and use terms such as prime, square, cube, square root, cube root, multiples and factors. | Find all the primes between 0 and 100. Is there a pattern? |
| | • recognise patterns in numbers through spatial arrangements. | Recognise square and triangular numbers and the relationship between them. |
| | • follow simple sets of instructions to generate sequences. | Produce a sequence in which the third or any subsequent number is the sum of the previous two numbers. Understand the program: 10 FOR NUMBER = 1 TO 10 20 PRINTNUMBER*NUMBER 30 NEXT NUMBER 40 END. |

## TABLE 38 Maths AT6: Algebra

Pupils should recognise and use functions, formulae, equations and inequalities.

| Level | Statements of attainment | Example |
|---|---|---|
| | Pupils should: | |
| 2 | • understand the use of a symbol to stand for an unknown number. | Find the number to be inserted in the box to make the statement $3 + \square = 10$ true. |
| 3 | • deal with inputs to and outputs from simple function machines. | INPUT (machine) OUTPUT $3 \rightarrow 5$ $7 \rightarrow 9$ $4 \rightarrow 6$ Describe what is happening to the left-hand numbers to get the numbers |

| Level | Statements of attainment | Example |
|-------|--------------------------|---------|
| | | on the right-hand side. (What is the function?) <br> Use doubling and halving, adding and subtracting, FORWARD and BACKWARD (in LOGO) etc, as inverse operations. |
| 4 | • understand and use simple formulae or equations expressed in words. | Recognise the relationship (function) between the corresponding members in the sets: <br> $\{ 2,3,10 \} \rightarrow \{ 21,31,101 \}$ <br> (ie multiply a number by 10 and add 1). <br> Solve a problem such as: 'If I double a number, then add 1 and the result is 49, what is the number?' |
| | • recognise that multiplication and division are inverse operations and use this to check calculations. | Know that if $43 \times 8 = 344$ then $344 \div 8 = 43$. |
| 5 | • understand and use simple formulae or equations expressed in symbolic form. | Use the fact that the perimeter $p$ of a rectangle is given by $p = 2(a + b)$ where $a$ and $b$ are the dimensions. |
| | • express a simple function symbolically. | Know that $a \times b$ is written as ab. If cakes cost 15p each then write $c = 15 \times n$ (or 15n) where $c$ pence is the total cost and $n$ is the number of cakes. |

## Measurement

The study of measurement is concerned with developing an understanding of the sizes of units needed to measure quantities such as length, area, volume, capacity, weight and time. It is important that children recognise the limitations of the accuracy of measurement – all measurement is approximate, even when sophisticated measuring equipment is used.

Children begin learning measurement by making direct comparisons without using units, for example comparing length of sticks, height of children, weight of two parcels. The next stage is often to match quantities using

---

## TABLE 39  Maths AT7: Algebra

Pupils should use graphical representation of algebraic functions.

| Level | Statements of attainment<br>Pupils should: | Example |
|---|---|---|
| 4 | • know the conventions of the coordinate representation of points; work with coordinates in the first quadrant. | Plot points; draw diagrams. Create shapes by using DRAW and MOVE commands in BASIC in the appropriate graphics mode, or by using LOGO commands. Draw graphs as required by other attainment targets. |
| 5 | • understand and use coordinates in all four quadrants. | Plot points and draw lines and figures, using the four quadrants. |

---

non-standard units such as handspans, footsteps or drinking straws, then standard units like centimetres or kilograms.

The best measuring tasks will have a genuine purpose which the children can understand, for example finding the best value for money by comparing chocolate bars. Understanding measurement involves choosing an appropriate unit and suitable measuring device. For example what would you choose to measure the playground, the length of a book or the weight of a tin? Since some imperial units such as miles and gallons are still in use, children will need to become familiar with these as well as with metric units. They will need to know imperial/metric equivalents, for example that there are approximately 30 cm in 1 foot, 5 km in 8 miles, 25 g in 1 oz and 5 litres in one gallon.

Children need help in recognising the nature of what is being measured, for example by understanding properties of conservation – that when an object changes shape it is as heavy as before. Which is heavier – a ton of feathers or a ton of potatoes? They will need to be introduced to a range of measuring equipment and taught how to 'read off' measures in both digital form (such as digital clocks or electricity meters) and analogue form (clock faces, linear scales and dials). They will need to devise ways of measuring non-standard items such as wavy lines, and understand that measurement is never exact and that different degrees of accuracy are needed in different circumstances. (What do you do with the 'bit left over'?) They will need practice in estimating and predicting measurements – and in ways of checking results.

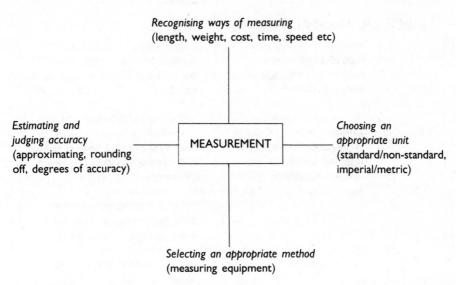

Figure 15 Measurement

---

## TABLE 40  Maths AT8: Measures

Pupils should estimate and measure quantities, and appreciate the approximate nature of measurement.

| Level | Statements of attainment<br>Pupils should: | Example |
|---|---|---|
| 1 | • compare and order objects without measuring, and use appropriate language. | *Use language such as: long, longer than, longest; tall, taller than, tallest; heavy, light; before, after; hot, cold.* |
| 2 | • use non-standard measures in length, area, volume, capacity, 'weight' and time to compare objects and recognise the need to use standard units. | *Use handspans, strips of paper, conkers, etc. as measures.* |
|  | • know how to use coins in simple contexts. | *Handle money – shopping activities in the classroom.* |

| Level | Statements of attainment | Example |
|---|---|---|
| | • know the most commonly used units in length, capacity, 'weight' and time, and what they are used for. | Suggest things which are commonly measured in metres, miles, litres, pints, pounds, seconds, minutes, hours etc. |
| 3 | • use a wider range of metric units. | Use centimetre, kilometre, gram. |
| | • choose and use appropriate units and instruments in a variety of situations, interpreting numbers on a range of measuring instruments. | Use an appropriate tape/ruler to compare lengths that cannot be put side by side. |
| | | Read digital clocks correctly and analogue clocks to the nearest labelled division. Read a speedometer on a car or bicycle correctly. |
| | • make estimates based on familiar units. | Estimate the height of a door in metres, the capacity of a bottle in litres, or a period of time. |
| 4 | • understand the relationship between units. | Use two units such as millilitres and litres to measure the capacity of the same jug. |
| | • find areas by counting squares, and volumes by counting cubes, using whole numbers. | Find the approximate area of a leaf; work out the approximate volume of a small box. |
| | • make sensible estimates of a range of measures in relation to everyday objects or events. | Estimate the length of a car, the capacity of a teacup, the 'weight' of a school bag. Use timetables to anticipate time of arrival. Estimate the time taken to complete a task. |
| 5 | • understand the notion of scale in maps and drawings. | Draw a plan of a classroom on a scale of 1 cm to 1 m. |
| | • use Imperial units still in daily use and know their rough metric equivalents. | Recall that 1 kg is about 2 lb, 8 km is approximately 5 miles, 1 litre is about 1.75 pints. |
| | • convert from one metric unit to another. | Work out that 2.4 kg is equivalent to 2400 g. |
| | • measure and draw angles to the nearest degree. | |

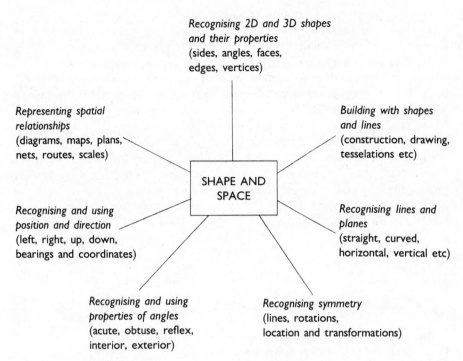

Recognising 2D and 3D shapes
and their properties
(sides, angles, faces,
edges, vertices)

Representing spatial
relationships
(diagrams, maps, plans,
nets, routes, scales)

Building with shapes
and lines
(construction, drawing,
tesselations etc)

SHAPE AND
SPACE

Recognising and using
position and direction
(left, right, up, down,
bearings and coordinates)

Recognising lines and
planes
(straight, curved,
horizontal, vertical etc)

Recognising and using
properties of angles
(acute, obtuse, reflex,
interior, exterior)

Recognising symmetry
(lines, rotations,
location and transformations)

Figure 16 Shape and space

## Shape and space

The exploration of shape and space is the subject matter of geometry. Shape involves the study of the special properties of solids (3D shapes), figures (2D shapes) and lines, and what can be done with them. From their earliest years children explore the properties of shapes and spatial relationships by playing with shaped objects, building with them, moving them and fitting them together – as well as demolishing and breaking them.

Children find many ways to describe shapes – 'it's sort of loopy all round!'. Gradually as they get older their descriptions become more refined, less ambiguous. 2D shapes are eventually described in terms of their faces (flat surfaces), edges (where two faces meet) and vertices (corners). For example at the end of the junior stage a child should be able to define a cube in terms of it being a regular solid, having six square faces, eight vertices and 12 edges of equal length.

The child's exploration of space begins with activities like moving, climbing, touching, sliding, finding how to get into, out of, round and through things. The language of position gradually develops – 'next to', 'in front of', 'behind' – and becomes more refined. Children are able to communicate direction and position with greater precision and power of expression. *Where is it? How do you get there?* are questions which encourage this.

One way for children to explore space is to use the computer, tracing the path of a moving point using a screen or floor turtle (LOGO). Computer programs such as LOGO can show geometric transformations such as translation (sliding along), reflection (mirror images), rotation (turning), or enlargement and reduction of shapes and objects in space.

Children need to be taught how to choose and use geometrical instruments to measure, draw or construct with accuracy, for example drawing circles, measuring lines and angles. By the end of the junior stage children should be able to draw and name parts of shapes, for example the parts of a circle (centre, radius, diameter, circumference, chord, arc, sector and segment).

## TABLE 41  Maths AT9: Using and applying mathematics

Pupils should use shape and space and handle data in practical tasks, in real-life problems, and to investigate within mathematics itself.

| Level | Statements of attainment | Example |
|-------|--------------------------|---------|
| | Pupils should: | |
| I | ● use materials provided for a task. | Make a collection of 3-D shapes from linking cubes. |
| | ● talk about own work and ask questions. | Make up and tell stories about the 3-D shapes; ask questions such as: 'Which is the longest?' |
| | ● make predictions based on experience. | Gain experience of the pattern of the school day; predict when the class will be in the hall for music and dance. |
| 2 | ● select the materials and the mathematics to use for a task. | Sort and classify a collection of coloured plane shapes using own criteria. |
| | ● describe current work, record findings and check results. | Describe how the classification of shapes was made and check the results. |
| | ● ask and respond to the question: 'What would happen if . . .?' | Discuss a block graph showing the ways children in the class came to school that morning; respond to the |

| Level | Statements of attainment | Example |
|-------|--------------------------|---------|
| | | question: 'How will the graph change if there are no buses running tomorrow?' |
| 3 | • select the materials and the mathematics to use for a task; check results and consider whether they are sensible. | Design and make a weather vane which involves reflective symmetry; test the weather vane and modify if necessary. |
| | • explain work being done and record findings systematically. | Keep a record of wind direction over a period of time; display the results in an appropriate chart and discuss the findings. |
| | • make and test predictions. | Experiment with a collection of dice with different numbers of coloured faces; predict the outcomes of rolling each die 50 times and test the predictions. |
| 4 | • select the materials and the mathematics to use for a task; plan work methodically. | Classify a set of plane shapes by considering line and rotational symmetry; present the results on a suitable display or chart. |
| | • record findings and present them in oral, written or visual form as appropriate. | Plan alternative layouts of furniture for the classroom, making use of squared paper; use coordinates to record the results. |
| | • use examples to test statements or definitions. | Use linking cubes to explore the variety of 3-D shapes that can be made from a given number of cubes; test the validity of various statements such as: 'There are two different shapes that can be made from three cubes'. |
| 5 | • select the materials and the mathematics to use for a task; check there is sufficient information; work methodically and review progress. | Devise a survey to investigate the ages of cars passing the school by noting registration numbers; carry out the survey, discuss awkward cases (eg personalised number plates) and analyse results. |
| | • interpret mathematical information presented in oral, written or visual form. | Collect and display a range of charts, diagrams and graphs gathered from newspapers; interpret the information |

| Level | Statements of attainment | Example |
|---|---|---|
| | | contained in the display; discuss possible headlines to accompany different graphs. |

| Level | Statements of attainment | Example |
|---|---|---|
| | ● make and test simple statements. | Make and test a statement such as: 'Most cars passing the school are over 3 years old'. |

# TABLE 42  Maths AT10: Shape and space

Pupils should recognise and use the properties of two-dimensional and three-dimensional shapes.

| Level | Statements of attainment | Example |
|---|---|---|
| | Pupils should: | |
| 1 | ● sort 3-D and 2-D shapes. | Sort a collection of objects of various shapes and sizes. |
| | ● build with 3-D solid shapes and draw 2-D shapes and describe them. | Make various constructions from a range of materials. |
| 2 | ● recognise squares, rectangles, circles, triangles, hexagons, pentagons, cubes, rectangular boxes (cuboids), cylinders, spheres, and describe them. | Create pictures and patterns using 2-D shapes or 3-D objects. Select from a collection of 3-D objects those which have at least one flat surface. |
| | ● recognise right-angled corners in 2-D and 3-D shapes. | |

| Level | Statements of attainment | Example |
|---|---|---|
| 3 | • sort 2-D and 3-D shapes in different ways and give reasons for each method of sorting. | *Sort shapes with a square corner, shapes with curved edges, shapes with equal sides or faces.* |
| 4 | • understand and use language associated with angle. | *Know acute, obtuse and reflex angles, parallel, perpendicular, vertical and horizontal, etc.* |
| | • construct simple 2-D and 3-D shapes from given information and know associated language. | *Construct triangles, rectangles, circles, nets for cubes, pyramids and prisms.* |
| 5 | • understand congruence of simple shapes. | *Group together congruent shapes from a range of shapes.* |
| | • explain and use angle properties associated with intersecting and parallel lines and triangles, and know associated language. | *Identify equal angles in a diagram.* |

## TABLE 43  Maths AT11: Shape and space

Pupils should recognise location and use transformations in the study of space.

| Level | Statements of attainment | Example |
|---|---|---|
| | Pupils should: | |
| 1 | • state a position using prepositions such as: on, inside, above, under, behind, next to, etc. | |
| | • give and understand instructions for moving along a line. | *Follow directions in a PE lesson.* |
| 2 | • understand the notion of angle. | *Rotate body through 1, 2, 3, 4 right-angles.* |
| | • give and understand instructions for turning through right-angles. | *Turn to left or right on instruction (PE games or LOGO).* |
| | • recognise different types of movement: straight movement (translation); turning movement | *Explore patterns in art and PE.* |

| Level | Statements of attainment | Example |
|---|---|---|
| | (rotation); flip movement (reflection). | |
| 3 | • recognise the (reflective) symmetry in a variety of shapes in 2 and 3 dimensions. | Study shapes and identify some lines and planes of symmetry. |
| | • understand eight points of the compass; use clockwise and anti-clockwise appropriately. | Describe wind direction from a weather vane. |
| 4 | • specify location by means of coordinates (in first quadrant) and by means of angle and distance. | Locate features on an ordinance survey map, given their grid references; use LOGO commands for distance and direction. |
| | • recognise rotational symmetry. | Turn shapes using tracing paper. |
| 5 | • identify the symmetries of various shapes. | Find the centres, axes and planes of symmetry in a variety of plane and solid shapes. |
| | • use networks to solve problems. | Find the shortest route for a person delivering post. |
| | • specify location by means of coordinates in the four quadrants. | Plot the vertices of a triangle (3,2), (−1,5), (−2, −6). |

## Data handling

Data handling is concerned with collecting, recording and processing statistical information, and in assessing probabilities. You can help children to develop an interest and skill in statistical work by involving them in activities which have a meaning and purpose. Topic work will often provide opportunities to gather statistics. With your help the children need to:

- establish their purpose for gathering statistics
- decide what data they require
- discuss how accurate it needs to be or can be

- find out where they can get it from
- plan how to collect the data
- decide on how to record it
- analyse, summarise and interpret their results

Once the data has been stored, children can be encouraged to formulate questions or hypotheses that they can answer by searching through, sorting and selecting from their collected data. You will need to help them develop their skills in representing the outcomes of their searches through varied forms of representation such as diagrams, charts, tables, and graphs. Computers can be a great help here in providing simple database facilities and in providing a powerful means of displaying results.

Children's statistical judgement can be developed by providing opportunities for them to analyse the data collected by others, and comparing it with their own, for example as a result of doing opinion surveys in class. Children can also be introduced to statistics published in newspapers, reference books (*The Guiness Book of Records* is a mine of information) and magazines. Discuss the quality of the data, and look for evidence of bias and distortion. Should you believe everything you read?

In human affairs and the physical world some events are certain (it will get dark tonight), some are impossible (I will be 21 tomorrow), and with most there is a degree of uncertainty (is it going to rain tomorrow?). Children should be helped to understand, estimate and calculate varying degrees of probability, for example they could collect weather statistics for a particular month and work out the probability of having rain on any particular day. What are the chances of tossing a coin to get heads twice in a row? By the end of the junior stage children should be able to justify their estimates of probabilities in a range of events, and understand the probability scale from 0−1:

```
0                            |              1
_____|_____

    no chance  poor chance   even chance   good chance   certain
```

What for example is the probability that the next car to pass the school will be a British car? What is the probability of picking an orange Smartie from a box of Smarties?

# TABLE 44 Maths AT12: Handling data

Pupils should collect, record and process data.

| Level | Statements of attainment | Example |
|---|---|---|
| | Pupils should: | |
| 1 | • select criteria for sorting a set of objects and apply consistently. | |
| 2 | • choose criteria to sort and classify objects; record results of observations or outcomes of events. | Identify those children who walk to school and those who travel by bus or car. |
| | • help to design a data collection sheet and use it to record a set of data leading to a frequency table. | Record the number and type of birds visiting the bird table:<br>Blackbird   XX        2<br>Sparrow    XXXXX  5<br>Robin       X          1<br>Blue Tit    XXX      3 |
| 3 | • extract specific pieces of information from tables and lists. | Read off a value from a table, the cost of an item in a catalogue, etc. |
| | • enter and access information in a simple database. | Handle weather statistics or personal data, such as height, date of birth, age, etc. |
| 4 | • specify an issue for which data are needed; collect, group and order discrete data using tallying methods with suitable equal class intervals and create a frequency table for grouped data. | Find and record the number of pupils born in each month of the year. |
| | • understand, calculate and use the mean and range of a set of data. | Calculate the means to compare the scoring records of two hockey teams which have played different numbers of games. |

| Level | Statements of attainment | Example |
|-------|--------------------------|---------|
| | • interrogate data in a computer database. | |
| 5 | • design and use an observation sheet to collect data; collate and analyse results. | *Devise a simple habitat recorder for an ecological survey.* *Conduct a survey of cars passing with one, two, three, . . . occupants.* |
| | • collect, group and order continuous data using equal class intervals and create a frequency table for grouped data. | *Collect information about height of children in a year group.* *Handle data arising through experiments or measurements in science, geography and CDT and from published sources in other areas of the curriculum.* |
| | • insert and interrogate data in a computer database and draw conclusions. | *Draw conclusions from census data about the effect of an epidemic.* |

## TABLE 45 Maths AT13: Handling data

Pupils should represent and interpret data.

| Level | Statements of attainment | Example |
|-------|--------------------------|---------|
| | Pupils should: | |
| 1 | • record with real objects or drawings and comment about the result. | *Draw a simple picture to represent 'Children at our table'.* |
| | • create simple mapping diagrams showing relationships; read and interpret them. | *Link children's names to pets owned.* |

| Level | Statements of attainment | Example |
|---|---|---|

**2**

- construct, read and interpret block graphs and frequency tables.

**Means of transport to school**

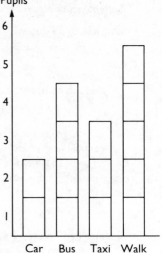

- use diagrams to represent the result of classifying using two different criteria.

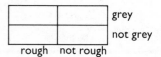

**3**

- construct and interpret bar charts.

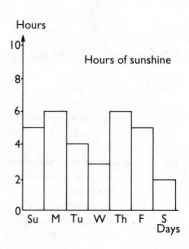

| Level | Statements of attainment | Example |
|---|---|---|

Statements of attainment

- create and interpret graphs (pictograms) where the symbol represents a group of units.

Example

Number of raffle tickets sold by each class

☐ = 20      ⊏ = less than 20

class A  ☐ ☐ ☐ ⊏

class B  ☐ ☐ ☐

class C  ☐ ☐ ☐

class D  ☐ ☐ ☐ ☐ ⊏

**4**

- create a decision tree-diagram with questions to sort and identify a collection of objects.

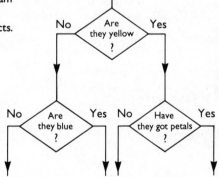

- construct, read and interpret a bar-line graph for a discrete variable (where the length of the bar-line represents the frequency).

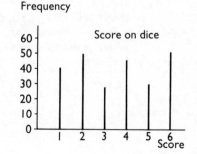

| Level | Statements of attainment | Example |
|---|---|---|

• construct and interpret a line graph and know that the intermediate values may or may not have a meaning.

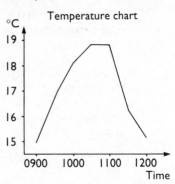

Temperature chart

• construct and interpret a frequency diagram choosing suitable class intervals covering the range for a discrete variable.

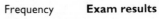
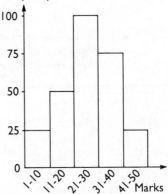

Exam results

**5**

• construct and interpret a pie chart from a collection of data with a few variables; interpret pie charts already presented in journals or newspapers.

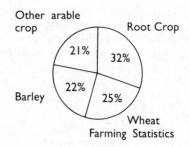

Farming Statistics

| Level | Statement of attainment | Example |
|---|---|---|
| | ● construct and interpret conversion graphs. | *Devise and use conversion graphs for different currencies, and for converting thermometer readings from Fahrenheit to Celsius.* |
| | ● construct and interpret a frequency diagram choosing suitable class intervals covering the range for a continuous variable. | |

| Class intervals | Frequency |
|---|---|
| $120 \leqslant h < 125$ | 2 |
| $125 \leqslant h < 130$ | 4 |
| $130 \leqslant h < 135$ | 6 |
| $135 \leqslant h < 140$ | 8 |
| $140 \leqslant h < 145$ | 5 |
| $145 \leqslant h < 150$ | 3 |
| $150 \leqslant h < 155$ | 1 |

$h$ = height (centimetres)

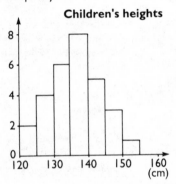

# TABLE 46  Maths AT14: Handling data

Pupils should understand, estimate and calculate probabilities.

| Level | Statements of attainment | Example |
|---|---|---|
| | Pupils should: | |
| 1 | ● recognise possible outcomes of simple random events. | *Realise that a new baby will be either a boy or a girl.* |

| Level | Statement of attainment | Example |
|---|---|---|
| 2 | • recognise that there is a degree of uncertainty about the outcome of some events and other events are certain or impossible. | *Recognise that it is:* <br> *certain    that 'it will get dark tonight';* <br> *impossible  that 'I will be 20 tomorrow';* <br> *uncertain   whether 'it will rain tomorrow'.* |
| 3 | • place events in order of 'likelihood' and use appropriate words to identify the chance. | *Decide for each of these statements if they are: 'very likely', 'likely', 'unlikely' or 'very unlikely':* <br> *'I shall arrive at school on time tomorrow'; 'I shall be a millionaire someday'; 'My favourite television star will visit my school'; 'I shall support the school team tonight'.* |
| | • understand and use the idea of 'evens' and say whether events are more or less likely than this. | *Recognise that if a die is thrown there is an equal chance of an odd or even number but the chance of getting a particular number (say 5), is less than an even chance.* |
| | • distinguish between 'fair' and 'unfair'. | *Recognise that if a 'fair' coin is tossed then there is an equal chance of a head or tail.* |
| 4 | • understand and use the probability scale from 0 to 1. | 0                              1 <br> ————————————+———————— <br> *No    Poor   Even   Good   Certain* <br> *chance chance chance chance* |
| | • give and justify subjective estimates of probabilities in a range of events. | *Recognise that when a 'fair' coin is tossed the probability of heads is 1 out of 2 or ½.* <br> *What is the chance of it raining today?* |
| | • list all the possible outcomes of an event. | *List the different ways of scoring a total of 7 when throwing 2 dice.* |
| 5 | • know that, when repeating the same experiment, different outcomes may result. | *Know that you do not always get 5 heads in 10 tosses of a 'fair' coin and that very occasionally there will be none.* |
| | • distinguish between estimates of probabilities based on | *Know that a sound estimate of the probability that the next car passing* |

| Level | Statement of attainment | Example |
|-------|------------------------|---------|
| | statistical evidence and those based on the assumptions of symmetry. | the school would be a British car could be made by first doing a traffic survey. |
| | ● know that if each of $n$ events is assumed to be equally likely the probability of one occurring is $1/n$. | Know that if the names of the 5 most common makes of car are put into a bag, the probability of picking a particular make of car is $1/5$. |

## Task 33 Planning for progression in maths

Plan a programme of study in maths for your children for a chosen period of time. Elements to consider include:

● your aims and intentions (including attainment targets)
● time allocation for the work
● resources, books and materials to be used
● sequence and differentiation of activities
● grouping of children to meet individual needs
● links with other curricular areas
● ways of assessing/recording pupil progress

Discuss with a colleague the way your plans fit in with overall school policy. Think of ways of communicating your expectations to children and to parents.

# Unit 9

# SCIENCE

If science is finding out about the world, where do you begin?
It's a big apple ... Student teacher

In developing a programme of study for science you may need to consider some of the following questions:

- Why teach science?
- How do children learn science?
- What science is right for our children?
- How is this embodied in the National Curriculum?
- How do we develop an atmosphere and environment for learning science?
- Where can we get help in teaching science?
- How do we assess the effectiveness of our teaching and of children's learning?

## Why teach science?

Science provides children with a means of understanding the natural, physical and technological world in which they live. It provides both knowledge about the world and a method – the scientific method – for investigating, checking and finding out more. For children, and for many adults, it is a long journey towards understanding. Before setting out on this journey we need to ask: *why* are we going? *which way* are we going? and *how* are we going to get there? There is a need to identify and communicate our broad aims and objectives. Figure 17 outlines some broad aims, arising out of the *Science 5/13* project (Schools Council, 1972).

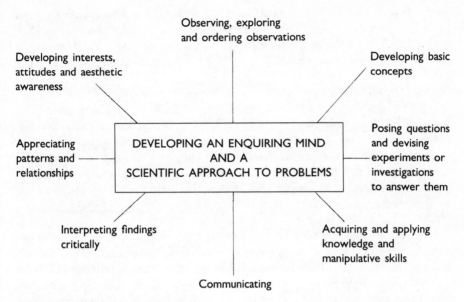

Figure 17 Developing an enquiring mind

## Task 34 Identifying aims in science teaching

Consider and list the aims you are hoping to work towards through the teaching of science.
Try to put your aims into some order of priority.
Compare your aims with those of colleagues.
Discuss these aims with your class.
Find out what your children think about science.

# How children learn science

Everyday life presents children with some puzzling experiences to explain:

What makes the water left in the open jar disappear 'into thin air'?
Why does metal go rusty when left outside?
What makes some plants grow fast and others wither and die?
Why can we hear some sounds that come from a long way away?

None of these are simple to explain in scientific terms, yet because children come across them so often they want to understand them. To do this they construct their own ideas, which may or may not be scientific. These ideas are not simply plucked out of the air, they are intuitive attempts at explanation.

The Primary SPACE (Science Processes and Concept Formation) Project has been working with teachers to find out what ideas children bring with them to the classroom, and ways in which school science can help develop their understanding further. One nine-year-old for example explained rust as 'a metal inside another metal. I think that the rain makes it come and the paint wears off and you can see it.' An eleven-year-old explained evaporation as 'The sun acts as a magnet and brings the water up drop by drop.' A ten-year-old explained the reason why you cannot see things grow with the idea that living things only grow at night.

In teaching science where do you start? A good way is to find out first what children already know. This is important, for their own intuitive ideas make sense to them and provide good explanations. Any new experience will have to link to and make sense in terms of their current understanding. Children's own ideas may not be very scientific but they are useful for them, and once expressed (through discussion, writing or drawing) can form the basis for testing and investigation.

In one class of second-year juniors the teacher asked them to think how they could explain 'drying' to someone from outer space. This led the children to devise ways of investigating and showing what happened when something dried. Two children made a plan which involved placing two equal-sized wet pieces of paper in desks, one with lid open, one closed. They expected the paper in the closed desk to dry first, and were surprised to find their predictions wrong. Further questioning by the teacher helped the children to make sense of their observations, and to relate what they had found out to what they had thought before.

Knowing a scientific term like 'evaporation' does not guarantee understanding. Children need to be helped not only to clarify their ideas, but also their vocabulary. Exploring with children what they mean by a particular word will help them make sense of the world, and will also help you to assess their understanding.

 ## Task 35  Exploring children's concepts in science

Choose a scientific concept that you wish your class to study. Present the concept in the form of a question. For example:

*Evaporation*:   What makes water left in an open jar disappear?
*Rust*:   What makes some metal things go rusty when left outside?
*Growth*:   What makes some plants grow fast, and others wither and die?

Ask the children to suggest answers to your question. Compare their answers (hypotheses). Encourage them to discuss ways of testing their ideas.

# What science is right for our children?

It is up to teachers and schools to design their own teaching schemes within the overall framework of the National Curriculum. This scheme or policy needs to be right for your own school and class, and fitting for the 5–16 continuum of science education. Table 47 lists some principles against which to judge your scheme of work.

---

## TABLE 47 Ten principles of science education

A scheme of work should have:

- *Breadth*: introduce all pupils to the main skills and concepts from the whole range of science
- *Balance*: achieve a balance between acquiring scientific knowledge and practising scientific method
- *Relevance*: draw on children's everyday experience, and prepare them for the adult world
- *Differentiation*: cater for the differing needs of all pupils, including the most able and those with special needs
- *Equal opportunities*: actively seek ways of exciting the interest of all children, including those (often girls) who find the subject unappealing or intimidating
- *Continuity*: link in with work being done in feeder infant and local secondary schools
- *Progression*: design the scheme to lead on to deeper understanding and greater competence
- *Links across the curriculum*: encourage cross-curricular links through common topics, themes or projects
- *Teaching methods*: teach in practical ways, through investigative and problem-solving activity
- *Assessment*: assess in ways that show what children know and can do

# Science in the National Curriculum

The National Curriculum prescribes 14 attainment targets for science that relate to children in the primary years (Key Stages 1 and 2):

| | |
|---|---|
| AT1 | Exploration of science |
| AT2 | The variety of life |
| AT3 | Processes of life |
| AT4 | Genetics and evolution |
| AT5 | Human influences on the Earth |
| AT6 | Types and uses of materials |
| AT9 | Earth and atmosphere |
| AT10 | Forces |
| AT11 | Electricity and magnetism |
| AT12 | The scientific aspects of information technology |
| AT13 | Energy |
| AT14 | Sound and music |
| AT15 | Light |
| AT16 | The Earth in space |

What follows is a summary of these attainment targets, and examples of classroom activities, which may help in planning a programme of study that suits you and your children.

*Note*: Junior science (Key Stage 2) in the National Curriculum includes ATs 1–6 and 9–16, levels 2–5.

---

## TABLE 48 Science AT1: Exploration of science

| Level | Statements of attainment |
|---|---|
| | Pupils should: |
| 1 | • observe familiar materials and events in their immediate environment, at first hand, using their senses. |
| | • describe and communicate their observations, ideally through talking in groups or by other means, within their class. |
| 2 | • ask questions and suggest ideas of the 'how', 'why', and 'what will happen if' variety. |

| Level | Statements of attainment |
|-------|--------------------------|

- identify simple differences, for example, *hot/cold, rough/smooth*.
- use non-standard and standard measures, for example, *hand-spans and rulers*.
- list and collate observations.
- interpret findings by associating one factor with another, for example, *the pupils' perception at this level that 'light objects float', 'thin wood is bendy'*.
- record findings in charts, drawings and other appropriate forms.

**3**
- formulate hypotheses, for example, *'this ball will bounce higher than that one'*.
- identify, and describe simple variables that change over time, for example, *growth of a plant*.
- distinguish between a 'fair' and an 'unfair' test.
- select and use simple instruments to enhance observations, for example, *a stop-clock or hand lens*.
- quantify variables, as appropriate, to the nearest labelled division of simple measuring instruments, for example, *a rule*.
- record experimental findings, for example, *in tables and bar charts*.
- interpret simple pictograms and bar charts.
- interpret observations in terms of a generalised statement, for example, *the greater the suspended weight, the longer the spring*.
- describe activities carried out by sequencing the major features.

**4**
- raise questions in a form which can be investigated.
- formulate testable hypotheses.
- construct 'fair tests'.
- plan an investigation where the plan indicates that the relevant variables have been identified and others controlled.
- select and use a range of measuring instruments, as appropriate, to quantify observations of physical quantities, such as volume and temperature.
- follow written instructions and diagrammatic representations.
- carry out an investigation with due regard to safety.
- record results by appropriate means, such as the construction of simple tables, bar charts, line graphs.
- draw conclusions from experimental results.
- describe investigations in the form of ordered prose, using a limited technical vocabulary.

**5**
- use concepts, knowledge and skills to suggest simple questions and design investigations to answer them.

---

Level    Statements of attainment

- identify and manipulate relevant independent and dependent variables, choosing appropriately between ranges, numbers and values.
- select and use measuring instruments to quantify variables and use more complex measuring instruments with the required degree of accuracy, for example, *minor divisions on thermometers and forcemeters*.
- make written statements of the patterns derived from the data obtained from various sources.

---

Note: The National Curriculum statements of attainment for Science do not include examples. The examples suggested on pp 143–157 have been devised by the author.

Examples of investigations that you can undertake with children to explore science include such problems as:

- Design a bag to contain the largest amount of flour possible using a given piece of paper. Design a fair test to gauge the strength of the bag.
- Design an aeroplane out of a sheet of paper to fly as far as possible. Can you make it glide to right or left?
- Design parachutes. Which takes the longest time to fall from a set distance? What factors affect its fall?
- Design a test to find out which magnet from a set is the strongest. Which part is the strongest?
- Design a test to find out which glue, from a selection, is strongest.
- Build a raft out of A4 paper to hold as many marbles as possible.
- Make a piece of Plasticine float. How many centi-cubes will it support?
- Make a bridge span a 40 cm gap using dried spaghetti and Sellotape.
- Design some tests to find out which brand of paper towel is best value for money.
- Design a fair test to find out which kitchen foodstuffs (from a selection) dissolve. Predict first, then test.
- Design a fair test to see if one type or colour of elastic band is stronger than another.
- Design a tent by folding a sheet of paper. Predict, then test, which shape is strongest.
- Test the best ratio of sand to cement to produce the strongest material when set.
- Use ten sheets of paper and glue to construct the tallest tower to support a play person.
- Make a maze and test to see if an ant can find the way to a food source.

● Devise fair tests for the germination of seeds under differing growing conditions.

These activities should encourage the ability to:

1  plan, hypothesise and predict
2  design and carry out investigations
3  interpret results and findings
4  draw inferences
5  communicate exploratory tasks and experiments

---

## TABLE 49 Science AT2: The variety of life

| Level | Statement of attainment | Example |
|---|---|---|
| 1 | ● know there is a wide variety of living things, which includes human beings. | *Visit local nature reserve to observe birds, plants, insects, and other small land and pond creatures.* |
| 2 | ● know that plants and animals need certain conditions to sustain life. | *Grow cress in different conditions.* |
|  | ● understand how living things are looked after and be able to treat them with care and consideration. | *Keep a diary of your care of plants and minibeasts such as snails, worms and spiders as well as small mammals.* |
| 3 | ● be able to recognise similarities and differences among living things. | *Visit school grounds, parks, field centre, zoo, to compare living things.* |
|  | ● be able to sort living things into broad groups according to observable features. | *Use photos, pictures and specimens for sorting, eg leaves, insects.* |
|  | ● know that living things respond to seasonal and daily changes. | *Long-term study or diary record of living things such as trees or birds through the seasons.* |
| 4 | ● be able to recognise similarities and differences both within and between groups of plants and animals. | *Make simple keys to identify and classify living things like leaves, eg broad/narrow, smooth/serrated, shiny/ not shiny.* |

| Level | Statement of attainment | Example |
|-------|------------------------|---------|
| | • understand the key factors in the process of decay (temperature, microbes, compactness, moisture) and how this is important in the re-use of biological material in everyday life. | *Study biodegradable materials such as bread, leaves, paper, apple, under different conditions.* |
| | • understand that plants and animals can be preserved as fossils in different ways. | *Study fossils, make plaster casts of leaves.* |
| 5 | • understand that the differences in physical factors between localities, including differences in seasonal and daily changes, are reflected in the different species of plants and animals found there. | *Study two differing localities to see how plants and animals are affected by environmental changes.* |
| | • be able to assign organisms to their major groups using keys and observable features. | *Observe and identify local plants, insects, birds, etc.* |
| | • be able to support their view about environmental issues concerned with the use of fertilisers in agriculture and horticulture, based on their practical experience. | *Collect and discuss news items from newspapers and magazines.* |
| | • understand predator–prey relationships. | *Study food chains, eg in pond life.* |

## TABLE 50 Science AT3: Processes of life

| Level | Statement of Attainment | Example |
|-------|------------------------|---------|
| 1 | • be able to name or label the external parts of the human body or of plants, eg arm, leg, flower, stem. | *Draw round child and label parts, draw and label parts of flowers.* |

| Level | Statement of attainment | Example |
|---|---|---|
| 2 | • know that living things reproduce their own kind. | *Make a book 'About Me', including photos/pictures of baby, child, parents, grandparents etc.* |
|  | • know that personal hygiene, food, exercise, rest, safety, and the proper and safe use of medicines are important. | *Make charts of good/bad foods, dental hygiene, visit by nurse.* |
|  | • be able to give a simple account of the pattern of their own day. | *Make pictorial chart of 'My Day', discuss sequences of events.* |
| 3 | • know that the basic life processes – feeding, breathing, movement and behaviour – are common to human beings and other living things they have studied. | *Keep and study pets or minibeasts.* |
|  | • be able to describe the main stages in the human life cycle. | *Make booklets or charts showing growth of humans, sequence pictures of families.* |
| 4 | • be able to name the major organs and organ systems in flowering plants and mammals. | *Careful observing, drawing and labelling of plants and mammals.* |
|  | • know about the factors which contribute to good health and body maintenance, including the defence systems of the body, balanced diet, oral hygiene and avoidance of harmful substances such as tobacco, alcohol and other drugs. | *Plan a campaign to promote good health habits and to counter drugs and smoking.* |
|  | • understand the processes of reproduction in mammals. | *Study audiovisual resources, eg TV programmes, on reproduction.* |
|  | • be able to describe the main stages of flowering plant reproduction. | *Make long-term plant study, collect and study varieties of seeds.* |
| 5 | • know that living things are made up from different kinds of cells which carry out different jobs. | *Study cell structures through audiovisual resources and microscope, eg cross section of stems.* |

| Level | Statement of attainment | Example |
|---|---|---|
| | • understand malnutrition and the relationships between diet, exercise, health, fitness and circulatory disorders. | *Visit by dental nurse, nutritionist or doctor to discuss and answer questions on aspects of good health.* |
| | • know that in digestion food is made soluble so that it can enter the blood. | *Draw and label digestive system.* |
| | • understand the way in which microbes and lifestyle affect health. | *See microbes through microscope, study benefits of cleanliness.* |
| | • be able to describe the functions of the major organ systems. | *Use video/TV programmes for 'My Body' project.* |

# TABLE 51 Science AT4: Genetics and evolution

| Level | Statement of attainment | Example |
|---|---|---|
| 1 | • know that human beings vary from one individual to the next. | *Survey children, compare similarities, differences.* |
| 2 | • be able to measure simple differences between each other. | *Measure height, weight, hand area, foot length etc and record, eg bar charts.* |
| 3 | • know that some life forms became extinct a long time ago and others more recently. | *Study dinosaurs and fossils, visit a natural history museum.* |
| 4 | • be able to measure variations in living organisms. | *Compare leaves, study leaf areas, number of prickles on holly, lobes on oak leaf, leaflets on chestnut etc.* |
| 5 | • know that information in the form of genes is passed on from one generation to the next. | *Grow seeds, compare growing plants, children with relatives, pets and their young.* |

# TABLE 52 Science AT5: Human influences on the Earth

| Level | Statement of attainment | Example |
|---|---|---|
| 1 | • know that human activities produce a wide range of waste products. | Survey litter in class, park and home. |
| 2 | • know that some waste products decay naturally but often do so over a long period of time. | Observe decay, over a period, in various materials. |
|  | • be able to keep a diary, in a variety of forms, of change over time. | Observe and record local building development, decay in food. |
| 3 | • know that human activity may produce local changes in the Earth's surface, air and water. | Study building site, local river/pond pollution. |
|  | • be able to give an account of a project to help improve the local environment. | Plan a litter project, eg 'Keep our school tidy', or environmental development, eg tree planting. |
| 4 | • know that some waste materials can be recycled. | Collect for recycling in bottle bank, paper bank etc. Make recycled paper. |
| 5 | • be able to describe the sources, implications and possible prevention of pollution. | Discuss news item/TV programme on pollution. |
|  | • be able to classify waste products as biodegradable and non-biodegradable. | Study, survey and classify dustbin contents (using plastic gloves!). |
|  | • be able to argue for and against particular planning proposals in the locality, which may have an environmental impact. | Study and discuss local news item/ environmental issue. |

# TABLE 53 Science AT6: Types and uses of materials

| Level | Statement of attainment | Example |
|---|---|---|
| 1 | • be able to describe familiar and unfamiliar objects in terms of simple properties, for example, shape, colour, texture, and describe how they behave when they are, for example, squashed and stretched. | Collect, sort and display materials and objects. |
| 2 | • be able to recognise important similarities and differences, including hardness, flexibility and transparency, in the characteristics of materials. | Study similarities and differences in sets of objects. |
| | • be able to group materials according to their characteristics. | Find out what floats/sinks, dissolves and is magnetic. |
| | • know that heating and cooling materials can cause them to melt or solidify or change permanently. | Cook simple recipes, make ice lollies, study melting ice. |
| 3 | • know that some materials occur naturally while many are made from raw materials. | Compare natural and manufactured objects, visit a factory. |
| | • be able to list the similarities and differences in a variety of everyday materials. | Sort, observe and test materials using senses, measuring instruments and forces such as magnets, water etc. |
| 4 | • be able to make comparisons between materials on the basis of simple properties, strength, hardness, flexibility and solubility. | Devise tests for materials, eg floating, dissolving, magnets, conduction etc. |
| | • be able to relate knowledge of these properties to the everyday use of materials. | Use materials to solve problems, eg make a boat waterproof. |
| | • know that solids and liquids have 'weight' which can be measured and, also, occupy a definite volume which can be measured. | Weigh and measure competing products to find best value for money. |

| Level | Statement of attainment | Example |
|---|---|---|
| | • understand the sequence of changes of state that results from heating or cooling. | *Make ice, record melting, heat water, record evaporation and condensation.* |
| | • be able to classify materials into solids, liquids and gases on the basis of their properties. | *Devise tests to show properties, whether solid, liquid or gas.* |
| 5 | • know that gases have 'weight'. | *Compare balloons on a balance, inflated and deflated.* |
| | • be able to classify aqueous solutions as acidic, alkaline or neutral, by using indicators. | *Test safe household liquids, eg vinegar, using indicators such as cabbage water or litmus paper.* |
| | • be able to give an account of the various techniques for separating and purifying mixtures. | *Try methods of cleaning dirty water, separating salt and sand, sugar and flour.* |

## TABLE 54 Science AT9: Earth and atmosphere

| Level | Statement of attainment | Example |
|---|---|---|
| 1 | • know that there is a variety of weather conditions. | *Record weather changes.* |
| | • be able to describe changes in the weather. | *Discuss daily observations.* |
| 2 | • know that there are patterns in the weather which are related to seasonal changes. | *Observe seasonal weather over longer periods.* |
| | • know that weather has a powerful effect on people's lives. | *Study clothing for different weather conditions.* |
| | • be able to record the weather over a period of time in words, drawings and charts or other forms of communication. | *Record weather in a variety of ways.* |
| | • be able to sort natural materials into broad groups according to observable features. | *Collect natural materials and sort into groups.* |

| Level | Statement of attainment | Example |
|---|---|---|
| 3 | • be able to describe from their observations some of the effects of weathering on buildings and landscape. | *Make observations on field trips, nature trails and school site.* |
| | • know that air is all around us. | *Investigate blowing up of balloons (how many breaths?), flight of spinners, darts, parachutes, kites, bubbles etc.* |
| | • understand how weathering of rocks leads to different types of soil. | *Collect and study soil and rock samples.* |
| | • be able to give an account of an investigation of some natural material (rock or soil). | *Classify rock samples by colour, texture, hardness, mass, displacement etc.* |
| | • be able to understand and interpret common meteorological symbols used in the media. | *Study and compare forecasts from TV, newspaper and own forecasts. Devise weather symbols.* |
| 4 | • be able to measure temperature, rainfall, wind speed and direction, and explain that wind is air in motion. | *Study weather using instruments, eg rain gauge, thermometer, wind vane, anemometer, wind-sock etc.* |
| | • know that climate determines success of agriculture and understand impact of occasional catastrophic events. | *Build mini-landscapes to show how plants grow under different conditions, investigate drought and flood.* |
| 5 | • know that landscapes are formed by agents including Earth movements, weathering, erosion and deposition over different time scales. | *Study AV aids showing change over time, visit geological museum.* |
| | • be able to explain how earthquakes and volcanoes are associated with the formation of landforms. | *Illustrate volcanic activity using charts or models.* |
| | • be able to explain the water cycle. | *Investigate water changing to steam, condensation and evaporation. Chart water cycle.* |

# TABLE 55 Science AT10: Forces

| Level | Statement of attainment | Example |
|---|---|---|
| 1 | • know that things can be moved by pushing them. | Construct and play with moving toys. |
| 2 | • understand that pushes and pulls can make things move, speed up, swerve or stop. | Push vehicles down, and pull them up a variety of slopes. |
| 3 | • understand that when things are changed in shape, move or stop moving, forces are acting on them. | Build simple moving models, and use 'force' to push and pull them. |
| | • understand the factors which cause objects to float or sink in water. | Make boats from various materials, load and weigh various cargoes. |
| 4 | • understand that the movement of an object depends on the size and direction of the forces exerted on it. | Investigate elastic and wind-powered models, eg land yachts or cotton reel/tin can buggies. |
| | • understand that the greater the speed of an object the greater the force and/or time needed to stop it, and the significance of this for road safety. | Toys and slopes – how far does a car roll? |
| | • understand that things fall because of a force of attraction towards centre of the Earth. | Test stability of cups etc on inclined plane at different angles. |
| | • be able to recognise that weight is a force, and know it is measured in newtons. | Weigh various objects using spring scales calibrated in g, kg and newtons. |
| 5 | • understand that when an object is not moving, or is moving at a steady speed, there are balanced forces acting on it. | A car standing at rest on the surface of the Earth. |
| | • be able to give an account of an investigation of the strength of a structure. | Build bridges using weak materials, test/record load-bearing capabilities. |
| | • be able to measure forces, distance and time. | Make a timing device, experiment with length and time instruments in toy car investigations. |
| | • be able to describe the effect of friction on moving objects. | Slide objects on different surfaces, investigate friction and improving efficiency. |

# TABLE 56  Science AT11: Electricity and magnetism

| Level | Statement of attainment | Example |
|---|---|---|
| 1 | • know that many household appliances use electricity, but that misuse could be dangerous. | *Collect pictures from magazines of electrical household appliances, make safety posters.* |
| 2 | • know that magnets attract certain materials but not others and can repel each other. | *Test familiar objects to see whether or not they attract magnets.* |
|   | • understand the danger associated with the use of electricity and know appropriate safety measures. | *Discuss electrical safety in the home and safety posters.* |
| 3 | • know that some materials conduct electricity well while others do not. | *Test which materials will/will not complete a battery-powered circuit.* |
|   | • understand that a complete circuit is needed for an electrical device, such as a bulb or buzzer, to work. | *Using given components make a bulb light and buzzer work.* |
| 4 | • be able to construct simple electrical circuits. | *Select components to make a simple circuit to light bulb, work buzzer or run motor.* |
| 5 | • be able to describe and record diagrammatically simple electrical circuits they have made. | *Record pictorially, using symbols, how to make a circuit.* |
|   | • be able to vary the flow of electricity in a simple circuit and observe the effects. | *Investigate use of multiple bulbs and batteries (fresh and old).* |

# TABLE 57  Science AT12: The scientific aspects of information technology

| Level | Statement of attainment | Example |
|---|---|---|
| 1 | • know about some everyday devices which receive text, sound and images over long distances, using information technology. | *Observe and discuss radio, television and telephone.* |
| 2 | • know there is a variety of means for communicating information over long distances. | *Make a telephone with string and tin cans.* |
| | • know that information can be stored using a range of everyday devices including the computer. | *Explore use of computer (including concept keyboard) use of database and wordprocessing.* |
| 3 | • be able to store information using devices, for example, a tape recorder and a digital watch. | *Children record stories, songs, plays, poems onto tape.* |
| | • know that information can be stored electronically in a variety of ways, for example text, number, pictures and sound. | *Store information on tape and computer database.* |
| | • be able to retrieve and select text, number, sound or graphics stored on a computer. | *Retrieve information from a computer database.* |
| 4 | • know about the range of uses of microelectronic devices in everyday life. | *Visit a supermarket, observe and discuss automatic barriers, doors, checkouts, barcodes.* |
| | • be able to detect and measure environmental changes using a variety of instruments. | *Use a variety of measuring instruments in weather studies.* |
| 5 | • understand the function of and be able to use switches and relays in simple circuits. | *Make and use model with switches, eg lighting circuits or alarms.* |
| | • understand logic gates and their use in decision making and simple control circuits. | *Make flow diagram of control circuit.* |

# TABLE 58 Science AT13: Energy

| Level | Statement of attainment | Example |
|---|---|---|
| 1 | • understand that they need food to be active. | Collect and discuss adverts for food. |
| | • be able to describe, by talking or other appropriate means, how food is necessary for life. | Discuss good and bad foods for different living things, humans and other animals. |
| 2 | • understand the meaning of hot and cold relative to the temperature of their own bodies. | Discuss clothes worn on hot and cold days. |
| | • be able to describe how a toy with a simple mechanism which moves and stores energy works. | Investigate simple clockwork toys using a variety of mechanisms. |
| 3 | • understand, in qualitative terms, that models and machines need a source of energy in order to work. | Identify energy sources in toys, models and machines. |
| | • know that the temperature is a measure of how hot (or cold) things are. | Use thermometer to measure temperature of air, water, soil and sand. |
| | • be able to use simple power sources (electric motors, rubber bands) and devices which transfer energy (gears, belts, levers). | Use construction kits with motors, gears, levers and drive belts. |
| 4 | • understand that energy is essential to every aspect of human life and activity. | Discuss and observe energy in the environment, eg food, heat, electricity, wind etc. |
| | • know that there is a range of fuels which can be used to provide energy. | Find out about fuel industries, eg petrol, gas, coal, electricity. |
| | • understand that energy can be stored and transferred to and from moving things. | Show how moving air, from fan or balloon, can move sails, windmill or land yacht. |
| | • be able to measure temperature using a thermometer. | Use thermometer to measure body temperature, temperature of various liquids and air. |
| | • be able to give an account of changes that occur when familiar substances are heated and cooled. | Record changes occurring during cooking and cooling food, at different temperatures. |

| Level | Statement of attainment | Example |
|-------|------------------------|---------|
| 5 | • understand the need for fuel economy and efficiency. | *Investigate and record fuel consumption, assessing costs, over time.* |
| | • understand the idea of global energy resources and appreciate that these resources are limited. | *Research energy sources worldwide and the use of alternative technologies.* |

# TABLE 59 Science AT14: Sound and music

| Level | Statement of attainment | Example |
|-------|------------------------|---------|
| 1 | • know that sounds can be made in a variety of ways. | *Identify various tape-recorded sounds.* |
| 2 | • know that sounds are heard when the sound reaches the ear. | *Compare sounds heard with and without ears covered.* |
| | • be able to explain how musical sounds are produced in simple musical instruments. | *Make a variety of simple instruments and discuss sounds made.* |
| 3 | • know that sounds are produced by vibrating objects and can travel through different materials. | *Investigate sound vibrations, eg using string telephone or tuning fork.* |
| | • be able to give a simple explanation of the way in which sound is generated and can travel through different materials. | *Listen to a ticking clock through a tube, tank of water, table top etc.* |
| 4 | • know that it takes time for sound to travel. | *Investigate echoes and the time they take to return from a distant wall.* |
| 5 | • understand that the frequency of a vibrating source affects the pitch of the sound it produces. | *Investigate the pitch of instruments with strings of different length and diameter.* |
| | • understand the relationship between the loudness of a sound and the amplitude of vibration of the source. | *Investigate sounds caused by vibrating a ruler extended at various lengths over a desk.* |
| | • understand the importance of noise control in the environment. | *Tape-record various environmental sounds, discuss noise pollution and insulation.* |

## TABLE 60 Science AT15: Using light and electromagnetic radiation

| Level | Statements of attainment | Example |
|---|---|---|
| 1 | • know that light comes from different sources. | Collect and discuss pictures and objects displaying a variety of light sources. |
| | • be able to discriminate between colours and match them or, where appropriate, demonstrate an understanding of colour in the environment. | Collect and sort pictures of various things by colour. |
| 2 | • know that light passes through some materials and not others, and that when it does not shadows may be formed. | Test and sort materials which are transparent or opaque. Make silhouettes of children. |
| | • be able to draw pictures, showing features such as light, colour and shade. | Draw light, dark and rainbow-coloured pictures. |
| 3 | • know that light can be made to change direction and shiny surfaces can form images. | Collect, observe and discuss things with shiny surfaces. |
| | • be able to give an account of an investigation with mirrors. | Use mirrors to reflect light and complete half-drawn pictures (symmetry). |
| 4 | • know that we see objects because light is scattered off them and into our eyes. | Look into darkened box with torch to locate objects. |
| | • know that light travels in straight lines and use this to explain the shapes and sizes of shadows. | Use OHP or other light source to investigate silhouettes and shadow effects, eg shadow puppets. |
| 5 | • understand how light is reflected. | Construct a periscope using mirrors. |

## TABLE 61 Science AT16: The Earth in space

| Level | Statement of attainment | Example |
|---|---|---|
| 1 | • be able to describe through talking, or other appropriate means, the seasonal changes in weather and in living things. | Collect and sort seasonal pictures. |

| Level | Statement of attainment | Example |
|---|---|---|
| | • know the danger of looking directly at the sun. | *Discuss and make warning posters.* |
| | • be able to describe, in relation to their home or school, the apparent daily motion of the Sun across the sky. | *Observe, discuss and illustrate where Sun is in morning, lunchtime and hometime.* |
| 2 | • be able to explain why night occurs. | *Demonstrate using globe or models how the Earth turns.* |
| | • know that day length changes throughout the year. | *Discuss and measure daylight hours throughout the year.* |
| | • know that we live on a large, spherical, self-contained planet called Earth. | *Observe globe, collect photographs of Earth from space.* |
| | • know that the Earth, Moon and Sun are separate bodies. | *Demonstrate through models or role-play the position and movements of Earth, Moon and Sun.* |
| 3 | • know that the inclination of the Sun in the sky changes during the year. | *Measure shadow lengths of a measure at noon at different times of year.* |
| | • be able to measure time with a sundial. | *Make a simple sundial and use it to tell the time.* |
| 4 | • know that the phases of the Moon change in a regular and predictable manner. | *Observe Moon face from home and record its shape on a nightly chart.* |
| | • know that the solar system is made up of the Sun and planets, and have an idea of its scale. | *Make a model of the solar system, visit a planetarium.* |
| | • understand that the Sun is a star. | *Make and discuss a star chart.* |
| 5 | • be able to relate a simple model of the solar system to day/night and year length, changes of day length, seasonal changes and changes in the inclination of the Sun. | *Prepare an illustrated talk to explain day length and seasonal changes.* |
| | • be able to observe and record the shape and surface shading of the phases of the Moon over a period of time. | *Discuss ways of charting the phases of the Moon over a period of time.* |

# How do we develop an atmosphere and environment for learning science?

Although attitudes are not specified as targets to be assessed in the National Curriculum they form an important element in learning. The attitudes of children will affect their willingness to respond to objects, situations and activities in science, and towards you as their science teacher. What attitudes and personal qualities do you wish to develop in children? Table 62 lists some suggestions.

---

**TABLE 62** Attitudes in science education

The following attitudes and personal qualities are important at all stages of science education:

- curiosity
- respect for evidence
- willingness to tolerate uncertainty
- critical reflection
- perseverence
- creativity and inventiveness
- open mindedness
- sensitivity to the living and non-living environment
- cooperation with others

---

These attitudes are developed through encouragement and example, through first-hand experience which stimulates and satisfies curiosity, through the use of children's interests and cultural background, through the use of questions and discussion, through personalising science topics and involving children in the planning of investigations.

Developing a stimulating environment for science involves gathering a range of resources to encourage and aid investigation. Teachers need to be collectors of interesting objects, gadgets, materials, books and pictures for use in the classroom. They need to make the most of whatever central bank of resources is available in the school, as well as a 'basic set' of classroom resources such as magnifiers, nature viewers, magnets, tweezers and collecting pots. Make the most of what children bring in. One of the pleasures of teaching science is that it helps to keep alive your own wonder and curiosity about the world, and the opportunity to share with children the excitement of discovering something new.

## Task 36  Preparing an environment for science

Select a topic you wish to cover in science over a specific period of time. Think of ways of preparing your classroom environment to maximise children's opportunities for learning. Factors to consider include:

- your aims/intentions (including attainment targets)
- the skills (eg use of equipment, testing and recording techniques)
- knowledge (eg use of reference materials, audio-visual aids)
- attitudes (eg use of children's interests and first-hand experience) you wish to develop through the topic work
- the teaching strategies you will use
- the outcomes that will provide a record of work (and possible audience)
- ways of assessing/recording pupil progress

Think of who can help in this research project – colleagues, parents, outside bodies (see below) – and your children – how will you find out and build upon what they already know?

# Where can we get help in teaching science?

As in all teaching, problems may arise, but there is now a surprisingly wide range of help and support in primary science. There will be sources of help within your school, from local advisory teachers, and other local schools. The ASE (Association for Science Education) is a body of primary and secondary science teachers who help and support each other, sharing expertise and ideas through a national and regional framework and their journal, *Primary Science Review*.

# How do we assess the effectiveness of our teaching and of children's learning?

Part of your task as a teacher will be to record the teaching you have undertaken and to develop a system of continuous assessment for children.

## Task 37  Assessing learning in science

Plan or review your record keeping and assessment in science. Questions to ask include:

- How do you record your teaching in science?
- How do you assess targets and levels for each child?
- How are these records communicated to colleagues and to parents?
- In what ways are children involved in the recording/assessing process?

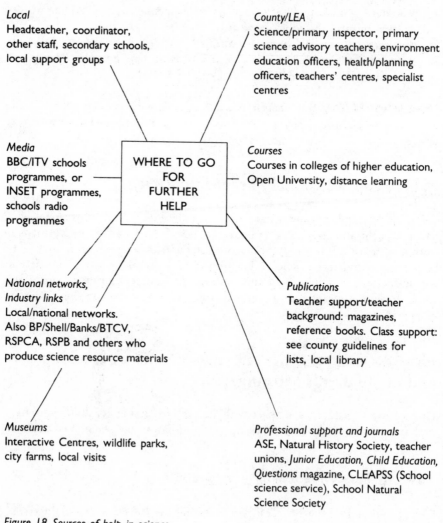

*Local*
Headteacher, coordinator, other staff, secondary schools, local support groups

*County/LEA*
Science/primary inspector, primary science advisory teachers, environment education officers, health/planning officers, teachers' centres, specialist centres

*Media*
BBC/ITV schools programmes, or INSET programmes, schools radio programmes

WHERE TO GO FOR FURTHER HELP

*Courses*
Courses in colleges of higher education, Open University, distance learning

*National networks, Industry links*
Local/national networks. Also BP/Shell/Banks/BTCV, RSPCA, RSPB and others who produce science resource materials

*Publications*
Teacher support/teacher background: magazines, reference books. Class support: see county guidelines for lists, local library

*Museums*
Interactive Centres, wildlife parks, city farms, local visits

*Professional support and journals*
ASE, Natural History Society, teacher unions, *Junior Education, Child Education, Questions* magazine, CLEAPSS (School science service), School Natural Science Society

*Figure 18 Sources of help in science*

When I write about an
experiment I use these
headings.

The problem

What I think will happen

What I used

What I did

What happened

What I found out

*1st year Junior child (Year 3)*

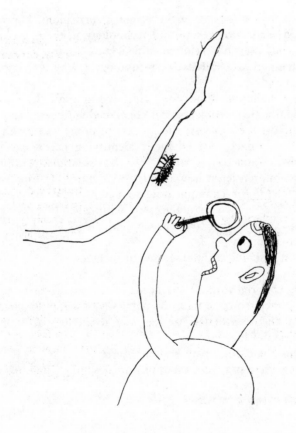

# Unit 10

# TECHNOLOGY

Science tells you what is, design and technology is about what
might be ...                                      Primary inspector

Technology is a new subject in the primary curriculum. For years teachers
have included aspects of design and technology in their work with infants
and juniors, but they have not identified it as a subject as they have say
English, maths and art. So what is 'technology'? Why is it important? How
should it be taught?

Technology challenges pupils (and teachers) to apply their knowledge and
skills to solve practical problems. It is concerned with perceiving and answer-
ing human needs. It is not just the process of doing and making things like
model cars or bridges, but is about identifying needs, generating ideas,
planning, making and testing *to find the best solutions*. Through technological activity children learn how to explore, control and improve aspects of
their environment, for example how to eat healthily or to recycle waste
materials. Technology is very much to do with *capability*, giving children the
'knowhow' to answer their own needs, and the needs of others in a given
context or environment.

The *aims* in teaching technology might include:

- preparing children to meet the needs of the twenty-first century
- equipping them to cope with the demands of a rapidly changing society
- increasing their awareness of the way technology is changing homes,
  workplaces and lifestyles
- stimulating their originality and enterprise
- developing their practical capability in designing, making and problem
  solving

In the National Curriculum technology is divided into two aspects (or profile components):

- design and technology capability
- information technology capability

The reference to capability emphasises that technology as a subject is concerned with practical action, and will relate to a wide range of subjects. Traditionally craft and design activities have been associated with 'art and craft', and technology with science. Technology, however, has a close relationship with a number of subject areas, including:

- science – fair testing of products and theories
- mathematics – data collection and analysis
- art – aesthetic evaluation of products, graphic design
- English – discussion and communication of ideas

In primary school technology is usually taught through topics and projects, which can link all subjects, including *cross-curricular themes* such as:

- economic and industrial understanding, business and enterprise education
- environmental education – conservation and quality of life
- health education – planning healthy systems and environment

# Design and technology capability

Technology is a new and important subject area that aims to give children the power to improve the quality of life. Because the subject matter of design and technology is so wide, and can be related to all human activity, there is no content specified for it in the National Curriculum. What the attainment targets set out is the *process* through which children can attain design and technology capability.

The design process is illustrated in Figure 19. Note that children can start from any point in the design process, beginning for example by evaluating a product and seeking their own ways to improve it.

Design and technology capability in the National Curriculum has four attainment targets, as follows:

*AT 1: Identifying needs and opportunities* through investigations related to home, school, recreation, local community, business and industry, or imaginary contexts, for example by devising a questionnaire about what pupils like or dislike about a local issue such as the playground and identify a need or opportunity for change.

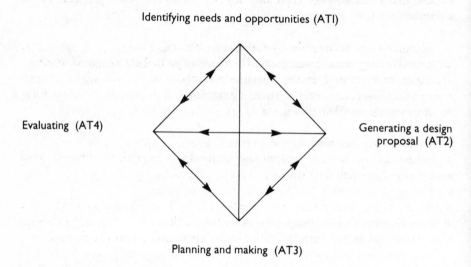

Figure 19 The design process

## Task 38 Identifying needs and opportunities for technological activity

There are many possible contexts for technological activity, for example:

- home
- school
- recreation
- local community
- business and industry
- imaginary contexts

Identify design-and-make opportunities that relate to human needs in each of these possible contexts.

*AT 2: Generating a design* includes exploring ideas to produce a design proposal, and developing it into an appropriate and achievable design specification, for example record and explain chosen features of their different designs for a desk-tidy.

## Task 39  Generating a design

Choose one identified need (See Task 38) and produce a design proposal, by for example:

- identifying and defining the problem to be solved
- brainstorming ideas, bringing available knowledge to bear on the situation
- taking account of advantages and disadvantages
- deciding one solution/design to be attempted
- planning its development

*AT 3: Planning and making*

If they are to achieve design and technology capability, children need practice in designing and making:

- artefacts – different sorts of objects made by people, such as jewellery, a container, a shelter, a vehicle, furniture
- systems – a set of objects and activities designed to perform a task, such as a business enterprise, road routes, party plans, recycling project, distribution system
- environments – surroundings made or developed by people, such as an adventure playground, wildlife garden, housing estate, interior design, animal home

Artefacts, systems and environments can be interrelated (see Figure 20), for example a car is an artefact (object), a system (set of objects) and an environment (surrounding people).

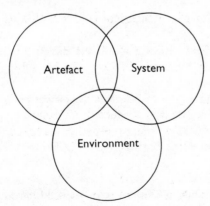

Figure 20 Artefacts, systems and environments

*Planning and making* includes working to a plan, and identifying, managing and using appropriate resources in making artefacts, systems and environments, for example in planning and making a puppet theatre for performing a play with puppets.

 ## Task 40  Planning and making

Using a design proposal (see Task 39), choose materials, tools and processess for your products, which could be made for example from:

- textiles
- graphic media (paint, paper, illustrations etc)
- construction materials (clay, wood, metal, plastic, etc)
- food

In planning your product take account of constraints such as costs, time available, experience and properties of materials. Decide which category/categories your product falls into: artefact, system or environment. Suggest criteria against which your product can be evaluated. Make or model your product, within the given constraints. Share your experience with your colleagues and children.

*AT 4*: Evaluating the processes, products and effects of their own design and technology activities, and those of others, including those from other times and cultures, for example in making their own board games and in comparing board games from different times and places.

 ## Task 41  Evaluating technological processes and products

Evaluation should occur at every stage in the design process, as well as after a product has been made. Evaluation should relate to:

- the outcomes of one's own work, and the processes used
- the work of others, including products from other times and cultures

Choose a product to evaluate. Suggest criteria against which it could be evaluated, for example:

- consider how well it satisfies the needs it should meet
- comment on the materials used

- review the process of making it, eg time and effort involved
- evaluate the economic cost of the product
- devise ways of testing it
- suggest ways in which it could be improved
- assess its social value

Which criteria do you think most important in evaluating the product and processes involved? How does your evaluation compare with that of your colleagues and children?

## Resources

Practical activity in the classroom will require the appropriate resources. A good set of tools available in the classroom or from some central base in the school could include the following: saws, hammer, drill, vice and G clamps, glasspaper and sanding block, screwdrivers, metal safety rules, pliers, scissors, adhesives.

A collection of materials available could include:

aluminium foil
balloons
bulldog clips
candles
cardboard
clay
construction kits
containers
corks
cotton reels
drawing pins
drink cans
electrical equipment: batteries, bulbs/
    bulb holders, buzzers, electrical
    wire
fabrics
green garden sticks
hooks
magnets
marbles
nails

papers, eg tissues
paper clips/fasteners
pipe cleaners
pipe offcuts
plastic bags/bottles/ties
Plasticine
polystyrene sheets/trays
propellers
pulleys
rubber bands
sticky tape
straws
string
syringes
tins/lids
washing up liquid bottles
wire
wood offcuts: dowel, plywood, balsa
    etc
yoghurt pots

# AT 5: Information technology capability

Information technology (IT) is about storing, processing and presenting information by electronic means. Over the past 40 years there has been an electronics revolution. From a time when computers took up the space of a classroom, and cost a fortune, we have moved to a society where microcomputers have been built into a wide range of everyday objects. They have become personal, portable and universal. Even if we may not know much about them, they know a lot about us. Computers store and process information about us all. They have also become powerful educational tools.

Children need to use IT in school

- to develop confidence, capability and control in the uses of IT;
- to enhance and extend learning in all areas of the curriculum.

Ideally each class should have a computer of its own so that children may have access to it on a regular basis. The range of software does not have to be large. It is better to master a few key programs and explore their use in some depth, than to be given brief exposure to a wide range of software options. This is true for both teacher and child.

New technology has particular benefits for language development, where the computer can provide stimulating opportunities for discussion. Working on the computer in pairs or small groups enables children to share, develop and review their ideas easily, for example when using a word processor or problem-solving maths program. For children with communication problems or severe learning difficulties the computer may provide the only viable means of access to the curriculum.

Using a database to sift and present information can free children from the laborious task of sorting large amounts of data, and enable them to focus on analysing the information, formulating hypotheses and drawing conclusions. Using adventure games can enable children to model or simulate problem-solving situations which can provide a focus for cross-curricular topic work. Using control programs like LOGO can enable children to program on-screen 'turtle' graphics, or to move turtle robots. Such experience will increase their understanding not only of the opportunities which IT provides, but also an awareness of the limitations of IT. IT capability is to do with trying to make the child the master and not the servant of the machine.

The various aspects of IT capability include:

1   Communicating information
2   Handling information
3   Modelling or simulation

4   Measurement and control
5   Applications and effects

## 1 Communicating information

IT should be seen not as a substitute for the experience of writing and communicating, but as a new medium for extending these experiences. Children can use word processors to compose and edit text, for example to create a class newspaper or stories for younger children.
Examples of word processing programs include Folio, Pendown, Word, Write, Caxton, Front Page Extra and Newspaper.

## 2 Handling information

Many children will first use databases when they are juniors. They should come to understand the power of computers in handling large amounts of data and in processing complex information. Few children will have the skill to construct a database unaided, but they should be able to ask questions of the data and obtain the information they need, for example about dinosaurs. Examples of database programs include Our Facts, Grass, Data Show, and Branch.

## 3 Modelling

By the end of Year 6 (top juniors) children should be able to use simple modelling programs to make predictions and be able to justify them, for example in considering possible alternative outcomes in an adventure program.
Examples of adventure/simulation programs include, for lower juniors – Albert's House, Dinosaurs, Granny's Garden; for upper juniors – Martello Tower, Fletcher's Castle, Suburban Fox, L Game, make and play adventures.

## 4 Measurement and control

Children will learn to devise and modify sets of instructions using a turtle graphics program, or a programmable robot, and give reasons for their instructions. Some pupils will progress to using IT to control models such as traffic lights or alarm systems.
Examples of programs include LOGO, LOGOTRON, control LOGO.

## 5 Applications and effects

As children become experienced in using IT they should be able to compare and contrast it with other ways of doing things. They should be able to give reasons for using IT in some situations and not in others, for example compare production techniques for producing a school magazine with and without using a computer.

Examples of creative application programs include Paintspa (art/design) and Compose (music). Can the computer help you to be creative?

As teachers we need to assess the widening range of software options carefully. Which programs will be best for our children? The following questions might help in assessing software:

- How good is this program?
- What is it offering children?
- What is the child learning?
- How is the child learning – by practice, problem solving or investigating?
- Is the program flexible enough to meet a wide variety of needs – slow learners and more able children?
- Does the program have possibilities for further learning?
- Can it be used in different ways?
- Has the program enough depth to create follow-up possibilities?
- How does the computer create/enhance learning possibilities?
- Could this learning be done effectively without the computer?

Planning for computer work will involve some important decisions. These include answers to the question:

*How shall I organise it in the classroom?*
1  Physical organisation – individual, pairs, groups or class use?
2  Timing – time allowed (remembering time for reflection/discussion)?
3  Teacher role – most effective role for teacher/helper?
4  Curriculum purpose – integrated into cross-curricular project or curriculum subject such as maths project or language skills?

5   Children's need
    - What skills/knowledge are needed to use this program?
    - Do children need any pre-screen experience?
    - What form should off-screen follow-up work take?

## Task 42  Planning information technology experience

Choose a topic theme or subject area in which a computer will be used to:

- enhance and extend children's learning
- give children confidence and capability in computer use

Plan experiences for children to include any or all of the following aspects of information technology:

- *communicating information*, eg wordprocessing, pictures, graphs, symbolic data
- *handling information*, eg enter and retrieve information using a database
- *modelling*, eg adventure programs using maps or physical models, use of LOGO
- *measurement and control*, eg programmable toys, models or turtle graphics
- *applications and effects*, eg use of IT in the home, office and community

# Unit 11

# HUMAN AND ENVIRONMENTAL STUDIES: HISTORY AND GEOGRAPHY

> When I began teaching I was told to teach them something about the world. 'Where do I begin?' I asked. I never got an answer.
>
> Primary headteacher

## Introduction

From an early age children are curious about the people, places, animals, plants and materials around them. They learn about their environment through first-hand experience, from parents, through the media and many other sources. The role of schools is to help children make sense of these experiences, and to extend their knowledge and understanding of the human and physical processes which shape the environment. 'Schools can also help foster a reasoned and sensitive concern for the quality of the environment, and for the management of the Earth's resources' (HMI, 1989).

Environmental education has links with all areas of the curriculum, to language through the skills of communication and research; to maths and science through the skills of scientific investigation and data handling; to technology; to aesthetic, religious, political and economic awareness; and to other cross-curricular themes like health, and multicultural, personal and social education. The key concepts however are those related to time and space, which form the subject matter of history and geography.

## Task 43  Planning for history and geography

Plan a course of work for one year for a particular class or age range, to cover environmental studies, including history and geography. The work may be undertaken through topics, subject-based study or a combination of both. Identify attainment targets (see pp 178 and 180–183) in your planning, as well as resources (see Table 28) and methods of inquiry (see Tasks 44 and 45).

# History

> History is full of problems ... Sarah, aged 8

The purpose of studying history is to help children develop an awareness and understanding of the past. The present is the product of the past and our knowledge, understanding and attitudes have been shaped by what has gone before. The study of history should be an important feature in any curriculum. HMI Reports however have suggested that history has been seriously under-represented in many primary schools, and that history teaching has often been patchy and unstructured. Children need to experience a planned programme of activities to help develop historical understandings.

The following are some ways in which the study of history can contribute to the school curriculum, whether taught in a topic or as a subject:

- giving children a *sense of identity* through learning about the development of their community, country and cultural origins
- passing on the *shared inheritance* of this society as well as putting diversity of cultures into a historical context
- *contributing to greater knowledge and understanding of other countries*, affirming toleration and respect for cultural variety
- *arousing curiosity*, raising questions, generating speculation and hypothesis testing
- *developing scientific methods of inquiry*, systematic analysis of evidence, and evaluation of argument
- *fostering imagination and empathy*, an awareness of human aspirations and endeavours in other times and places
- *preparing children for adult life*, giving them a range of reference, opportunities for an informed use of leisure, and a deeper understanding of the background of current affairs.

As in all teaching, the teacher's task is to make exploration of the past interesting, exciting and enjoyable. To achieve this teachers need to draw

## TABLE 63 Resources for history

- *Books* are still the most important single resource for studying history: stories, poems, biographies, textbooks, topic books, diaries, encyclopedias, magazines – a wide range of types of book.
- *Drama, role play and re-enactments* will help to bring alive, and give children insight into, the behaviour of people in the past, their motivations, reactions and relationships.
- *Audio and visual aids* can provide a vivid impetus to the study of history when they support specific topics and are appropriate to the interests of children.
- *Visits to museums and historical sites* (see Table 64) can include historic houses as well as industrial sites and places of local historical interest, and can help inspire children and reinforce what is learnt in the classroom.
- *Oral history* can include the spoken memories of local people as well as families, friends and members of the school community, adding colour and depth to historical studies.
- *Artefacts* and historical objects can offer children first-hand experience and opportunities to gather information about the past, to discuss and speculate on their origins and use.
- The *local environment* can provide an important source of historical evidence for study and in comparing the past with the present.
- *Archaeology* yields important evidence, shows ways of searching for and studying historical objects, and can introduce children to important methods of historical research.
- *Archives* can offer a useful means of extending the resources of the teacher beyond the classroom to explore the resources of local libraries, local history collections, exhibitions, facsimilies and reproductions, and text/film/sound archive materials.
- *Information technology* can provide powerful means of compiling, collating, and processing information. Computer databases, as well as simulation programs, can provide valuable tools for the study of history in schools.

upon a wide range of teaching materials and historical sources, such as those listed in Table 63.

## History across the curriculum

Many teachers of juniors integrate their history teaching into cross-curricular themes or topics. Sometimes the topic will have a particular historical focus, at other times the topic will focus on other areas of the curriculum. The cross-curricular process is two-way. History can directly contribute to a

# TABLE 64 Teachers' checklist for museum visits

*LEARNING STRATEGIES*

- How do the aims of the visit relate to the aims of the school and specific schemes of work in terms of knowledge, ideas, skills and attitudes?
- Is the visit an introduction, central stimulus or climax to class work?
- What preparatory work is needed by the class?
- What techniques will pupils use to observe and record?
- How will pupils be organised during the visit?
- How does the visit build on any previous visits undertaken by the pupils?
- What follow-up work will be done?
- How will the visit be evaluated?
- Will the outcome of the visit be shared with other classes or with the museum staff?

*PRACTICALITIES*

**What you need to know about the museum** (preliminary visit)

| Learning opportunities | Resources available | Facilities to check |
|---|---|---|
| appropriate displays for topic | museum plan | car/coach parking |
| A/V or tape commentaries | teachers' notes | reception point |
| reading level of labels | gallery guides | clip boards/stools |
| handling materials/loans | worksheets | sandwich room/picnic area |
| museum talks/activities | reading lists | cloakroom/lavatories |
| space for work near displays | archive documents | disabled access/WC |
| is photography allowed? | pre-visit slides/video | induction loop |

Museum's requirements on adult: child ratio

Admission charges (if any) and group concessions

Journey time from school

**What the museum needs to know about you**

| Teacher in charge of visit | Topic studied | Date and Times of |
|---|---|---|
| number of pupils | syllabus/radio/ETV | arrival/departure |
| age and ability | programme | museum staff |
| any special needs | preparation done | contact |
| number of other adults | aims of visit & follow-up | work in galleries |
| parking space | gallery displays needed | A/V booking |
| | handling/role play/activity | lunch booking |

Phone/write **AS FAR AHEAD AS POSSIBLE** to select date and time for visit. Confirm the booking in writing.

**At School**

Seek the Head's permission for the visit and liaise with colleagues at school for suitable dates. Contact parents for their consent and enlist helpers to conform with your LEA's (and the museum's) requirements of adult:child ratio. Negotiate transport arrangements whether by public transport, school minibus or hired coach.

Check on insurance and funding for the visits.

Enthuse the children about the visit and give them clear expectations about the purpose of the visit and the work and behaviour expected of them.

Brief the adult helpers and allocate specific children to each. Give the helpers plans of the museum, marking rendezvous points and give them guidance notes on the work expected of the children, together with a timetable of the visit.

From *Museums and the Curriculum* published by the Area Museums Service for South Eastern England, 1988

subject or theme of study, and it will benefit from drawing on the knowledge and skills of other subjects and cross-curricular fields.

The following are some of the links that can be made between history and other areas of the curriculum:

- *English* The study of history requires practice in the skills of talking and listening, reading and writing. Children will need study skills to analyse source materials and communication skills to report on their findings. All language has a history, words and place names have origins and change meanings through time. All literature too has a historical and social context.
- *Maths* The conventions of chronology and the passing of years are important elements in the study of history. To quantify historical phenomena – populations, prices, percentages, averages – numerical skills are needed. History involves the practical application of mathematical techniques and terms. Maths also has a history, drawn from different cultures.
- *Science* Methods of scientific inquiry have become important tools for historians: the formulation and testing of hypotheses, the ability to observe and record physical evidence, the use of materials, forces and sources of energy.
- *Design and technology* The achievements of designers, artisans and engineers have been a major influence in bringing about change in society. Through design and technology children can explore ways of representing the past, for example through making models.
- *Geography* All history relates to place and much of it has been about conflicts over the use of or possession of space. Children studying history

need a good grasp of physical geography and map-reading skills. Geography and history share many themes such as transport, clothes, houses, food, communication etc.

- *Art*  There are cultural and aesthetic aspects to any topic of study. The creative arts offer a rich range of primary resources for study of history, such as paintings, sculpture, music, dance and drama. All works of art have a historical and cultural context.
- *Music*  Music is a vivid source of evidence about the past with its many functions such as entertainment, telling stories or celebrating triumphs, and with its different forms − religious, martial, folk, popular, classical etc.
- *PE and movement*  Historical narrative can be expressed through movement, mime and dance. Dance forms and physical games form part of the human and cultural dimensions of history.
- *RE and moral education*  Religion and religious life are important aspects of human history. Much of the subject matter of history raises implicit or explicit moral questions, especially where human motivation and choice is concerned.
- *Personal and social education*  The values and attitudes implicit in historical interpretation are important in helping to prepare children for an active and informed life within their family and community. Other themes and dimensions related to history include: equal opportunities, multicultural education, environmental education, and education for democratic citizenship.

In planning a scheme of work for history, teachers need to select appropriate history study units from the National Curriculum programmes of study and to take account of the attainment targets (ATs) which can help inform teaching and learning.

## History in the National Curriculum

The proposed attainment targets for history within the National Curriculum are as follows:

*AT 1: Knowledge and understanding of history* is based on two aspects or strands of study:

a)  understanding the concept of time and changes which occur over time. For example children should learn how to sequence events by using time-lines or other diagrammatic representations to show the historic development of transport, buildings or writing
b)  understanding the concept of cause and effect through learning that

historical events have causes and consequences, for example the reasons for the Great Plague (1665) and the Great Fire of London, or the results of the factory system in Victorian England.

*AT 2: Interpretations of history.* Children should begin to recognise that there may be different versions of historical events, and that some interpretations may be more firmly based on evidence than others, for example different assessments of Boudicea (Boudicca), or of attitudes in World Wars.

*AT 3: The use of historical sources* is based on two strands:

a)  knowing about sources and acquiring information from them, for example extracting information from books, maps, visual and aural sources, statistics and databases, or a visit to a museum for a particular historical topic

b)  knowing how to evaluate sources of various kinds in order to find out about the past, for example by discussing which type of historical source might provide useful information for a historical enquiry into the voyages of Columbus or life in Victorian Times.

Children should express their historical understanding in a variety of ways, for example a local study could include recording an interview, making notes and fieldwork sketches, compiling statistical information from more than one source including use of IT (computer), writing of various kinds, drama, drawing and modelmaking.

The skills to be encouraged through the study of history are: asking questions, speculating and suggesting possible answers, connecting and comparing new with existing information, investigating and searching for clues and using evidence to stimulate the imagination.

*Note*   The programmes of study for history (NCC December 1990) specify nine study units for juniors (KS2).

The core study units are:

1  Invaders and settlers (Romans, Saxons and Vikings)
2  Tudor and Stuart times
3  Victorian Britain
and/or 4  Britain since 1930
5  Ancient Greece
6  Exploration 1450–1550

Supplementary study units include:

7  A thematic study, such as ships, food, houses, writing, transport or family life

8   A study of local history
9   Study of a non-European society eg Ancient Egypt.
The units should be studied chronologically where possible, and a scheme of
work planned across the four junior years.

## Historical enquiry and communication

Pupils should be helped to investigate historical topics on their own. They
should be shown how to organise and communicate historical knowledge and
understanding in a variety of ways.

They should have opportunities to:

- ask questions, choose sources for an investigation, collect and record
  information, for example: *plan how to use a visit to an historic house
  to find out about past ways of life; discuss with teacher and other pupils
  sources needed for an investigation; make notes and field sketches;*
- select and organise historical information, for example: *group material
  from different sources under headings; draw diagrams; analyse information in an IT database;*
- present results orally, visually and in writing, using a range of techniques,
  for example: *write narratives and descriptions; discuss with teacher and
  other pupils the results of an investigation in local history; make a model
  or collage; take part in an historical drama; use graphs and piecharts to
  present information from an IT database.*

## Task 44  Encouraging historical enquiry

This task may be undertaken by individuals, by pairs or by small groups of children:

1   Collect and give children up to six different historical resources. These can be:

- primary sources ie real artefacts of historical origin, or
- secondary sources ie pictures of historical objects, settings or events

2   Ask the children to study these resources and to formulate some questions
    about them.
3   Can the children put the resources *in order of historical age*, from earliest to
    most recent? Discuss results.

(This activity might lead on to the creation of a time-line, or a mini-museum. See
also: *A Teacher's Guide to Learning from Objects* (Durbin et al, 1990).)

# Geography

Can you teach Geography so as to make people think?
Dr Benjamin Jowett
(Quoted in the first issue of *The Geography Teacher*, 1901).

Geography explores the relationships between the Earth and its peoples through the study of place, space and environment. This includes both physical and human dimensions at local, regional, national, continental and global levels. A central concept in geography is that of *change*, not only where and what, but also how and why. Geography develops skills and knowledge essential to help understanding and solve the problems of the modern world.

The aims of geography include:

● to stimulate children's interest in their local environment, its surface features, human activities and weather and help them understand the changes taking place in their locality.
● to develop their awareness of the variety of physical and human conditions on the Earth's surface, and to be able to compare and contrast environmental conditions.
● to help develop an informed concern about the quality of the environment and the future of the human habitat.
● to enhance their sense of responsibility for the care of the Earth and its peoples.
● to acquire the knowledge, skills and understanding necessary for geographical enquiry and the investigation of issues relating to place, space and environment.

What ways are there of finding out about the environment? The following are some of the approaches to investigation that children should experience, and that can be incorporated into geographical aspects of topic work during the junior stage:

● mapwork – using a variety of maps and globes
● fieldwork – studying physical and human environments at first hand
● learning from material presented by the teacher or from visitors to the classroom
● using audio-visual material, such as video, pictures and tapes, as a stimulus for further study
● using language skills – reading, writing, talking and listening
● engaging in role play, drama and educational games
● using mathematical skills relating to statistics and data handling

- using a computer to store, analyse and retrieve information
- practical activities such as model making, drawing and painting

One of the challenges that teachers face is to plan work that will capture the child's imagination and interest. As HMI argue in *Geography from 5–16*, 'there is much to gain by focusing on comparatively small areas of study and exploring these in some depth' rather than looking at a region or topic in its entirety, for example studying a specific economic activity such as a farm, or factory, or limited area such as a short section of coastline (HMI, 1986). Table 65 shows some questions that can be asked about any geographical location which might help in preparing a study or in assessing a child's learning.

## Geography in the National Curriculum

The proposed attainment targets for geography in the National Curriculum are as follows:

*AT 1: Geographical skills*:

a) using and producing maps and diagrams, for example drawing a sketch map of a school, park or local shopping area
b) conducting fieldwork, for example studying different types of home, or land-use in town or country
c) using secondary sources, for example how to use an atlas to find out about places in the news

*AT 2: Knowledge and understanding of places* includes developing knowledge and understanding of the place where pupils live, around their home, their school and their locality, for example studying the main occupations, land use and patterns of settlement in their local area, and investigating recent changes or proposed developments.

- *The United Kingdom within the European Community* includes knowing and understanding more about the other regions and constituent parts of the UK, and of the European Community (EC), for example using simple maps to find out about different features, activities and journeys within the UK and Europe.
- *The wider world* includes knowing and understanding more about a variety of places and countries in different regions of the world with special reference to trade, development and human welfare, for example identifying and naming features on a suitable globe or map of the world, or studying changes wrought by tourism or natural disaster in a tropical or subtropical locality.

**TABLE 65** Questions about geographical location

- Where is this place?
- What does the place look like? What are the main features of the landscape — physical and cultural?
- Do many or few people live there and why?
- What is it like to live there?
- In what ways are people's activities and ways of life influenced by the character of the place and its location?
- How have people made use of or modified the environment?
- Do many people visit the place and for what purposes?
- What important links does it have with other places?
- In what ways is this place similar to, or different from, our own home area?
- What are the reasons for the main similarities and differences?
- Is the place changing in character and, if so, why?
- What do we feel about the place? What do we find attractive or unattractive about it?
- Do we think that the changes taking place are an improvement or not?
- What are the views of the people who live there?

H.M.S. Victory

*AT 3: Physical geography* includes developing knowledge and understanding of:

a)   weather and climate (atmosphere)
b)   rivers and seas (hydrosphere)
c)   land forms (lithosphere)
d)   animals, plants and soils (biosphere)

for example by studying plant growth in different environments and under different physical conditions (a strong link here with science).

*AT 4: Human geography* includes developing knowledge and understanding of:

a)   population
b)   settlements
c)   communication and movements
d)   economic activities

for example by studying reasons why very few people live in some areas while a great many live in others, including such factors as transport links, farming and industrial development.

*AT 5: Environmental geography* includes developing knowledge and understanding of:

a)   the use and misuse of natural resources
b)   the quality and vulnerability of different environments
c)   the possibilities of protecting and managing environments

for example discuss how some environments need special protection such as historical sites, conservation areas or wildlife habitats, or how to restore derelict land.

## Task 45 Encouraging geographical enquiry

This task may be undertaken by individuals, by pairs or by small groups of children:

1   Give children pictures illustrating two different geographical locations (colour magazines are good sources for such pictures).
2   Ask them to study these locations and to formulate some questions about them that are geographical.
3   Pass the pictures and questions on for other children to consider (or use the questions from Table 29).
4   What inferences and information can the children draw from the evidence? Discuss and reflect on their findings.

# Unit 12

# AESTHETIC DEVELOPMENT: ART, MUSIC, DRAMA AND DANCE

Creativity is not a special faculty with which some children are endowed and others are not. It is a form of intelligence and as such can be developed and trained like any other mode of thinking. The Calouste Gulbenkian Report *The Arts in Schools* (1982)

Aesthetic development includes the training of ear, eye and touch, the development of discrimination, of manipulative skills and creative expression. These areas are among the most difficult to plan, provide for and assess. Art, music, drama and dance make important contributions to a child's all-round development. They develop different aspects of a child's intelligence:

- art – visual/spatial intelligence
- music – aural/musical intelligence
- dance/drama – bodily/kinaesthetic intelligence

HMI surveys reveal that many teachers have not paid much attention in the past to long-term planning, nor assessment of progress in these areas. Now that art and music are foundation subjects in the National Curriculum there will more than ever be a need for teachers to have clear objectives, appropriate resources and training in relevant skills if they are to help children achieve their potential. In particular they will need to allow sufficient time for children to complete the creative work they have in hand. How then should you approach the planning of art, music, drama and dance?

---

**TABLE 66** Aims/objectives for the visual arts

In the visual arts the curriculum from five to 11 should enable children to:

1  experiment with different media – watercolour, crayon, paper, cloth, clay etc.
2  explore different techniques, tools, and modes of manipulation in each – modelling, brushwork etc.
3  understand the basic ideas of, for example, tone, colour, texture and contrast, and eventually more complicated ideas of, for example, balance, focus and proportion.
4  begin to respond to a variety of styles and forms of visual arts, including differences between cultural forms (eg Western, Oriental, African) and between historical periods (eg primitive, ancient, medieval, modern).
5  develop an awareness of the use of visual symbols to convey ideas and feelings.
6  develop an awareness of design – the relationships between materials, forms and functions of objects and constructions.
7  develop powers of observation and description.

---

# Art

Teachers need an agreed framework of aims and objectives to give meaning and coherence to their work. Table 66 suggests some objectives for teaching visual arts.

The majority of teachers integrate art and craft into project and other ongoing work, as well as teaching separate art lessons. Teachers usually try to offer a rich variety of media and techniques to children during the course of a year. Research in the Junior Project highlighted one particular characteristic common to many art lessons. They found that the teachers they saw communicated less with children during art activities than in any other curriculum area. The use of questioning during art sessions was extremely rare. Teachers devoted more time to routine matters of organisation and less on the content of what the children were doing than in any other type of lesson.

Sometimes art is seen simply as a form of therapy, but if teachers are to help children to express their feelings and ideas about experiences effectively, children will need to be taught a repertoire of skills and trained to apply a variety of techniques to the representation of their ideas. They need to be taught how to observe the real world very closely, how to select the appropriate tools and how to work at making the marks they make capture what they feel and see. They need to be encouraged to concentrate for lengthy periods on their artwork, with the support of teacher dialogue about the content and

---

## TABLE 67 An art curriculum checklist

| | |
|---|---|
| DRAWING | • Pencils – both hard (HB) and soft (B – 10B) |
| | • Crayons – wax, pastel, chalk, charcoal |
| | • Pens – biro, felt tips, fibre tips etc |
| | • Brushes – colour limited to black, white, ochres and browns |
| PAINTING | • Powder, liquid tempera, poster, oil and inks |
| | • Brushes of various sizes |
| | • Palettes for colour mixing and matching |
| PRINTING | • Potato and other vegetables |
| | • Miscellaneous – card, wood, string, clay, lino |
| COLLAGE | • Paper, card, pictures, newsprint |
| | • Materials, fabric, threads, found objects, natural and man-made |
| TEXTILES | • Weaving, applique, embroidery, needlework, collage |
| | • Fabrics, garments, tie/dye etc |
| THREE-DIMENSIONAL | • Modelling materials – clay, Plasticine, papier mache etc |
| | • Carving – wood, clay plaster, polystyrene etc |
| | • Construction – card, wood, metal, plastics, wire, sculpture, mobiles etc |
| | • Puppetry – hand, rod, string and shadow |
| RESPONSE TO ARTEFACTS | • Displays of illustrations and objects |
| | • Visits to art galleries, exhibitions and museums |
| | • Visits by artists and craftsmen |

---

techniques of their art activity. Children should sometimes be encouraged to return to paintings, drawings, clay and fabric work over a number of working sessions to take the time to achieve a satisfying result. The checklist in Table 67 can be used when considering the breadth and balance of experience in basic areas of two- and three-dimensional artwork.

The classroom should have access to art books, postcards, posters, cartoons and advertisements as well as a variety of illustrated books. We need to give children the opportunity to assess both 'high art' and pop culture, and not simply surround them with the work of their peer group. It is a mistake for teachers to prejudge what children will respond to or how they will respond. Children should be allowed to think, feel, respond and discriminate in their own way and at their own level. The following task offers an opportunity to see how children respond to a variety of images.

Matthew Roche

## Task 46  Assessing children's response to paintings

Collect ten colour reproductions of diverse subject matter, ancient and modern, all approximately the same size, mounted and numbered 1 to 10. Spread them on a surface where they can easily be seen. Tell individual or groups of children, '*I want you to look very carefully at these pictures*'. Allow time for child or group to view each picture, then ask the following questions:

- Which one do you like best?
- Which do you like second best?
- Which do you like third best?
- Which one do you think I like best?
- Are there any you do not like?

Then ask why the child or group gave each answer. Allow free discussion, influencing it as little as possible. Adapted from Morgan, 1989, p 93.

# Music

Music, like art, is a foundation subject of the National Curriculum and as such should be taught in schools to all pupils. At the nursery and infant stages, and in the early junior years, music should be an integral part of every child's daily experience. More specialised music teaching, often with the support of a music consultant, is generally introduced after the age of eight.

In half the schools studied in the Junior Project class teachers were responsible for taking their own music lessons. Sometimes other teachers were involved, particularly with instrumental tuition. Most schools offer the opportunity for juniors to learn the recorder. Nearly half the schools studied offered guitar tuition. The sorts of instrumental tuition offered in schools varies widely, from percussion, steel bands, violin and cello to wind instruments like the flute. All schools offer singing as a group activity and most offer some extra-curricular musical activity and periodic musical entertainments or festivals.

Why is music important in the primary curriculum? For the child, music can be the source of:

- personal pleasure, enjoyment and enrichment
- self-confidence and and self-esteem
- self-discipline and self-reliance
- social development through shared music making
- therapeutic and emotional development through self-expression
- aural discrimination through listening, singing and playing
- visual discrimination through reading music
- cultural awareness of local/national musical forms
- multicultural/global awareness through varied musical experience
- intellectual challenge and problem-solving skills

The following model identifies three areas of music education for children which are closely inter-related:

- *making sounds and music*
  voices through singing;
  instruments through experience of a range of musical instruments
- *understanding sounds and music*
  elements of music, reading music
  shape, form and texture of music, musical appreciation
- *music and culture*
  folk, classical and popular music
  music in the arts, community and differing cultures

As a class teacher you may be asked to implement the curriculum in music for your class, or this job may be shared with specialist teachers. In most primary schools there is at least one teacher with more expertise in music than his or her colleagues. Such a teacher may have designated responsibility for music throughout the school, coordinating musical activities in and out of class, and offering much needed help and advice to less musically experienced teachers. The school should have a written scheme of work for music, suggesting possible methods of approach for the non-specialist teacher. The following task presents one way of reviewing your school curriculum guidelines for music:

## Task 47  Reviewing curriculum guidelines in music

In reviewing your curriculum guidelines for music, consider the following questions:

1   Is there a written scheme of work?
2   Has it been discussed with all teachers who teach music?
3   Does it identify aims in the teaching of music?
4   Are these aims translated into objectives which provide realistic guidelines for lesson planning?
5   Does it offer a good balance of musical activity linked with the acquisition of necessary skills, concepts, attitudes and ideas?
6   Does it cater for pupil differences in terms of age, ability, interest and family and cultural background?
7   Does it give clear guidance as to content, method and assessment?
8   Does it list organisational needs (adequate time, resources, grouping, accomodation) for successful implementation of the activities?
9   Is it reviewed from time to time?
10  Are careful records kept? What happens to these records? Are programmes of work and individual pupil records passed on?

What should children have experienced and achieved in music by the time they leave the junior school? The HMI (in HMI, 1985) has offered a checklist of experiences which children should be offered through their programmes of study in music (see Table 68).

# Drama

Drama relies on the striking human ability to pretend to be someone or something else. Through acts of imagination children can explore how people

# TABLE 68 Objectives in teaching music

By the age of eleven, children should have had musical experiences which enable them, with varying degrees of skill and understanding, to:

- demonstrate an awareness of sounds of every kind, including those produced electronically;
- identify, collect and imitate sounds of various kinds; to classify and to describe them; create new sounds and combinations of sounds;
- be able to recognise and discriminate between the various elements of music such as pitch, rhythm, dynamics, timbre, melody, solo, accompaniment, chord, ostinato, drone etc;
- know from memory and be able to join in with a wide-ranging repertory of songs appropriate to the age group in as many as possible of the following categories:

  ○ traditional folk songs and ballads
  ○ songs from other lands and other cultures
  ○ songs from former times
  ○ modern songs including some 'pop'
  ○ songs for all seasons
  ○ songs for assembly
  ○ simple descants, ostinati and second parts in conjunction with the above
  ○ rounds and cannons
  ○ music in and for drama;

- accompany singing on tuned or untuned instruments by playing remembered rhythms, melodic phrases, drones, repeated chord sequences and added parts;
- improvise and compose original music (employing voices and/or instruments) with or without recourse to a direct stimulus such as a picture, movement, a narrative, a poem, a lyric, a mood, a situation, drama etc; make a permanent record of such compositions by means of tape recorder and/or the appropriate musical notation;
- play by ear and perform simple pieces (both notated and otherwise) individually and as a member of a group;
- listen with attention and understanding to live and recorded music and to be able to describe what has been heard (in respect of mood, style, instrumentation, structure, origin etc) both orally and on paper, using appropriate vocabulary;
- discover relationships between music and other studies;
- recognise something of the evocative and expressive qualities of music.

Source: *Music from 5–16* (HMI, 1985)

in particular circumstances might behave now and at different times and places. The dramatic experience of children in schools includes:

- free and structured play
- classroom improvisations
- performance of specially devised material (plays or playlets)

Drama is a valuable educational tool and can be a potent means of developing a child's imaginative thinking. As part of the English curriculum it offers language experience in programmes of study for attainment targets in:

- speaking and listening – as participants and observers of drama
- reading – as readers of plays and scripts
- writing – as writers of plays, dramatised stories and re-enactments

Drama links with other arts, particularly music, movement, visual and technical arts. It can enrich work in many subjects across the curriculum such as history, geography and religious education. The design and making of props, costumes and scenery provides opportunities for links with technology and science. Different ages and abilities can take part in creative dramatic ventures. Drama can provide a powerful unifying force within a class, children working and cooperating together, making decisions and solving problems.

What should we be aiming to achieve through children's experiences of drama? The booklet *Drama from 5–16* (HMI, 1989) gives a list of objectives that teachers and children should work towards achieving by the end of the primary phase (see Table 69).

In many primary schools drama features in class presentations for assembly, perhaps involving only a group of children. Teachers tend to approach drama as a class lesson involving all children with great caution. They may feel that problems of control, of structuring the work and of trusting in the children's response presents too many risks. What characterises successful class teaching of drama?

In planning drama for children the following elements may need to be considered:

- *focus* or issue:   What is the problem or situation?
  What might happen next?
- *place* or situation: Where are you? What is it like? Who is there?
- *roles* or identity: Who are you? What are you doing there?

Finding a focus which will hold the interest of the class is very important. Sources of good ideas include:

- *stories* from class or school library
- *illustrations*, pictures of places, characters, events etc
- *artefacts*, interesting objects such as a key or old chest
- *costumes and props*
- *tapes/video* to record and play back play readings and improvisations
- *puppets*

---

**TABLE 69 Objectives in teaching drama**

By the age of 11 pupils should be able to:

- invent and develop convincing roles in specific situations
- create and take part in improvised scenes in order to explore particular issues which could, for instance, have a practical social or moral dimension
- know how to structure dramatic sequences in order to convey meaning
- carry out dramatic intentions with a clear but unforced control over movement and voice
- organise and deploy physical materials, colour, light and sound to create a space for drama
- be able to use artefacts or properties as symbols in dramatic action
- experience the power of ritual and display and other structural means in order to appreciate the contribution these make to dramatic meaning
- select and use first-hand material which is relevant and dramatically significant
- recognise good work in drama through a detailed and critical observation of the characters created, the issues involved and the processes employed

---

Drama provides obvious opportunities for group collaboration. These group efforts in drama can be shown to the teacher, the class, other classes, the whole school, to parents or other community groups. What you will need to make clear to pupils and audience is the *purpose of the learning and experience* so that all understand what they are doing and why they are doing it.

## Task 48 Planning opportunities for drama

- Select a class topic, or lessons planned over a period of time.
- Think where elements of drama might fit into your programme of study.
- Identify objectives or attainment targets you may wish your children to achieve.
- Note ways in which you will record and assess what takes place.
- Relate what you plan to school or LEA drama guidelines.

# Dance

Dance focuses on the expressive use of the body to convey ideas, experience and emotion. This is achieved through the use of gesture, rhythmic movement and patterns made by the body to communicate a message or to express feeling. Music can be a powerful stimulus to movement, as can literary experience, for example retelling a story through mime and movement. Ideas to stimulate movement and dramatic response can stem from classwork or natural happenings like a fall of snow or a windy day. Children can be helped to refine their vocabulary of movement and gesture through creating their own sequences, rhythms and patterns of movement. Experience should include individual and group work (for example building different robotic movements into a class 'machine'). This focus on developing flexibility, mobility, strength and grace in movement is an important contribution to the child's physical education.

# Unit 13

# PHYSICAL EDUCATION

> The dread of beatings! The dread of being late! The dread of games!  John Betjeman *Summoned by Bells* VII

Physical education includes many activities that primary children enjoy pursuing in their leisure time, such as team games, swimming, dance, athletics and gymnastics. No wonder that a survey in London schools found that 34 per cent of primary school children identify physical education as their favourite subject. This was the highest percentage recorded for any subject. PE in school is not simply physical recreation, playing games and keeping fit, it also provides opportunities for children to face challenges, solve problems and develop skills, knowledge and attitudes that contribute to their physical, emotional, social, aesthetic and intellectual development. In so doing it helps the development of personal qualities like self-confidence and self-reliance, and of an understanding of ways of maintaining physical health. In our teaching of PE, what should we be aiming for? The HMI have identified aims for PE (in HMI, 1989), shown in Table 70.

 ## Task 49 Developing understanding of health-related exercise

PE has much to contribute to health education. How do you plan to highlight health-related exercise with your children? Ways to explore children's understanding of the importance of exercise in maintaining a healthy life include encouraging children to:

- brainstorm in groups a topic like 'Good Health' or 'Healthy Exercise'
- plan a 'Keep Fit' campaign

---

## TABLE 70 The aims of physical education

The aims of physical education are to:

- develop a range of psycho-motor skills
- maintain and increase physical mobility and flexibility
- develop stamina and strength
- develop understanding and appreciation of the purposes, forms and conventions of a selection of physical activities
- develop the capacity to express ideas in dance forms
- develop the appreciation of the concepts of fair play, honest competition and good sportsmanship
- develop the ability to appreciate the aesthetic qualities of movement
- develop the capacity to maintain interest and to persevere to achieve success
- foster self-esteem through the acquisition of physical competence and poise
- develop self-confidence through understanding the capabilities and limitations of oneself and others
- develop an understanding of the importance of exercise in maintaining a healthy life.

---

Source: *Physical Education from 5–16* (HMI, 1989)

- survey the exercise habits of others
- devise a training schedule for themselves
- interview an experienced sports or medical expert
- study bodily responses to exercise – lungs, heart, muscles etc
- develop their own routine (to music?) of health-related exercise

(Note: You may like to undertake one or more of these activities for yourself or with colleagues!)

To achieve a balanced physical education for all pupils, teaching programmes might include the following elements:

- gymnastics using floor and apparatus
- games skills
- athletics
- creative movement and dance
- swimming

# 1 Gymnastics

The distinctive contribution of gymnastics lies in its structure of increasingly complex skills of body movement and control. It offers children of this age physical challenge as well as opportunities to be inventive and creative. When well taught, gymnastics makes demands on children's strength, flexibility and stamina which help maintain and develop their physical capacities at a crucial stage of their development.

The task of the teacher is to create the environment and set situations which stimulate the child to draw on its own resources in response. Having explored movement ideas on the floor, children should be given the opportunity to apply their knowledge to the use of apparatus. Many teachers like to build their lessons around a central movement idea or theme which is then investigated and extended in different situations. The following is an example of how a gymnastics lesson may be planned:

1 *Introductory activity* – the theme is introduced and developed on the floor using the whole space without apparatus. Children are given opportunities to experiment, to develop and repeat actions and sequences, until they become skilful. *For example*: the theme of 'balance' is introduced by children taking their weight on different parts of the body.

2 *Apparatus work* – the children cooperate in carrying and assembling the apparatus before working on it in small groups, practising their floorwork skills on the apparatus. *For example*: children practise activities involving balance in different kinds of apparatus.

3 *Finishing activity* – at the end of the lesson when the children put the apparatus away they all take part in a finishing activity to bring the lesson to a calm, controlled and relaxed ending. *For example*: children in groups work together on a sequence of movements involving balance and display their sequences to others.

To ensure that the lesson goes smoothly it is necessary for the teacher to:

- plan beforehand the activities and placing of the apparatus
- have the apparatus ready at hand before the lesson
- ensure that the children know how to lift and carry the apparatus
- check the safe assembly and fixing of all apparatus before children start
- keep working groups small, eg four, to avoid queuing up for an activity
- ensure children are properly changed and that watches and jewellery are removed before the lesson
- be a role model, wearing suitable clothes and safe footwear

Gymnastics is a challenging activity, and safety should be a prime concern. Activities should be included that enhance the safety of children, for example learning how to fall in a variety of ways, how to recover balance and how to land easily. Various award schemes, such as the BAGA awards, may provide ideas for progression in gymnastic skills, though a special course of training will be needed to teach gymnastic skills to a high level.

# 2 Games skills

There are certain basic skills essential to all games playing. These skills include running, jumping, catching, fielding, throwing, bouncing, hitting and so on. Such skills will be found in most of our major games. As they get older children become more interested in adult forms of recognised games, and wish to play 'the proper game'. In games lessons, whether children are competing one against one, in small or large groups, or teams, the emphasis should be on the application of practised physical skills, and the development of the skills of cooperation and team play.

Figure 21 shows some of the skills/techniques involved in ball games.

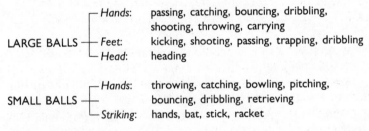

| | Hands: | passing, catching, bouncing, dribbling, shooting, throwing, carrying |
| LARGE BALLS | Feet: | kicking, shooting, passing, trapping, dribbling |
| | Head: | heading |

| | Hands: | throwing, catching, bowling, pitching, bouncing, dribbling, retrieving |
| SMALL BALLS | Striking: | hands, bat, stick, racket |

Figure 21 Ball skills

Mastery of the skill can be taught through:

1 *individual experiment and challenge* – how far? how many times? how high? etc
2 *work with a partner* who serves or returns the ball
3 *introduction of opposition* – the need to dodge, mark, intercept
4 *practice in a games situation* with groups or teams

The games played in school fall into three categories:

● *invasion games* such as soccer, netball, mini-hockey, mini-rugby, mini-basketball, or skittleball
● *net games* such as short tennis, softball, volleyball and badminton
● *batting/fielding games* such as rounders, cricket, stoolball and longball

Children should be introduced to the skills and techniques of each category as well as inventing their own games.

*Inventing games* involves working cooperatively on formulating rules, scoring, equipment and extent of playing area. When the game is developed and refined, children can show it to others, explain it and help others to play.

Games at this stage should have teams and playing areas that ensure maximum involvement, in which all children can experience success and satisfaction. The following is an example of how a games lesson might be planned:

1 *Introductory activity* – warm-up with a class activity, for example a dodging game or free use of small equipment such as bats and balls
2 *Skills practice* – a time for teaching and practising specific games skills, individually and in small groups, such as throwing, catching, batting, fielding, kicking, dodging etc
3 *Games practice* – using skills practised in a variety of small sided games using two to five players, as well as larger team games

# 3 Athletics

Children's natural capacity to run, jump and throw can be developed through athletic experience and training. Athletic activities are often taught as part of the games programme, particularly in spring and summer. The aim of the athletics lesson is the involvement of every child. The development of gifted individuals for competitive events, as in other areas of sport, is best left to clubs in out-of-school hours. Competition at this age, in its most beneficial form, will be against the child's own self.

Suitable athletics activity includes:

*running*    sprints (max. 80–100 metres)
relays: shuttle (back and forth) or baton activity races such as ball-bouncing, skipping, walking, obstacle, hurdle, leapfrog etc
long distance for upper juniors, under 1200 metres (use stopwatch, record times)
*jumping*    long jump and standing broad jump
high jump using natural movements, refer to safety regulations for landing areas
*throwing*    a cricket ball, rounders ball, tennis ball and soccer ball or netball using sideways technique, stationary and with run-up

(Measure jumps and throws with a partner using a tape measure.)

Various athletics award schemes, some sponsored commercially, may provide useful resources for planning activities. Children usually learn best when they are organised in small groups with each group spending a few minutes at several activities.

# 4 Creative movement and dance

In this aspect of the PE programme the focus is on creative, expressive and rhythmic forms of movement. Dance has instrumental and expressive elements closely allied to gymnastics and drama:

DANCE
- gymnastics: control, coordination, and versatility in movement of body (instrumental)
- drama: gestures to convey feelings, ideas and moods (expressive)

Much of the children's experience at this stage should consist of responding spontaneously to a variety of well-chosen stimuli. Examples of such stimuli include:

- *percussion* – tambourine, drum and cymbal can be used to accompany any movement required
- *words* – action words like 'creep', 'twist', 'leap', 'drag', 'lightly', 'smoothly', 'freeze' can create rhythm, sequence and drama
- *poetry and stories* – offer a wealth of material for movement ideas and expressive response
- *records and tapes* – extracts of music, or prerecorded radio programmes
- *class or topicwork* – using class themes and children's work as starting points
- *environmental stimuli* – such as seasons, the sea, machinery, occupations, toys, fireworks, circus, natural disasters, puppets, transport – can spark off dramatic movement experience
- *aerobic dance* – rhythmic response in coordinated sequence created by groups of children
- *folk dance* – traditional dances from many countries

Children should be encouraged to create and invent for themselves as individuals, in pairs, and in small and large groups. As with other forms of expression, providing a purpose and an audience for the activity may help in creating a sense of sharing and enjoyment, and in developing an inner discipline.

## Task 50  Planning opportunities for creative movement

Identify a topic or theme for your children to study. Think of ways in which creative movement or dance may be used to explore aspects of the topic. Look at links with other subjects or cross-curricular areas, for example:

- subject links with language, music or maths
- cross-curricular links with equal opportunities (eg boy/girl involvement), environmental or health education

What form(s) will the creative movement take? What purposes will it serve? (Audience? Outcome?)

# 5  Swimming

All children should have the opportunity to learn to swim, and our aim as teachers and parents should be that by the end of primary school each child is capable of swimming confidently and efficiently in deep water.

To teach swimming, a teacher should be suitably experienced and qualified. During swimming lessons it is essential that an adult, not necessarily the teacher, be present who is capable of rescuing a child in difficulties, can apply resuscitation and has a qualification in life-saving techniques. No child should be allowed in a pool area, whether a public or school pool, without supervision.

Safety precautions must be taught to children and strictly adhered to, for example no child should enter the water without permission and signals must be obeyed immediately. Teachers should have a whistle available and teach the routine: STOP – LOOK – LISTEN.

The first requisite for teaching children is that they should become 'at one' with the water. The importance of water confidence cannot be overstressed – and exploration strategies should be set which keep them moving in different ways through the water.

Schools usually have access to a range of swimming certificates or badges designed to encourage swimmers at different levels of competence. Once children have achieved buoyancy and propulsion through the water, then teaching the four main strokes (front and back crawl, breast stroke and butterfly) can begin. Children should learn other skills such as surface diving, diving from the side and jumping in from a height.

The ability to swim confidently will enable children to participate in a variety of water sports such as canoeing, sailing, water skiing, diving, snorkelling and surf-boarding. More important, it may help to save their own lives and perhaps the lives of others.

*Outdoor pursuits* such as camping, canoeing, sailing, hill walking etc may also be seen as part of the PE programme. It will not be easy to provide for this, given lack of facilities and curriculum time, however many schools try to give such experiences through extra-curricular clubs or residential trips.

A well balanced PE programme should meet the physical and social needs of all children, and provide opportunities to enrich other areas of work – for example spatial aspects of mathematics and language development. Means of assessing and recording will need to be developed across the whole school to monitor progression and continuity in each child's development. The National Curriculum guidelines will provide a framework for assessment and the development of comprehensive schemes of work.

## Task 51  Devising a programme for PE

Devise an outline programme of activities in physical education covering a school year for a chosen class or age range. Try to offer a balance across the year in:

- gymnastics, including named skills such as handstands
- games skills – such as ball skills and a variety of games
- athletics – including activities and opportunities for self-assessment
- creative movement and dance – including a range of stimuli and purposes
- swimming (if facilities are available)

Discuss your programme with colleagues and children.
Compare your suggestions with their ideas.

# Unit 14

# RELIGIOUS AND MORAL EDUCATION

Religion is about things you can't always put in words.
Religion is not always taken seriously in this day and age.
Religion is weird ... I don't understand it.

                                        Three primary children

Religious education is the education of children about religion. It is not primarily social education or education in social relationships, although there are opportunities for both these within this area of the curriculum. Nor should religious education be confused with moral education. Responsibility for moral education should run across the whole curriculum. Religious education does overlap with moral education when children explore the ethical teaching of religious traditions and the moral conflicts that can arise in the lives of religious believers.

## What is religious education?

Religious education is concerned with the spiritual growth of the individual, with feelings and beliefs that arise out of experience and influence the search for meaning and purpose in life. For some this experience will be interpreted in religious terms. The spiritual development of children is the concern both of the school and of faith communities. The family and faith community will encourage spiritual growth in accordance with its own tradition. The task of the school is to help children become aware of the wide range of religious interpretations of personal experience, and of the importance to believers of their religious way of life. There is no sole definition, but there are certain common elements of religious experience, illustrated in Figure 22.

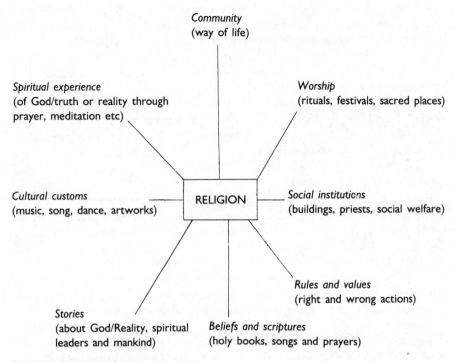

*Figure 22  Elements of religious experience*

## Task 52  Exploring the syllabus for RE

1  Investigate the syllabus for RE relevant to your children. This may involve consulting:

- the school RE policy and/or
- the LEA/SACRE locally agreed syllabus

2  Look at the way common elements of religious experience (Figure 22) feature in the syllabus. See how the syllabus:

- reflects the fact that the religious traditions in Great Britain are in the main Christian and
- takes account of the teaching and practices of other major religions

3  Plan a programme of study, identifying the aims, or attainment targets, you wish your children to achieve.

Religious education must include the study of Christianity. It is the religion that has most influenced our culture, giving rise to institutions, moral codes and patterns of behaviour; it may also be the religion most readily available for study. Religious education must also help develop an understanding of major world religions, and of the beliefs and ways of life to be found in a multi-faith society like Britain today. There is a source of possible tension here between the rights of parents to educate children according to their own religious traditions and the role of the school in preparing children for living in a multicultural democracy. The law safeguards the rights of parents to withdraw children from religious education lessons. It also safeguards the rights of teachers not to teach RE. What then is the status of RE in the school curriculum, and how should it be taught?

Religious education is not a core or foundation subject in the National Curriculum, but is a basic subject alongside the others. RE should be for all pupils, taught in a non-denominational way and in accordance with local Agreed Syllabuses. Unlike other subjects in the National Curriculum, RE is under *local* control. The local bodies set up to formulate Agreed Syllabuses for schools in their area are called Standing Advisory Councils in Religious Education (SACREs), which are made up from local representatives of Christian and other religious denominations, teachers and the local education authorities.

The Agreed Syllabus must 'reflect ... that religious traditions are in the main Christian whilst taking into account the teaching and practices of other principal religions in Great Britain.' Whilst there will be no nationally agreed attainment targets in RE, a local syllabus can include targets recommended by the SACRE.

# Classroom approaches to RE

Religious education can be taught through different organisational patterns: through topic work and through timetabled lessons.

## 1 Integrated topic work

Religious expression involves language, art, music, drama, mime and ritual. Religious traditions have a historical, social and geographical dimension. RE is therefore ideally suited to being part of an integrated project since it relates to a variety of subjects. For example Figure 23 shows a topic plan for studying a religious building, such as a parish church.

Many topics can be enriched by using a religious element. A study of India would be enriched by reference to Hinduism, Buddhism, Sikhism and Islam.

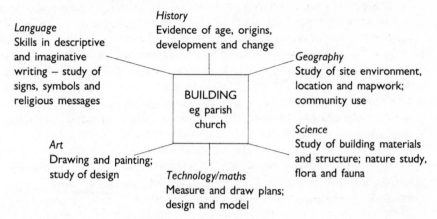

*Figure 23 Topic plan – parish church*

The theme of communication could include the study of signs and symbols, and of holy books. Beware of tokenism, of using religious elements that do not contribute in a meaningful way to the study of topic or religious education – such as the class studying a topic on water and asked to retell (not for the first time) the story of Jonah and the Whale. Better to have one RE-based project where a theme can be studied in depth, than passing reference in a number of uncoordinated topics.

## 2 Timetabled RE lessons

Some junior teachers prefer to ensure provision of RE by means of a specific timetabled allocation. The danger here is that insufficient time will be allowed for children to explore in depth a particular religious theme or activity. The following checklist highlights a range of learning experiences that can support RE:

- *Story-telling*  Stories lie at the heart of religion, and contain many layers of meaning; the story of Rama and Sita for example can lead to a discussion about evil and ways of symbolising it.
- *Talk*  Research evidence points to the value of talk in all learning, for example in introducing the idea of worship, children in groups discuss what is of real worth (worthship) and value to them.
- *Visits*  These can be a powerful stimulus, particularly if children are given the opportunity to meet people and talk of their experience, as well as seeing buildings and artefacts.

- *Visitors* Visitors can be a useful resource, provided the visit is well planned, with a preparatory lesson in which children have time to work out their own questions.
- *Visual aids* Resources that allow children to observe, raise questions and reflect on situations being illustrated include books, posters, videos, slides and filmstrips.
- *Art, drama and mime* Children need opportunities to express religious stories and ideas, and to celebrate festivals and worship in appropriate ways.

RE teaching could include both the *implicit* approach through the study of certain life themes such as family, friends, light, journeys, nature, harvest, helping others, and the *explicit* approach involving teaching about different religious traditions and ways of worship.

Children will have their own view of religion and what it means to be religious. Task 53 offers one way of exploring what religion means to your children.

 ## Task 53 Exploring what religion means to your children

There is no one single definition of religion. The word 'religion' means different things for different people. This activity attempts to make clear some of the meanings your children ascribe to religion. It may also help children to appreciate the different meanings which are present in the class, and to reflect on those meanings.

Divide children into four groups of about six children. Each group is given a large sheet of paper and felt pen. Each group appoints a scribe who writes the word 'RELIGION' clearly in the centre of the paper. Give the groups 15 minutes to brainstorm their ideas and associations with the word. Children take turns. All ideas are recorded. No child is allowed to discuss, criticise or laugh at any word or phrase written down. Analyse and discuss which are related to family, which taught in school.

# Assemblies

There must be daily collective acts of worship in all state-maintained schools, the majority of which must be 'wholly or mainly of a broadly Christian character'. These may be at any time in the school day, and be organised for separate groups of children. The responsibility for planning and organising assemblies lies with the headteacher, but often teachers will be invited to

contribute and in many schools classes or teachers are timetabled to lead certain assemblies. These present opportunities for children to share their work, learning and concerns with others in the school, and to develop a sense of community and shared endeavour. Assemblies can therefore play an important role in planning for and in fostering the aims of RE, as well as in personal and social education (PSE).

## Moral Education (PSE)

Like RE, moral education is an important aspect of personal and social development (PSE). Children often have a clear moral code and sense of justice ('It isn't fair'). Different levels in the development of a child's moral judgement are identified in Table 71.

The aim of moral education is to help children move from egocentric, individualistic and conventional judgements to principles governed by their own sense of reason and fairness. In the classroom we as teachers will be striving for a consensus or reasonable agreement about how to behave and respond to each other. Children will become involved in moral conflicts both within and outside the classroom, and these can provide a rich source of discussion. In our dealings with children, are there moral values we should seek to impose?

## TABLE 71 Stages of moral development

| Level | | |
|---|---|---|
| 1 | Egocentric | – doing what is right to avoid punishment, considering only one's own interests |
| 2 | Individualistic | – recognising rules of fairness, doing right to serve one's own needs |
| 3 | Mutual/conventional | – recognising the need to be good and to follow rules laid down by others |
| 4 | Social/conventional | – fulfilling social duties, with a developing sense of conscience |
| 5 | Social/principle | – having a utilitarian sense of laws, rules and rights for self and others in society |
| 6 | Universal/principle | – following and committed to self-chosen ethical principles of universal human rights |

Adapted from Lawrence Kohlberg's six stages of moral development (L Kohlberg (1984) *The Psychology of Moral Development* Harper and Row)

The question whether there are universal moral values has been long debated. The following list gives some of the values that appear most consistently in the great religious and moral teachings of the world. Figure 24 shows some areas of moral concern.

- *respect for persons* – expressed through personal relationships
- *fairness* – allowing equal rights and opportunities for others
- *truthfulness* – being a reliable witness and truth telling
- *trustworthiness* – keeping promises, being reliable
- *helping others* – friendship, charity towards others

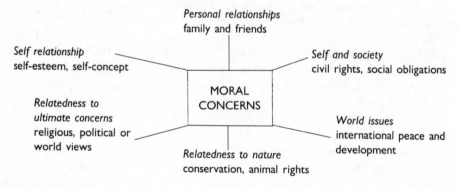

Figure 24 Moral concerns

In all aspects of moral education there may be a gap between judgement and action, between theory and practice. We do know that children learn from example, perhaps more from the example we set than from what we say. The importance of the moral climate in the classroom, the ethos of the school, the expectations that are built up through the interactions of others, are all important. So too are opportunities to raise moral questions, to prompt reflections and discussion, to challenge assumptions and the unfairness of certain attitudes and actions. Such opportunities will include:

- *discussion* of moral dilemmas and problems as they arise, eg bullying, name calling, sharing, helping
- *stories for thinking*: all good literature has a moral dimension, pick an issue from a current book for discussion, reading and writing
- *drama and role play* of conflicts, for example family disputes
- *pictures* as a source of questions, discussion. What is happening, why, what should be done?
- *debating* an issue of current concern, eg should children smacked, what rules should we have in the classroom, should children go to school?

 ## Task 54  Raising moral questions

Indentify some moral choices that may confront children, for example:

- Should/do you always tell the truth?
- Should/do you ever take things which don't belong to you?
- What should/would you do if you found a £5 note?
- What should/would you do if your best friend told you he or she had stolen £5 from home?
- Should/would you stop bullying if you saw it in the playground?
- Should/do you share things with your friends?
- Should/do you always keep a secret?

Ask the children to discuss a chosen dilemma in small groups. Each group should report back on their group discussion. Ways of reporting could include writing, drawing or taping a discussion.

# Unit 15

# ASSESSING PUPIL PROGRESS

> We are assessing all the time as teachers. And of course while we are assessing, our children are assessing us.　　Junior teacher

A key task of teachers is to assess and record the progress of each child in their class. To the new teacher, and sometimes the old teacher, it can present a daunting prospect. How with all this assessing and recording are they going to get any teaching done? Who are the records for? And what sorts of records or assessments are needed?

Assessing pupil progress is part of the wider process of evaluation that goes on in the school. Assessment relates not only to what children have learnt and need to learn, but also to the effectiveness of our teaching and the quality of the curriculum we have to offer. As teachers we need to evaluate our own work. Others who are part of this evaluation process are our colleagues, parents, governors, other interested parties and of course those for whom the whole enterprise is undertaken – the children.

## How should children be assessed?

There are, broadly speaking, two ways of approaching the assessment of children in the classroom. One way is through *tests of ability*, which aim to measure a child's underlying ability in a particular area, for example like the old-fashioned arithmetic and reading tests. These are called *norm-referenced* tests, since they aim to judge children against some assumed 'norm' of progress. There are several weaknesses in this form of assessment. The norms of tests are often statistically unreliable. Give a child two different traditional reading tests and she or he is likely to come out with different 'reading

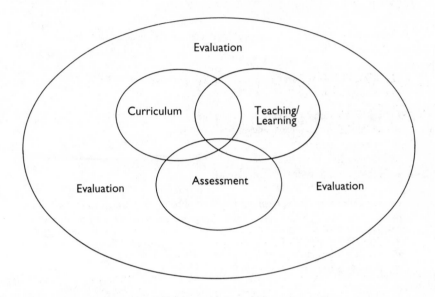

Curriculum

Teaching/
Learning

Evaluation

Assessment

Evaluation

Evaluation

*Figure 25 Evaluation*

ages'. The tests are often separate from and unrelated to what the child is learning in the classroom. They are often 'one-off' rather than part of a continuous process of assessment. Their purpose is often to rank children rather than identify what particular successes the child has achieved in his or her learning.

The TGAT Report argued that if assessment was aimed at helping in the learning process it should be continuous, and that it should focus on the child's current achievement. Judgements should not be made about a child's potential in terms of ability, which is always hazardous, not least because it tends to label a child, but relate to the child's observed performance at regular intervals. This form of assessment is called *criterion referenced*, for it relates to specific criteria of attainment for the individual child. The problem in the past has been, against what criteria of performance should the child be judged?

Teachers are now helped in the process of assessment by having clearly stated criteria, in the form of statements of attainment, against which to judge progress and achievement. They 'provide a framework in which educational objectives may be set and pupils' progress charted and expressed. It can

---

## TABLE 72 Principles of assessment

Assessment is at the heart of the process of promoting children's learning.                                    TGAT Report, para 3

1   *The first principle of assessment* is that it should help children in their learning. Assessment should therefore:

- tell us something about individual progress
- enable us to diagnose individual weaknesses
- draw out strengths
- identify future targets
- provide motivation

2   *The second principle of assessment* is that it should assist the teacher to evaluate her teaching and the children's learning. To achieve this, assessment should:

- indicate the strengths and weaknesses of our curriculum
- provide information on teaching methods and materials
- provide a basis for future planning

3   *The third principle of assessment* is that it should provide a means of communicating with legitimate parties. The asessment process is needed to inform:

- children on how they are doing
- class teacher about children's learning needs
- parents about the progress of their child
- headteacher and other teachers in the school
- teachers in receiving schools for the next phase of education
- governors about the progress of groups of children
- LEA inspectors
- national bodies, including HMI

---

yield a basis for planning the next educational steps in response to children's needs. By facilitating dialogue between teachers it can enhance professional skills and help the school as a whole to strengthen learning across the curriculum and throughout its age range' (TGAT Report, para 3). The attainment targets provide a common language for teachers in assessing children, one that can be shared with children, parents and other professionals.

A common consequence of formal testing or public exams is that the experience is competitive and is often stressful for the child. In informal assessment the child may not know he or she is being assessed, it forms a

TABLE 73 Old and new models of assessment

*Old model*
Traditional public examinations are *norm-referenced*, and have the following character-istics.

- Tests are secret beforehand.
- Children are all asked the same questions.
- Normal classroom work is suspended.
- Total marks are related to other children's scores, and allow for a simple ranking system.

*New model*
Teacher assessments recommended for the National Curriculum differ from class-room 'testing' in the following ways.

- Teacher assessment is continuous.
- Assessment is part of the normal life of a classroom.
- Children are assessed in relation to the criterion of an AT, not in comparison with other children.
- Assessment tasks are related to a child's learning needs and can be repeated.

natural part of classroom activity, with the teacher choosing from time to time to record how children are tackling particular learning tasks, such as a maths problem or aspect of project research.

The criterion-referenced approach to assessment should help the shy or quiet child, the child who does not stand out from the others and who sometimes may get overlooked. Old reports and record cards often contained such vague generalisations as 'about average', 'tries hard', or 'could do better', which gave little idea as to what the child had or had not achieved. Assessment under the National Curriculum should help teachers move away from such descriptions towards comparing the child's progress against agreed standards of attainment. The aim is to assess what the child *can do*, and where the child has achieved success.

What steps are involved in teacher assessment of children? The Schools Examination and Assessment Council (SEAC) say that teacher assessment is designed to INFORM teachers' decisions on planning the way forward for their pupils, and to offer ways in which children themselves can think about their attainments. They identify six stages in the process of teacher assess-ment, shown in Table 74.

---

## TABLE 74 The process of teacher assessment

The INFORM process of teacher assessment is as follows:

- Identify the statements of attainment (ATs) your lesson plans will promote.
- Note carefully opportunities for the child to demonstrate attainment.
- Focus on the performance, looking for evidence of achievement.
- Offer the child the chance to discuss what has been achieved.
- Record what you have identified as noteworthy.
- Modify future lesson plans for the child accordingly.

As this assessment process is cyclical, there is no first or last step, only decision points in a continuous process.

---

This process of continuous assessment is called *formative assessment*. Its purpose is so that the day-to-day achievements of a child can be recognised and the next steps planned. In addition there is *summative assessment*, where the overall achievement of a child is assessed at the end of a given stage, for Key Stage 2 at the age of 11. Both formative (continuous) and summative (end-stage) assessments have other purposes, illustrated in Figure 26. These include:

- *diagnostic*, so that learning difficulties can be identified and appropriate help given
- *evaluative*, so that aspects of the work of the teacher and the school can be assessed
- *informative*, so that information can be appropriately obtained, recorded and reported

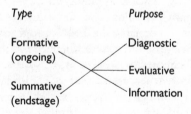

Figure 26 Types and purposes of assessment

The task of assessing children against a whole range of attainment targets is a huge one. To cope with this teachers have had to learn new ways of assessing and recording pupil progress. What techniques can help us in our assessment of children?

# What assessment techniques should we use?

Assessment techniques can be broadly grouped into four categories:

1  systematic observation
2  the gathering of evidence
3  the development of manageable recording systems
4  the use of other assessments

## 1 Observation

Systematic observations can be made at certain fixed points in the programme of activity, for example when the bulk of the class are engaged in independent study and you wish to observe a specific task undertaken by a group of children or an individual who is next on your list. During your observation of the activity there may be many features of it that could be assessed or recorded. There is a need therefore to *focus* on the specific aspect or aspects of the performance you wish to record. Beware of expectations that might cloud your judgement. There may be a 'halo' of success or failure which illuminates your image of certain children. A child may be 'labelled' in your mind as someone who can/cannot be expected to succeed. Try to have clear objectives in mind, and to look for evidence of actual achievement.

## 2 Evidence

The gathering of evidence is an important aspect of assessment, and needs to reflect the range of work done by the child in the classroom. The evidence that you will need to collect in support of your assessment will include samples of children's work. One way to organise this is to open a portfolio or file for each child, in which samples of work can be stored. This portfolio could form part of a Record of Achievement (see p 220) for each child.

## 3 Recording systems

In developing a manageable recording system the following points are important. Records should be:

---

**TABLE 75** Evidence for assessment

Evidence for assessment could include:

WRITTEN   story, letter, report, diary/log, essay, questionnaire, notes/drafts display, newspaper, magazine, storyboard

ORAL      role play, performance, recorded conversation, recorded discussion, interview, debate, taped 'radio' programme

VISUAL    picture, poster, design, photo, film, video, graph, chart, diagram, computer printout, model, sculpture, artefact

---

- *simple* to complete, so that they are manageable in a classroom setting
- *relevant*, so as to inform decisions about future actions
- *meaningful*, so that they can be used to communicate and report progress clearly
- *accessible* to pupils, colleagues, and parents

Some recording systems involve checklists, using ticks or other symbols or colour codes. This is a useful shorthand method of gaining a general impression of the experience or mastery of an attainment target. But these will need to be augmented by fuller description, perhaps on a notebook with a double-page spread for each child, which will be needed as evidence of assessment. This might include one or more of the following:

- a note of what happened (and dated)
- a note of a child's relevant comment
- a teacher's descriptive comment
- a sample of work, where appropriate

## 4 *Other assessments*

Other assessments which might contribute to the child's record of achievement include test results and evidence supplied by other teachers involved with the child, as well as by the child's parents. At the end of each year a summary of these assessments will need to be given to parents in the form of a school report. At the end of the Key Stage at age 11 a *summative assessment* will be made which will be a balance between teacher assessment and specially devised Standardised Assessment Tasks (SATs). SATs will provide the teacher with tasks explicitly related to ATs; they will be common to the assessment of children in schools across the country. The National Curriculum Council will provide clear and detailed guidance on the ways these summative assessments are to be carried out.

### Task 55  Teacher assessment: gathering information

This activity focuses on gathering information in order to assess children's performance in common kinds of classroom work.

1  Plan a lesson in one core area of the curriculum – English, maths or science.
2  Identify up to three attainment targets you think you will have the opportunity to observe during the lesson.
3  Choose up to four children you will aim to assess.
4  Carry through your lesson plan, ensuring that the three children work with the rest of the class as normal.
5  Talk with the children afterwards about their work, and decide whether each child has achieved the statement of attainment.
6  Decide what to record and, on the basis of their work, what the child should do next.

## Assessment in action in the classroom

Opportunities for assessment can arise in different types of classroom organisation. For example:

1  *Group work*: The class is engaged in one subject area, such as maths. The children are working in three or four groups. The teacher begins by briefing the whole class. Each group is given a task matching their level of achievement. The teacher shares her time between the groups, supporting their learning, and assessing the progress of certain individual children.
2  *Integrated activities*: The class is engaged in three or four different activities. The teacher aims to concentrate on children in one particular group, while keeping an eye on the others.
3  *Individual work*: The children are working on activities chosen by themselves such as artwork, research and reading. The teacher uses some of the time to discuss with and record the progress of individual children.
4  *Classwork*: The teacher presents an openended activity to the children in the class, such as a writing assignment, to gather evidence on the different levels of achievement of individual children.

Assessment and the recording of progress should take place as a normal part of teaching and learning. It may be problematical, but should not be seen as a separate burden.

## What problems might arise in assessment?

The attainment targets provide a framework for assessment, but problems will arise in judging whether a child has achieved a particular level of attainment. Difficulties may arise in:

● assessing an individual child
● assessing group work

One problem that can arise is that a child's performance and response may vary from day to day according to changes in mood or circumstances. This may indicate that the attainment target has not been fully or confidently mastered. In any case it suggests a need for repeated assessment, and for the teacher to be sensitive to the optimum conditions for talking with a child about the task being assessed. Remember that assessment is 'of the moment' and does not provide 'the truth' of that child for all time!

There may be ambiguity inherent in the wording of certain statements of attainment, for example in the use of such terms as 'understand', 'know', 'appreciate' and 'use'. In this situation there is a need for agreement with colleagues (part of what is called the *moderation* process) about the nature of evidence to be used in such circumstances, and to discuss examples of work in which judgement seems problematic. There needs to be a policy of agreed definitions in a school for assessing attainment targets.

*Assessment of group or collaborative work* may present special problems, particularly when children are sharing or copying ideas. The initial approach might be to gain a general impression of the activity, and then to focus on individuals, looking for some *detailed evidence* of achievement – in written, diagrammatic or verbal form. Talking with the child after the group task can often clarify what the child has understood about the activity. Table 76 is a checklist of points to look out for in assessing groupwork.

The challenge for teachers is in focusing on and recording something about individual children, while keeping track of the group, and not losing sight of other groups in the class. Some children do not perform well in a group situation. The group may not generate stimulating interaction, or individual involvement – it may be dominated by particular individuals or a child may simply be ignored by the rest of the group. Ensuring beforehand that each child has a definite role to play can help overcome these difficulties. Children can also be assessed on different kinds of output, for example spoken report,

TABLE 76 Assessing groupwork: a checklist

To help assess the work of a group, questions to consider include:

- Do all members of the group contribute to the task?
- Who is producing questions and suggestions that take the task further?
- Who in the group does not work well with others? Why?
- How much time is spent off the task, and by whom?
- What have individual children shown they can achieve during the task?

drawing, modelling, or tape recording, and not just on one form such as a written record.

## Task 56  Assessing individual children in a group

This activity focuses on assessing individual children when they are working collaboratively in a small group.

1  Plan a lesson which includes children working in small groups.
2  Choose two of the quietest children in the class to be assessed. Think how in their groups your chosen children will have a chance to show what they can do.
3  Identify the attainment targets you will seek to assess.
4  Carry out the lesson plan, taking time to assess what your 'quiet ones' are achieving in their group.
5  Talk with the children afterwards about their work.
6  Decide what to record for these, and for other children as appropriate – and what their work should lead on to next.

# What records should be kept?

Teachers generally keep two kinds of records:

1  *Class teaching plans*, which summarise the schemes of work, or programmes of study, to be followed over a period of time, perhaps in the form of weekly forecasts. More detailed lesson plans would derive from these.
2  *Individual records*, which record the achievements and attainments of individuals in the class, either on separate record sheets which can be

fitted together, or in a record book, for example with a double page spread for each subject area.

This information will help form the basis of an annual report to parents. Your records are confidential except to those who have the right of access to the information you record about the children, namely:

- parents, who have a statutory right to view records concerning their children
- teachers who are to receive pupils into their class
- headteachers, who need to monitor the work of the school and respond to queries from parents
- governors of the school
- LEA inspectors, who review and monitor the work of the school

## Records of achievement

Teachers need to record the progress of all children in the subject areas of the National Curriculum. The National Curriculum is not of course the whole of the curriculum. In the last few years, Records of Achievement have developed to provide a means of recording achievements of the whole child, both inside and outside school.

A Record of Achievement is compiled by the *teacher*, *child* and *parent*. It provides a profile of achievement, which can form a focus for parent–teacher discussion, and can help the child reflect on, evaluate and make judgements about his or her own achievements. The record becomes the shared property of the child and the school, and it goes with the child through the school and is transferred to the child's new school. What might a Record of Achievement include? Table 77 makes some suggestions.

Teacher records need to be kept on a *regular* basis; they need to be *complete* in the sense of covering all aspects of the school curriculum (including National Curriculum subjects); they need to be *work related* and include evidence to support the records in terms of samples of work; and they need to relate to *agreed standards* in schools. Children's learning does not take place evenly, so it is important to record their achievements systematically over a long period. There should, therefore, be continuity and progression in record keeping throughout the school – providing positive feedback for children, parents and colleagues in school.

It is important that standards in schools are clear and are shared by all. The process of moderation can help promote a common interpretation of standards and encourage discussion of children's work as it is experienced by all concerned. Task 57 may help this process.

## TABLE 77  Recording achievement

Evidence of achievements could be collected in a loose-leaf file or folder and might include:

- National Curriculum attainments
- statements about personal and social skills and attitudes
- extra-curricular learning and activities, such as certificates of achievement, heritage languages etc
- samples of children's work, dated (could include photos, tapes etc)
- records of discussions with parent or child on child's achievements and targets
- teacher's assessments and comments (including annual summary)
- child's comments and self-assessments
- parents' comments

## Task 57  Agreeing on standards

The process of moderation seeks to achieve agreement on standards of attainment.

1   Collect samples of work of children across a range of ability.
2   Through group discussion, try to achieve agreement as to the levels of attainment shown in each piece of work.
3   Agree samples of work which accord to different levels of attainment.
4   Retain a portfolio of examples, identifying attainment targets for reference and for discussion with other colleagues.

*Note*: For more on assessing and recording children's achievement, see R Fisher (1991) *Recording Achievement in Primary Schools* Blackwell

# Unit 16

# CATERING FOR SPECIAL NEEDS

I try to put myself in the place of my special needs children, and ask 'What would I want?' if I was sitting there as this particular child in the class'. Special needs coordinator in a primary school

All children are different and have their own individual needs. Most should cope with programmes of study appropriate for their age and stage of development with reasonable success. Some children however may experience particular difficulties in coping with the normal programme of classroom tasks. These children may be said to have 'special educational needs'. The teacher needs to identify these difficulties, and plan ways to overcome them so that all her children can experience success in learning.

The Warnock Report (1978) concluded that 20 per cent of pupils will experience difficulties of one kind or another at some time in their school career. In the past such children were thought of as being handicapped and beyond the professional scope of the ordinary teacher. Often they were withdrawn from the classroom setting and taught by specialist teachers, and labelled as 'slow learners' or 'remedial' children. This usually meant that they missed out on the full range of lessons in the normal classroom. Instead they may have been given simple repetitive drill and practice exercises. This approach sometimes entailed giving them more of what they were failing in and reinforcing their sense of failure. The progress of children in remedial classes was often disappointing. Could there be a better way of trying to meet their needs?

The 1981 Education Act abolished the category of handicap and replaced it with the concept of 'special educational needs'. With its focus on the needs of individual children, it was quickly adopted in primary and secondary schools, replacing such concepts as 'slow learner' and 'remedial'. The teacher's responsibility was now seen as extending to all children in her class, including those with special needs. But how should a teacher plan to meet all the varying needs of *all* the children in her class?

Questions that need to be asked include:

- Who are the children in my class with special needs?
- What are their problems?
- How do I cope with them?

## Task 58  Reviewing children with special needs

Look at a list of the names of children in your class. Pick out all those you think have special needs. Record their names, assess their needs and suggest possible ways of meeting these needs. One way of listing your findings is as follows:

| Name | Special needs/problems | Possible courses of action |
|------|------------------------|----------------------------|
|      |                        |                            |

Coping with children with special educational needs is not different from coping with the variety of needs of other children in the class, but it can often present a complex and time-consuming challenge. There is a need for *support* from others, and for *professional development* in coping with problems. Having identified the children, we need to identify and assess their learning problems (see Figure 27). The process of identifying, observing, informing, teaching and assessing is a continuous one, and requires careful recording at every stage.

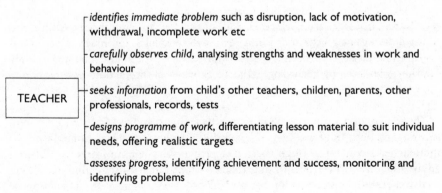

*Figure 27  Assessing problems in learning*

There are various danger signals to be aware of, particularly relating to children with emotional or behaviour problems. These include sudden deterioration in work, an inability to concentrate, unprovoked aggression, irritability, sulkiness, delinquent acts such as stealing, attention-seeking behaviour, nervous symptoms (such as a speech defect), excessive daydreaming, fluctuating moods, failure to make or keep friends, or a high sensitivity to criticism. Some children who display behavioural/emotional problems are very visible in the classroom, others may be relatively invisible. 'Visible' children make themselves known by their loud, attention-seeking behaviour. They seek enhanced status in the class through their behaviour, while invisible children wish to avoid the teacher's attention.

- *visible children* – lively, outspoken, extrovert, disturbed or immature, the self-proclaimed 'stars' of the class
- *invisible children* – shy, anxious, introvert, withdrawn, unsociable, the survivors on the margins of the class

## Task 59 Identifying visible and invisible children

- Identify the children in your class who are 'visible' and who attract a lot of attention (for positive and negative reasons), and the children who are 'invisible' and attract little attention to themselves and make little impact on the classroom.
- Record the number of interactions you have with each child, ie responses and spoken comments, during one day, for example by a tick list:

| Sam | √ | √ | √ | √ | √ | √ |
|-----|---|---|---|---|---|---|
| Jo  | √ | √ | √ |   |   |   |

- Decide if there are strategies you might try to ensure that visible and attention-gaining behaviour is not rewarded by gaining too much of your time, and that invisible children are given more of your attention. You might check this again later by recording again the number of interactions you have with each child.

There are many factors that can affect the responses of children with learning or behaviour problems. The child's social setting at home is not in the teacher's control, though there is a professional responsibility to inform, advise and support parents or guardians of children with special needs. There is also a responsibility to monitor and record any evidence of physical abuse inflicted on the child outside of school. What are the procedures in your

**TABLE 78** Classroom variables that can affect a child's response to learning

| | Variable | Example | Reaction |
|---|---|---|---|
| 1 | Behaviour of teacher | Teacher finds it hard to like a child | Child reacts accordingly, seeking attention |
| 2 | Behaviour of other children | Children reject/ encourage child | Child responds to peer expectations |
| 3 | How child perceives teacher | Child dislikes teacher | Child resents demands |
| 4 | Content of lesson | Child is bored by lesson | Child seeks distractions |
| 5 | Language used in classroom | Child does not understand | Child loses interest |
| 6 | Child's understanding of task | Child is confused | Child fears failure |
| 7 | Teaching methods and materials | Child does not enjoy | Child rejects work |
| 8 | Physical setting of classroom | Child feels uncomfortable | Child is restless |
| 9 | Management of class | Child unclear about rules | Child is unsure |
| 10 | Organisation of lessons | Child has too little or too much time | Child gets left behind or becomes bored |

school for recording and reporting to other professionals incidents that might affect a child's physical or emotional well-being?

Learning difficulties may arise through some physical disability like deafness, poor eyesight, or brain damage. These factors are also outside the teacher's control, although there may be a responsibility to ensure appropriate medical checks are carried out. The 1981 Act established the need for multi-professional assessment and review of children with special needs, with a record kept for each child.

There may be many factors relating to special needs (SEN) children that teachers cannot change. What is directly under their control is what happens in the classroom, in particular the factors that may trigger disruption, or failure of learning. Table 78 lists some of the variables that are under teacher control and are open to change.

There are various positive ways in which we can respond to a child's learning difficulties, for example by:

- *varying task demands* – not necessarily by giving simpler activities, but by planning smaller steps between targets to account for differing levels of ability
- *offering more structure* – providing a more structured framework, or support materials to aid the child
- *varying the approach* – offering ways into the activity in which the child feels confident and can achieve success
- *providing flexibility in time demands* – giving more time to complete a given amount of work
- *working through a child's interests* – relating work to the individual interests of the child
- *working with support groups* – using other children in cooperative learning or an adult helper in paired or group working
- *using varied resources* – working with support of learning aids like the computer
- *setting clear targets* – being clear to the child what he or she is to and can achieve
- *being aware of a child's strengths and weaknesses* – so that strengths can be built on and weaknesses supported with special help
- *valuing individual contributions* – giving praise, where appropriate, for effort made and work achieved

Research by Brophy and Good highlighted ways in which the responses of some teachers tended to restrict the progress of low achievers, as compared to the way other teachers encouraged it. These included:

- *waiting less time for an answer*, then giving the child the answer or asking others
- *criticising more and praising less often*, being less friendly with less eye contact and feedback than with higher achieving children
- *interacting less frequently* and sitting them further away from the teacher's desk

Children learn best when they feel valued and their achievements are recognised. What implications does this have for the teacher? Perhaps one implication is that rather than looking for problems and evidence of failure we should look for success and achievement in our children. But how can we encourage children to succeed in class?

## Encouraging classroom success

We cannot guarantee that children will achieve success in their tasks but we can plan for it and we can look for it. To do this we need to provide:

1  *effective motivation* for children to make an effort and
2  *cognitive support* while they are on task

1  We are more likely to motivate children if we are able to:

- *increase self-confidence*, giving them a sense of competence, of 'can do', so that they become more willing to tackle unfamiliar challenges
- *increase independence*, by giving them some control over their work, making them more responsible for their learning and so helping them to develop a sense of independent mastery over things
- *increase active learning*, giving them variety in their approaches to learning rather than repetitive low-level drill and practice tasks

2  In planning support for their efforts we need to:

- *communicate our expectations*, so that children are clear about the nature and purpose of their work and can answer the question, 'Why am I doing this?'
- *ensure work is relevant*, by matching tasks and materials to individual children, so that they can answer the question, 'Why am I doing it this way?'
- *provide support and feedback*, by offering our help or collaboration with others, so that the child can answer the question, 'Where can I get help if I need it?'

Collaborative work, tackling tasks with others, helps foster understanding, but is not always easy to organise. One common fault is that groups working together are too large – so that children with special needs become marginalised or lack opportunities to contribute. Two or three children are sufficient to begin collaborative learning. Another mistake sometimes made is not to vary the composition of groups, so that children have an opportunity to work alongside varied partners. Collaborative working needs to be introduced gradually, starting with pairs engaged on a familiar task, and the demands increased over time. Good results can often occur when older pupils act as 'tutors' in short, focused sessions, for example in reading. Older children with emotional or behavioural problems may also benefit themselves by acting in the role of 'tutor' to younger children.

There are various teaching resources that can help in supporting 'special needs' children with their individual programme of work. Table 79 suggests some possibilities.

# Very able children

In any large group of children some will be much more able or gifted than others. The very able child may stand out because she or he has:

---

**TABLE 79** Support and resources for teaching special needs children

Possible sources of support which may help in catering for children with special needs include the following:

| | |
|---|---|
| • parents | – to support at home and in school |
| • classroom assistants | – to help implement specific teaching programmes |
| • special needs coordinators | – to advise on school resources and policy |
| • advisory/support teachers | – to provide curriculum support |
| • educational psychologists | – to consult on child's problems/disabilities |
| • other teachers in school | – to offer information and advice |
| • headteacher | – to monitor assessment and progress |
| • students/voluntary helpers | – to assist under guidance of teacher |
| • other children in class/school | – to collaborate in learning/tutoring |
| • non-teaching staff | – to monitor welfare in and around school |

---

**TABLE 80** Some ways of helping able children

Have you given your able pupils opportunities to:

- work independently, following their own interests and at their own pace?
- tackle more challenging tasks?
- explore more demanding resource materials, including IT?
- investigate and solve open-ended problems?
- work with other able, perhaps older, children?
- think creatively, forming and testing hypotheses?
- pursue areas of interest at home and beyond the classroom?
- read widely on a topic, making judgements and drawing conclusions?
- justify their beliefs, both orally and in writing?
- analyse the strengths and weaknesses of their work?

---

- high intelligence
- high achievement
- specific talents

The teacher will need to assess and identify the needs of the very able child and plan accordingly. HMI reports have stressed the failure of many primary teachers to provide for children of high ability. Under the pressure of coping with large numbers of average and less able children, the teacher may well leave the very able child to 'coast along'. As one teacher remarked, 'the able child can look after himself (or herself), it's the less able that need the help.'

The able child however needs as much challenge, stimulus and 'stretching' as the less able. In particular, the National Curriculum highlights the need for all children to have targets at which to aim. We need therefore to identify the very able children in our classes, and to provide specific learning challenges or targets so that their potential for achievement can be fulfilled. How then can we help a child with exceptional ability, a child who may be more intelligent and talented than ourselves? Table 80 offers some suggestions.

## Task 60  Providing for the very able child

Identify from your class the child or children who are very able. Note the evidence of high achievement/ability on which you base your assessment. Plan ways in which you could offer specific support in your teaching for the very able child. The following chart offers one way of recording your assessment and provision:

| Name | Evidence of high ability | Teaching provision |
|------|--------------------------|--------------------|
|      |                          |                    |

# Unit 17

# ENSURING EQUAL OPPORTUNITIES

We're all different, but really we're all the same.

Ten-year-old-boy

The whole curriculum of a school goes far beyond the formal timetable. It includes the policies and practices that promote the personal and social development of the whole child, the recognition of individual differences and the fostering of positive attitudes and values. What are the values and attitudes we wish to encourage in our school? Among them must surely be:

- respect for self
- respect for others

The development of such attitudes should not be left to chance, but needs to be coordinated as part of a whole-school policy, and to permeate every area of the curriculum. We need to ensure equal opportunities for all children in educating them for life in a multicultural society. This will require the development of positive attitudes in children, and in ourselves, towards cultural diversity, gender equality and people with disabilities.

There are many ways in which children may be limited or disadvantaged in terms of their interests, achievements and self-esteem in the classroom. A teacher may have low expectations of certain children, or groups of children, have stereotyped expectations of certain racial, cultural or social groups ('they are from the estate, what do you expect?') or of boys and girls. Differences of race, culture and gender can be interrelated but should also be considered separately as important elements of an equal opportunities policy in terms of:

- multicultural/anti-racist education
- gender equality

TABLE 81 Values and attitudes relating to equal
            opportunities

Among the attitudes and values a school should help all children develop are:

*respect for self*
- a positive self-image
- a confident sense of their own identity
- a willingness to express their own thoughts, feelings and ideas
- a recognition of their own achievements
- a knowledge of the achievements of their own culture/gender/social group

*respect for others*
- accepting the uniqueness of each individual human being
- respecting the equal rights of others
- valuing the achievements of other individuals, social and ethnic groups, cultures and nations
- recognising the damaging effects of prejudice and discrimination on rejected individuals and groups
- understanding the dangers of stereotyping other individuals and groups

# Multicultural/anti-racist education

We do not live in a monocultural society. Many cultures and languages are represented in our communities, whether or not we have children from different ethnic groups in our classes. There is a need for children to become aware of the culture most immediate to them, and to develop an understanding of the diverse cultures in our own society as well as aspects of more distant human communities (see Figure 28).

From the child's growing awareness of the diversity of races, religious beliefs, traditions, art-forms and languages should come a broader understanding of cultural diversity, and a respect for and appreciation of its richness. Multicultural education aims to provide the child with access to diverse cultural forms, and foster an understanding between people of different racial and cultural groups. It will also aim at the active discouragement of adverse attitudes and activities, and in particular at combatting racism and racial discrimination.

Three principles of multicultural education form the basis of multicultural policies in many schools and classrooms. They are that:

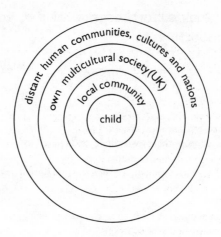

*Figure 28 The child's growing multicultural/global awareness*

1  multicultural education is a logical outcome of living in a pluralist society, and should be available for all children.
2  multicultural education seeks to improve the quality of life of young people by enhancing personal identity, developing responsible moral behaviour and a knowledge and understanding of the diverse cultural traditions represented in our society
3  multicultural education is not a separate subject but should permeate every area of the curriculum

Table 82 suggests some ways in which cultural diversity can be harnessed to enrich the curriculum. Teachers should become aware of the cultural background of each child in their care, and initiate activities which reflect a multicultural world.

 ## Task 61  Planning for multicultural education

Plan a programme of study, in curriculum areas or as topic work, for your class. Identify the elements within your plan of work which reflect multicultural dimensions in the curriculum.

Racist incidents such as harassment and name calling can happen in any school. The fact that in some schools children may lack the opportunity to

# TABLE 82 Multicultural aspects of the curriculum

The following checklist offers some starting points for exploring cultural diversity in the primary curriculum:

*English/language*
- survey languages spoken in your class/school
- list common words/phrases in different languages
- collect and investigate dual language books
- study naming systems, names in different languages
- practise calligraphy in non-English scripts
- share poems, stories, non-fiction books illustrating different cultures
- survey library books for multicultural interest/racist stereotypes

*Maths*
- study number systems in other cultures
- use of pattern/shape in other cultures, eg Arabic designs
- investigate board games from around the world

*Science*
- relate science topics to different cultural backgrounds
- use resources from different cultures eg ethnic food/clothes/artefacts

*Technology*
- study artefacts, systems and environments from different cultural traditions, eg cookery, toys, housing

*History*
- study units in European and World History

*Geography*
- study human and physical aspects of world geography

*Art*
- study arts and crafts of different cultures, materials and methods

*Music*
- study musical instruments, songs from around the world

*RE*
- study festivals and religious experience of different faiths and cultures

meet those of different ethnic origin does not mean that racist attitudes are not forming. The trigger for racist behaviour may be skin colour, or language or other cultural differences. Children who are subjected to name calling and insults because of their colour or physical appearance need the support of teachers, for such insults hurt.

Racist behaviour can take various forms, for example:

- physical assault or harassment
- verbal attack – name calling, ridicule, threats, insults, racist jokes, incitement to racial hatred
- graffiti – written abuse in public places
- racist comments in lessons, eg denigrating/stereotyping cultural groups
- refusal to cooperate with children from particular races or groups

The Elton Report (1989), *Discipline in Schools*, points out that: 'Bullying not only causes considerable suffering to individual pupils but also has a damaging effect on the school atmosphere. This is perhaps even more true of racial harassment . . .' Many schools will have anti-racist policies, which include such strategies for dealing with racist incidents as those listed in Table 83.

 ## Task 62 Identifying strategies to combat racism/bullying

Identify an incident from your school experience that involved racial harassment or insulting behaviour by one child towards another (or others). Consider how you dealt with the problem.

- What *short-term* strategies did you, or might you, have used?
- What *long-term* strategies did you, or might you, have used?
- In what ways did you/could you support the victim?
- In what ways did you/could you deal with the bully?
- In what ways would you seek support from other children, colleagues or parents in combatting racism/bullying?

# Gender equality

Teachers are becoming increasingly aware of the effect they have on a child's development through gender stereotyping. They cannot expect to undo all the conscious and subconscious indoctrination of the home, or others in society, that might be lowering expectations and limiting the horizons of children's lives. But as teachers we do need to make an effort to provide children with a positive view of their role in life. Of particular concern is the domination of

**TABLE 83 Dealing with racist incidents**

Strategies for dealing with racist incidents include:

1  Acting immediately when a racial incident takes place.
2  Making clear to children that racist behaviour is not acceptable.
3  Clearly identifying the racist behaviour and trying to determine how much of this behaviour is understood.
4  Offering support to the child who has been insulted or rejected.
5  Dealing firmly yet supportively with the child who was insulting, helping the children settle any argument.
6  Not side-stepping the issue, for example by saying that name calling does not matter ('Sticks and stones . . .' etc).
7  Involving other children in discussion or curriculum activities to help illustrate and resolve the problem.
8  Discussing such incidents with colleagues, and with parents if appropriate, so that ideas can be shared.
9  Monitoring carefully for future incidents, and assessing effectiveness of anti-racist policy.
10  Reinforcing the notion that it is the behaviour rather than the child that is unacceptable.

boys in certain curricular areas often regarded as of high value in society, such as maths, science and technology. The seeds of inequality in these areas can be sown in the primary years. The primary school environment can encourage the self-confidence and achievement of girls, and can foster attitudes in boys such as caring, cooperation and sensitivity, which challenge traditional stereotypes for both sexes.

How is gender equality to be achieved? Perhaps the best way is by being continually aware of the problem, and by creating a policy with colleagues in school aimed at ensuring equal opportunities. Such a policy might involve keeping a check on ourselves about the specific ways in which we can foster gender equality in the classroom (see Table 84).

There are various ways in the classroom that teachers can raise children's awareness of gender bias, and can help to confront and challenge it. The following are examples of activities that can be used to explore stereotyped attitudes and opinions:

- *brainstorming relevant concepts*, such as male/female, 'Girls are . . ./boys are . . .', 'stereotyping means . . .', 'sexism is . . .', as an individual or group activity for about ten minutes, to share and discuss afterwards.

## TABLE 84  A checklist on gender equality in the classroom

Questions to ask in evaluating gender equality in the classroom include:

- Do I sit girls and boys at separate desks/tables?
- Do I ever suggest it is a punishment for a boy to sit next to a girl or vice versa?
- Do I divide children by sex for activities such as PE or lining up?
- Do I record boys' and girls' activities in different ways?
- Do I expect different sorts of behaviour from girls and boys in the same situation?
- Do I check that school resources such as books, materials and displays are not sexist in nature?
- Do I challenge sexist attitudes and behaviour from children in the classroom?
- Do I ensure both sexes share tasks such as carrying things and tidying up?
- Do I allow for a balance of boys and girls in curricular and extra-curricular activities?
- Do I introduce information about the achievements of women as well as men?
- Do I monitor how I behave towards girls and boys in the class, trying to give children equal teacher time and attention?
- Do I provide opportunities for collaboration between girls and boys?

- *jobs and occupations survey*: children in groups to list occupations under three headings: Female/Male/Both. Discuss whether all jobs can be done by both sexes, and which occupations fall into stereotyped patterns. Survey the jobs that the pupils' parents do, or those that children would like to do. Discuss and compare results.
- *adjectives to describe people*: children in groups choose adjectives to describe boys/girls/either. Which adjectives would they use to describe themselves? Discuss any stereotyped assumptions promoted by language use.
- *survey of reading books*, to find the number of male and female characters, and the activities they are engaged in. Chart and discuss results.
- *survey of comics* that the children read. Children review comic features and decide who they are written for, and say what they liked and did not like about stories. Discuss how the sexes are portrayed in comics. Similar surveys could focus on adverts and discuss which are thought to be sexist or stereotyped.
- *playground survey* invites children to observe and comment on their school playground with reference to the space used and the activities of boys and girls. Groups discuss and design the ideal playground for equal sharing between boys and girls.

## Task 63  Exploring gender issues

Explore your children's perceptions of gender roles through one of the above activities or project work on families or jobs.

What differences are there in the perceptions of girls and boys?

Do they think your classroom provides equal opportunities for girls and boys? Do they have any suggestions on how opportunities in your classroom could be made more equal?

Cooking is for boys too

# Unit 18

# WORKING WITH THE COMMUNITY

> I like to think of our school as reflecting all that is best in the local community.
>
> Primary School Governor

Primary teachers serve a local community of parents and children, and most would see their schools as being part of that community. Just what the characteristics of that community are will vary considerably, given the location, situation and attitudes of the school. Some primary schools relate to geographically recognisable communities of which they are a part, for example village schools or those attached to housing estates. Church schools tend to see themselves as representing a parish of which they are a part. Other schools have no clear boundaries to their communities and see themselves as simply representing the shifting population of parents and children who have associated themselves with the school.

What community does your school serve?

 ## Task 64  Defining the community your school serves

Identify the local communities and groups which your school serves. These may include community groups relating to:

- areas of housing, eg housing estates
- religious groups, eg local churches
- workplaces, eg local factories, commercial centres, shops
- community associations, eg old people's home
- linked schools, eg feeder and follow-on schools

Consider the kinds of relationships you would wish to have with these groups, and ways in which these relationships may be developed by yourself and the school.

---

**TABLE 85** The responsibilities of school governors

Under the 1986 Act, school governors must:

- take general responsibility for the conduct of the school
- decide the content of the curriculum, taking account of the LEA curriculum policy, the National Curriculum and the advice of the headteacher
- decide whether sex education should be provided
- be responsible for the local management of the school, including the school budget
- lay down a policy on discipline and school uniform
- be responsible for selecting, and if need be dismissing, staff
- monitor the support given to children with special educational needs
- ensure that registers of attendance are kept
- ensure regular communication with parents, and report to parents at an annual meeting
- ensure schools make available to parents all curriculum policies and schemes of work used in the school

---

One formal link between the school and the community is the governing body, which will include representatives of the local community, of the parents and teaching staff of the school. Governors have specific responsibilities as guardians of the community interest in the school. (See Table 85.)

It is important for the class teacher to know who the school governors are, and what responsibilities they may be undertaking in the school, for example as link-governors attached to a class, or overseeing a particular area of the curriculum on behalf of the governing body. A governor may have a specific contribution which he or she could make to your class. You also have a responsibility to the governing body to make the needs of your class, and the results of your teaching, known to the governors. In what ways do you relate to your school governors?

Most schools engage in specific activities to encourage communication between teachers, parents and governors. These may include open days, Christmas plays, harvest festival services, sports days or exhibitions of work which have a specific purpose in their own right as well as serving the function of opening the school to the wider community. Parents may be invited to discuss the children's progress on a regular basis, perhaps once a term, or at the beginning and end of the school year. Some schools go further and invite parents into school during the normal day-to-day routine, to see assemblies and observe classroom activities. Parents may be invited to help

## TABLE 86 Ways of involving parents

The following are some ways of involving parents in the life of the school, and of encouraging them as partners in the process of helping children to learn:

- a newsletter for parents from the school and/or your class
- inviting parents in to see your class at work
- inviting parents and local residents to class concerts and assemblies
- displaying the work of the class for parents to see, eg in the school foyer or local library
- termly parents' evenings
- a regular after-school time when you are available to see parents, perhaps once a week for an hour
- encouraging parents to contribute to class activities, eg sharing a skill or hobby
- arranging for social gatherings where parents may meet
- informing parents of what you intend to teach, and showing them ways in which they can help at home
- providing in-service training for parents and parent-helpers

the teacher with individuals or groups of children in the classroom, perhaps to hear reading or help with computer work, or to assist with clubs, sports teams and outings. Some ways in which schools try to involve parents are listed in Table 86.

Schools often have programmes aimed at involving parents in the teaching of their children. Various research projects, such as the Haringey Research (Tizard et al, 1982) show the success of involving parents in the teaching of reading at home, even in areas of social deprivation, provided the parents involved receive support and training. Home–school reading schemes, whereby children take home reading books from school, are now common. Less common but receiving growing attention are home–school maths support schemes, following the pioneering IMPACT approach. Most schools provide periodic Curriculum Evenings when specific aspects of the curriculum are discussed, children's work displayed and questions answered on ways parents can help.

The question whether parents should be involved in the school and classroom often attracts strong feelings. Involvement is seen by some teachers as a natural and helpful extension of parental interest, others regard it as an intrusion and threat. Task 65 presents one way of examining the present position and the potential value of involving parents in the classroom.

# Task 65  Reviewing parental help in the classroom

Survey the actual and possible use of parental involvement in classroom activities by, for example:

1  Listing all the ways in which you *do* involve parents in your classroom.
2  Listing ways in which you *would be prepared* to involve parents in your classroom (it may help to identify any gaps in your curricular provision which parents may be able to provide).
3  Comparing your lists. Are there activities which you would like to involve parents in, which have at present no parental involvement? If so, consider for instance:

- Do parents know in which activities they may be involved?
- Do parents know which specific activities you would like help with?
- Are opportunities provided for parents to find out about ways of helping children in specific areas of the curriculum in the classroom or at home?

One of the key factors to consider when evaluating your relationship as a teacher with the local community is that of rapport or effective dialogue with members of the community who are not themselves professional educators. They may not share our professional background or speak our professional language, but they have legitimate interests and concerns. There is a need to speak *to*, and not *at* others, and to regard them not negatively as non-teachers but positively as what they *are*. As one headteacher put it, 'I try to remember that everyone knows something I don't know about teaching or children, and it's in my interests to find out whatever I can.' Finding time to speak to parents, governors, non-teaching staff and visitors to the school is not easy in a busy teaching day and with many outside pressures, but it can be time well spent in fostering that sense of community which is the hallmark of many good schools.

Another way in which teachers may seek to relate to the community is by reflecting that community in the curriculum. Environmental studies often appears as a component of the primary curriculum. Such studies aim at integrating historical, geographical and scientific perspectives within a study of the local area, offering an opportunity to apply linguistic, mathematical, artistic and technological skills to aspects of local interest and concern to pupils. Study of the local environment also provides opportunities for consideration of social and religious issues as well as the economic and industrial understanding which children need as future citizens. We would not wish to limit the horizons of pupils only to the local environment, but it is a powerful resource for learning and for study at first hand.

Task 66 reviews ways of extending children's understanding of the local environment and of involving the community in their learning.

## Task 66 Involving the local community in teaching and learning

Keep a diary or checklist of examples of community involvement with the school. This could include notes on visitors to the school, contacts with local shops and firms, outings to sports centres or the library, class or group visits to a local place of interest, speakers, classroom helpers and so on.

Further analysis, if possible with colleagues, could include:

1 Thinking back over a period of time, to review what input the school has sought and obtained from the local community.
2 Planning a study of the local environment to involve one or more classes. Such a project could involve maps, photographs, sketches, cuttings from old newspapers, tape recordings, writing, models and artwork, culminating perhaps in a public exhibition or display.
3 Listing all the individuals and local agencies which you think the school should have a relationship with. Identify those which are currently strong contacts, and those where new relationships might be established. Decide on ways of trying to make links with those in the local community who might be of benefit to the pupils and the school. Keep a register or diary of contacts.

Who in the local community can we help, and who can help us?

# Unit 19

# APPRAISING YOUR TEACHING

Teaching a class is like trying to keep a lot of plates spinning on the ends of long rods. Just when you've got one plate spinning, another needs attending to. The trick is to keep them all spinning, and to keep sane at the same time.                    Primary teacher

Teachers are constantly being observed and judged by other people, including colleagues, headteachers, advisers, parents and children. They are regarded as being in positions of trust and responsibility, and as such are accountable for their professional actions. The web of accountability can be illustrated as in Figure 29.

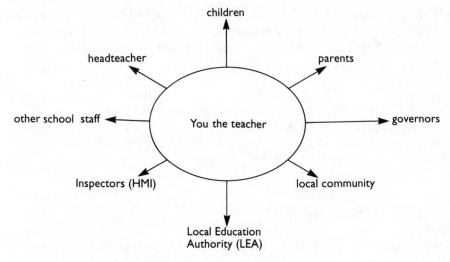

Figure 29 The web of accountability

# Self-assessment

Accountability begins with the teacher monitoring, assessing and evaluating her own teaching, asking questions like:

- What have I achieved today?
- What have I really taught?
- What have my children actually learned?
- What are my main strengths and weaknesses?
- What gives me greatest satisfaction?
- What are my greatest frustrations?
- How can I make a better job of what I do?

Self-assessment can help you be more effective in your teaching. Reflecting on your practice as a teacher can help in identifying weaknesses and in recognising and building on strengths. Teaching is a complex activity, and as valuable as general questions like this may be in focusing on important aspects of a professional role, you will need to consider elements of your teaching in more detail, to make sense of and assess more clearly your work as a teacher.

## Task 67 Agreeing principles of effective teaching

Write down three factors you identify as being the most important principles of effective primary teaching. Ask colleagues to do the same. Try to rank your chosen principles in order of importance. Compare and discuss the principles and priorities with your colleagues.

This activity can also be undertaken with any section of the self-assessment model shown in Figure 30, which specifies the basic elements of teaching under six headings. We begin by looking at those elements which establish the *context* of classroom learning, then consider the *content* of the curriculum and ways to assess and foster learning.

## 1 Relationships with children

All teachers need to build up and maintain relationships with the children they teach. The quality of such relationships can have a direct bearing on the success of teaching and learning. There are many variables involved in help-

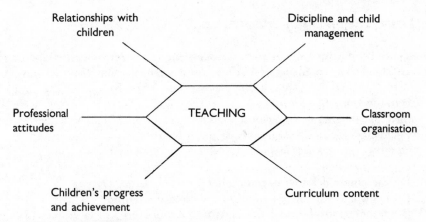

Figure 30 A model for self-assessment

ing each child develop to his or her own potential. This aim is easy to state but hard to achieve, particularly in a large class. Questions that teachers need to consider include:

- Do I offer all children similar opportunities as learners?
- Do I offer all children an equal amount of my time and attention over a specific time span?
- Do I try to develop positive relationships with all children?

---

## TABLE 87  Relationships with children

In developing and maintaining good relationships with children in my class, am I able to:

- understand the personality needs of each child?
- treat each individual child with consistent respect and courtesy?
- communicate easily with each child, with warmth and good humour?
- recognise the need to enhance in each child a positive self-image?
- encourage ideas and contributions to activities from each child?
- make time to listen to children and discuss their concerns?
- become aware of the child's background, interests and enthusiasms?
- understand the influence of the peer group on children's attitudes and behaviour?
- ensure there are equal opportunities for all children?
- provide a suitable model and example for children?

## 2 Discipline and child management

A teacher cannot function effectively unless she is in control of her class, and the children respond to her lead. This does not mean that children have to work in a hushed atmosphere. Busy classrooms often have a steady hum of background noise as children set about their tasks. There are many ways of establishing and maintaining order in the classroom. Much will depend on the personality and self-awareness of the teacher.

Questions to consider include:

- Do the children know exactly what I expect of them?
- Do I know what interests and motivates the children?
- Does the atmosphere of the classroom/school provide a framework in which children work hard and respect each other?

---

**TABLE 88** Discipline and child management

In maintaining a positive atmosphere of order and discipline in the class, am I able to:

- establish clear rules and boundaries in which children can operate?
- communicate my expectations clearly to the children?
- create and maintain a positive atmosphere conducive to learning?
- use praise and encouragement to reinforce good behaviour and work habits?
- employ a variety of strategies to motivate children?
- maintain a consistent and fair approach to dealing with children?
- involve children in classroom routines and policy decisions?
- monitor the whole class while working with individuals and groups?
- react calmly, confidently and decisively to disruptive behaviour?
- show flexibility in voice control in response to differing classroom situations (ignoring minor infringements where appropriate)?

---

## 3 Classroom organisation

Most of a teacher's working day is spent in the classroom. For the class teacher and for the children, their classroom is a home base, a workshop and a territory. It will reflect very much the personality and professional skill of

## TABLE 89 Classroom organisation

In the day-to-day running of my classroom am I able to:

- use a combination of individual, group and whole-class teaching to maximise the use of time?
- organise a variety of materials, apparatus and activities to cover all areas of the curriculum?
- provide a variety of materials, apparatus and activities to cater for all abilities?
- encourage the children to be responsible for the storage and retrieval of resources?
- ensure good use of time for children and self, avoiding time wasting and inactivity?
- use charts, pictures, objects etc to stimulate response, interest and learning?
- display the work of each child, over time, to the best advantage?
- maintain high standards in the presentation of work, for example in lettering and mounting?
- invite the children's involvement in the planning of classroom activity, organisation and displays?
- create an interesting, orderly and attractive classroom environment?

the teacher. The good practitioner takes pride in and responsibility for all that goes on there. The skills of classroom management, organisation and display are of primary importance in establishing an environment for learning.

Questions to consider include:

- Have I established efficient routines for the day-to-day running of my classroom?
- How does the way I organise my class reflect my priorities in teaching?
- Is my classroom a stimulating environment for my children?

## 4 Curriculum content

The school curriculum policy will provide the framework for the schemes of work you plan for your class. It is important to assess the planned outcomes of learning – the curriculum content – in any scheme of work, to ensure that the planned programme of study is broad, balanced and relevant to the needs of the children.

Questions to consider include:

---

## TABLE 90 Curriculum content

Do my schemes of work provide opportunities and resources for children at all levels
of development in:

- English (listening, speaking, reading and writing)?
- maths (using and applying maths, number, algebra, measures, shape and data handling)?
- science (exploration, and investigation of scientific knowledge, concepts, skills and attitudes)?
- technology (identifying needs, generating designs, planning and making, and information technology capability)?
- history (understanding, interpreting, evaluating and communicating historical information)?
- geography (geographical knowledge, understanding and skills)?
- art (artistic skills, knowledge and appreciation)?
- music (musical skills, knowledge and appreciation)?
- PE (gymnastics, games and movement skills)?
- religious education (knowledge and understanding of religious experience)?
- personal, social and moral education (including multicultural education and gender equality)?
- cross-curricular themes (economic and industrial understanding, environmental education, health education and citizenship)?

---

- Does the curriculum content reflect the needs of children, and the aspirations of their parents?
- Does the scheme of work for my class reflect the school curriculum policy?
- Does it reflect the requirements of the National Curriculum in its content and cross-curricular provision?

## 5 Children's progress and achievement

If our teaching is to relate to the needs of children, then our children's progress and achievements will need to be continually assessed. Gone are the days when assessment could be left to a few end-of-term or end-of-year tests. We need up-to-date knowledge of our children and their capabilities. To achieve this requires a day-to-day system of recording children's develop-

---

**TABLE 91  Children's progress and achievements**

In monitoring the progress and achievement of each child, am I able to:

- provide a variety of learning situations in which all children can succeed?
- match tasks to the needs of all children, including the most able and the least able?
- keep accurate and systematic records of children's progress?
- be up-to-date with setting, marking and responding to children's work?
- create opportunities to discuss activities, outcomes and achievements with individual children?
- collect evidence of children's achievements?
- encourage children to assess and record their own progress and achievements?
- offer time, encouragement and incentive for children to complete assignments satisfactorily?
- take time to observe children's approach to learning?
- ensure children know the aims and objectives of their learning activities?

---

ment. It is a demanding task and one we need to keep in manageable proportions. Assessment should be the servant of teaching, not the master or mistress.

Questions to consider include:

- Do I know the current levels of progress of each child in my class?
- Do I have an efficient and effective system of monitoring children's progress and achievements?
- Am I up-to-date with current thinking about methods of assessment?

## 6  *Professional attitudes*

What kind of teacher you are will depend in part on the ways you approach your duties and responsibilities, your professional attitudes and personality. Personal qualities such as enthusiasm, confidence and a sense of humour all contribute to your teaching style in the classroom. They affect your relationships with children, as well as with the wider community of colleagues and parents. To 'see ourselves as others see us' has always been one of the hardest forms of self-assessment. It is easier often to judge others than to judge our own qualities and attitudes.

Questions to consider include:

---

## TABLE 92 Professional attitudes

In your professional role as a primary teacher are you:

- regularly monitoring and evaluating your own performance?
- committed to and generally positive about your role as a teacher?
- able to convey enjoyment and enthusiasm to children?
- supportive to colleagues and receptive to new ideas?
- willing to contribute to staff discussion?
- able to build professional relationships with non-teaching staff, parents and community members?
- willing to encourage the interest of parents and discuss matters of concern with them?
- willing to take part in out-of-school activities of a social and educational nature?
- punctual, reliable and conscientious in your approach to professional duties?
- willing to undertake professional development, in-service training and appraisal by others?

---

- What qualities do I most admire in myself as a teacher?
- What qualities do I least admire?
- In what ways could I promote my own personal and professional development?

## Task 68 Self-evaluation: assessing your effectiveness as a primary teacher

For any chosen section of the self-assessment model, allocate yourself points, eg on a scale of 1–5 (or 1–10) for each subsection, with 5 (or 10) high. After a careful study of the section, apportion the points you think that a fair-minded evaluator who knew your work well would give you.

Often as teachers we tend to be too self-critical; giving yourself the marks you think someone who knows you and your particular context well would give, will help you arrive at a more balanced assessment. This profile should help you see what you are doing effectively and where your strengths lie. It may also highlight areas of weakness where further support or modifications in practice may be needed.

*Note:* On a ten-item list, adding each mark out of ten will give you a percentage rating for that section.

# Appraisal by others

While teachers are evaluating themselves, they are also being evaluated by others. Among those who will be appraising you as a teacher, will be the children you teach. What do they think are the qualities of a good teacher? Rowan Hayward, aged 10, had few doubts about the qualities needed by anyone aspiring to be a good teacher:

> A good teacher is: Someone who is a good storyteller, someone who laughs a lot, someone with good taste. Someone who children like and find amusing, who understands and likes children. Someone who is gentle and kind, firm but not strict. Neat and organised and who insists that the children are the same. Someone who doesn't frighten pupils and doesn't get too angry or pick on children or have favourites.
>
> Times Educational Supplement, 2 February 1990

What makes a good teacher? This could be an interesting theme for your children to discuss in groups, or to write about. Hopefully you will recognise some of your own qualities in the resulting survey of opinion!

Teacher appraisal schemes exist in many schools. If the proposals of the National Appraisal Project are put into effect, every teacher working in schools will be subject to periodic appraisal, usually by the headteacher or a senior colleague. Appraisal should be based on the teacher's job description and undertaken according to a policy agreed by the LEA or school governors.

The pattern of appraisal recommended is that teachers have a formal appraisal every two years, with a follow-up interview with the appraiser in the year between full appraisals.

A full appraisal could include six stages, as shown in Table 93.

If handled well, the appraisal process presents a positive opportunity for teachers to discuss at length their own professional development, as well as the management and organisation of the school. If handled badly, appraisal will become just an extra burden to cope with in an already demanding job.

# Coping with stress

Teaching is a stressful occupation. On an average day a teacher can experience up to 1000 personal encounters. For some teachers such encounters can offer a vital and rejuvenating challenge. Others find the multitude of daily encounters, with their inevitable points of friction, particularly wearing. Bertrand Russell wrote feelingly, 'Nobody who has not had a go at it can appreciate the expense of personal spirit it entails.'

# TABLE 93 Stages of teacher appraisal

The six stages recommended for appraisal are:

1  *The initial meeting*
- to discuss the purpose of appraisal
- to consider the teacher's job description
- to agree the scope and timetable for appraisal

2  *Classroom observation*
- a full briefing before observation
- classroom observation at agreed time(s)
- discussion with appraiser within two days of observation

3  *Collection of information*
- collection of information on teacher's performance, eg samples of work
- information relating to classroom teaching and any administrative responsibilities
- colleagues may be consulted on relevant professional matters

4  *Self-appraisal*
- self-appraisal should be part of the appraisal process
- all teachers should reflect on their own performance
- self-appraisal cannot be compulsory

5  *The appraisal interview*
- the central component of appraisal is an extended interview between appraiser and appraisee
- its object is to identify successes and training needs
- the results should include agreed targets for action

6  *The appraisal record*
- a record of main points that arose in interview to be agreed
- both appraiser and appraisee to sign the record
- records to be confidential to headteacher and LEA officers

The causes of stress can be many and varied, from the behaviour of children, to the heavy workload of assessment and marking, the problems of mixed-ability teaching, lack of support from colleagues and the government, the demands of parents, the pressures of constant change, lack of information, lack of non-contact time, lack of promotion opportunity, low salary, low status in society and so on. Table 94 suggests some ways of combatting the possible build-up of stress.

---

## TABLE 94 Ways of reducing stress

- Work no more than ten hours a day, take breaks and pace your effort.
- Have at least one day a week free from all school work, and some time 'away from it all' during every holiday period.
- Take some form of regular physical exercise, preferably outdoors.
- Cultivate a creative hobby such as gardening, painting, do-it-yourself; spend time on it – avoid boredom.
- Share your problems, and seek advice and support from others – avoid feeling isolated.
- Set realistic targets, sort out your priorities and avoid work overload.
- Recognise signs of stress and tension, and practise some techniques of relaxation.
- See work as a challenge, a problem to be solved, not as a threat. If you're in a rut, get out of it!
- Be positive; take personal responsibility for your own health and happiness.
- Learn to smile and laugh more. Try not to take your job or life too seriously.

---

## Task 69 Devising your own recipe for success as a teacher

- List, or discuss with a colleague, what you find most stressful in teaching.
- Reflect on and list what you find most satisfying and relaxing in your life.
- Keep a record of the ways which work for you in reducing stress and achieving satisfaction in your personal/professional life. Review this from time to time.
- Remember to reward yourself for the success you achieve in your professional role, and in the demanding and vital task of teaching juniors.

Only a mediocre teacher is always at his or her best. There will be times of success and times of failure in teaching. What works with one child, group or class may not work well with another. Outside pressures may deflect us from giving of our best, and there may be no-one to thank us for our efforts. It is not always easy to hold on to one's ideas and to retain a vision of what children might achieve. Much that we do may not bear fruit for many years. We need to keep our aims high and keep hold of our dreams. As the Reverend Edward Thring wrote over a hundred years ago, 'though law and public opinion make teaching impossible, dreams are beyond law.'

## Task 70 Reflecting on your philosophy of primary education

Imagine you are applying for a teaching post. The application form requires you to set out in about 500 words your philosophy of primary education. Draft out your response after due reflection.

# FURTHER READING AND REFERENCES

Here you will find references relating to the main text and suggestions for further reading grouped under each unit theme. This list is not intended to be comprehensive, but will provide an excellent basis for further professional study.

## 1 Thinking about teaching
Ashton P et al (1975) *The Aims of Primary Education: A Study of Teacher's Opinions* Schools Council/Macmillan
Claxton G (1990) *Being a Teacher* Cassell
Delamont S ed (1987) *The Primary School Teacher* Falmer
Kohl H (1976) *On Teaching* Methuen
Mortimore P et al (1988) *School Matters: The Junior Years* Open Books (study later referred to as Junior Project)
Nias J (1989) *Primary Teachers Talking* Routledge


## 2 Seeing how children learn
Ausubel D (1968) *Educational Psychology: A Cognitive View* Holt
Croll P (1986) *Systematic Classroom Observation* Falmer
Donaldson M (1978) *Children's Minds* Fontana
Galton M, Simon B & Croll P (1980) *Inside the Primary Classroom* Routledge (study later referred to as ORACLE)
Holt J (1984) *How Children Learn* Penguin
Junior Project: see references for Unit 1
Meadows S & Cashdan L (1988) *Helping Children Learn* David Fulton
Mills R W (1988) *Observing Children in the Primary Classroom* Unwin Hyman
Wood D (1988) *How Children Think and Learn* Blackwell

## 3  Developing a teaching style
Bennett N (1976) *Teaching Styles and Pupil Progress* Open Books
Cohen L & Manion L (3rd edn 1988) *A Guide to Teaching Practice* Holt
Davis R (1989) *Learning to Teach in the Primary School* Hodder
Fisher R (1990) *Teaching Children to Think* Blackwell
HMI Survey (1978) *Primary Education in England* HMSO
Jacobsen D et al (1981) *Methods for Teaching: a Skills Approach* Merril


## 4  Managing a classroom
Craig I (1988) *Managing the Primary Classroom* Longman
Dean J (1983) *Organising Learning in the Primary Classroom* Croom Helm
Kounin J S (1970) *Discipline and Group Management in Classrooms* Holt
Laslett R & Smith C (1985) *Effective Classroom Management* Croom Helm
Plowden Report (1967) *Children and their Primary Schools* HMSO
Wheldall K & Glynn T (1989) *Effective Classroom Learning* Blackwell


## 5  Promoting discipline and good behaviour
DES (1989) *The Elton Report: Discipline in Schools* HMSO
Docking J W (1987) *Control and Discipline in Schools* Harper
HMI (1987) *Education Observed 5: Good behaviour and discipline* HMSO
Gray J & Richer J (1988) *Classroom Responses to Disruptive Behaviour*
    Macmillan
Lawrence D (1988) *Enhancing Self-Esteem in the Classroom* Paul Chapman
Mongen D & Hart S (1990) *Improving Classroom Behaviour* Cassell
Robertson J (1990) *Effective Classroom Control* Hodder


## 6  Planning the curriculum
HMI (1985) *The Curriculum 5–16* HMSO
HMI (1987/88) *Annual Report on Schools* HMSO
Kerry T & Eggleston J (1988) *Topic Work in the Primary School* Routledge
NCC (1990) *Curriculum Guidance 3: The Whole Curriculum*
Schools Council (1981) *The Practical Curriculum* Methuen
Tann C S (1988) *Developing Topic Work in the Primary School* Falmer
Wray D (1988) *Project Teaching* Scholastic


## 7  English
Beard R (1984) *Children's Writing in the Primary School* Hodder
Beard R (1987) *Developing Reading 3–13* Hodder
HMI (2nd edn 1986) *English from 5–16* HMSO

Houlton D (1985) *All Our Languages* Arnold
Hunter-Carsch M, Beverton S & Dennis D eds (1990) *Primary English in the National Curriculum* Blackwell/United Kingdom Reading Association
Jarman C (1979) *The Development of Handwriting Skills* Blackwell
Martin T, Waters M & Bloom W (1990) *Managing Writing: Practical Issues in the Classroom* Mary Glasgow
NCC (1989) *English in the National Curriculum* HMSO
Southgate V et al (1981) *Extending Beginning Reading* Heinemann/Schools Council
The Journal of the National Oracy Project *TALK* HMSO

## 8 Mathematics

Brissenden T (1990) *Talking About Mathematics: Mathematical Discussions in Primary Classrooms* Blackwell
Burton L (1990) *Primary Mathematics: Patterns and Relationships* Blackwell
The Cockcroft Report (1982) *Maths Counts* HMSO
Fisher R & Vince A (1989) *Investigating Maths* Books 1–4 Blackwell
HMI (2nd edn 1987) *Mathematics from 5–16* HMSO
Hughes M (1986) *Children and Number: Difficulties in Learning Mathematics* Blackwell
NCC (1989) *Mathematics in the National Curriculum* HMSO
Woodman A & Albany E (1989) *Mathematics through Art and Design 6–13* Unwin Hyman

## 9 Science

ASE (1989) *The National Curriculum: Making it Work for the Primary School* Association for Science Education/ATM/NATE
Harlen W ed (1985) *Taking the Plunge* Heinemann
Harlen W & Jelly S (1989) *Developing Science in the Primary Classroom* Oliver & Boyd
HMI (1986) *Health education from 5–16* HMSO
NCC (1989) *Science in the National Curriculum* HMSO
Richards R, Collis M & Kincaid D (1989) *An Early Start to Science* Simon & Schuster
Schools Council (1972) *Science 5/13 Project* Macdonald
Ward A (1989) *1000 Ideas for Primary Science* Hodder

## 10 Technology

Crompton R ed (1990) *Computers and the Primary Curriculum* Falmer
Fisher R ed (1987) *Problem Solving in the Primary School* Blackwell

HMI (1985) *Home economics 5–16* HMSO
HMI (1987) *Craft, design and technology 5–16* HMSO
HMI (1989) *Information Technology 5–16* HMSO
Johnsey R (1990) *Design and Technology through Problem Solving* Simon & Schuster
NCC (1990) *Technology in the National Curriculum* HMSO
Richards R (1990) *An Early Start to Technology* Simon & Schuster
Straker A (1989) *Children Using Computers* Blackwell
Tickle L ed (1990) *Design and Technology in Primary School Classrooms* Falmer

## 11 Human and environmental studies – history and geography

Blyth J E (1988) *History in Primary Schools* Open University Press
Durbin G, Morris S & Wilkinson S (1990) *A Teacher's Guide to Learning from Objects* English Heritage
HMI (1986) *Geography from 5–16* HMSO
HMI (1988) *History from 5–16* HMSO
HMI (1989) *Environmental Education from 5–16* HMSO
Mays P (1985) *Teaching Children through the Environment* Hodder
Mills D ed (1988) *Geographical Work in Primary and Middle Schools* The Geographical Association
NCC (1990/91) *History in the National Curriculum* HMSO
NCC (1990/91) *Geography in the National Curriculum* HMSO
Pluckrose H (1991) *Children Learning History* Blackwell

## 12 Aesthetic development: art, music, drama and dance

Barnes R (1989) *Art, Design and Topic Work 8–13* Unwin Hyman
Britten A (1987) *Starting Points for Drama* Arnold
HMI (1985) *Music from 5–16* HMSO
HMI (1990) *Drama from 5–16* HMSO
Lowden M (1989) *Dancing to Learn* Falmer
Morgan M ed (1989) *Art 4–11* Blackwell
Salaman W (1983) *Living School Music* Cambridge University Press
See also National Curriculum reports on music and art (1991/92)

## 13 Physical education

ASA (1989) *The Teaching of Swimming* Amateur Swimming Association
Cooper A (1984) *The Development of Games Skills* Blackwell
Evans D A (1984) *Teaching Athletics 8–13* Hodder

HMI (1989) *Physical Education 5–16* HMSO
Roberts C (1987) *Go For It!: PE Activities for the Classroom Teacher* Oxford University Press
Trevor M D (1987) *The Development of Gymnastic Skills* Blackwell
Williams A ed (1989) *Issues in Physical Education for the Primary Years* Falmer
See also National Curriculum report on physical education (1991)

## 14 Religious and moral education

Bastide D ed (1990) *Good Practice in Primary Religious Education* Falmer
Fisher R (1981) *Together Today: Themes and Stories for Assembly* Unwin Hyman
HMI (1989) *Personal and Social Education from 5–16* HMSO
Holm J (1985) *Teaching Religion in School* Oxford University Press
Jackson R & Starkings D (1990) *The Junior RE Handbook* Stanley Thornes
Smith H (1990) *The Really Practical Guide to Primary RE* Stanley Thornes
Westhill RE Centre (1990) *Attainment in RE: A Handbook for Teachers*

## 15 Assessing pupil progress

ASE (1990) *Teacher Assessment: Making it Work for the Primary School* Association for Science Education/ATM/NATE
Connor C (1990) *Assessment and Testing in the Primary School* Falmer
Duncan A & Dunn W (1988) *What Primary Teachers should know about Assessment* Hodder
Gipps C (1990) *Assessment in Schools: A Guide to the Issues* Hodder
Shipman M (1983) *Assessment in Primary and Middle Schools* Croom Helm
See also other guidance issued by the School Examinations & Assessment Council (SEAC) to Teacher Assessment in the National Curriculum
TGAT Report (1988) *Task Group on Assessment and Testing* Report DES

## 16 Catering for special needs

Ainscow M & Tweddle D A (1988) *Encouraging Classroom Success* Fulton
Brophy J E and Good T L (1974) *Teacher-Student Relationships* Holt
Cohen A & Cohen L (1986) *Special Educational Needs in the Ordinary School: A Source Book for Teachers* Harper
Hegarty S (1987) *Meeting Special Needs in Ordinary Schools* Cassell
Leyden S (1987) *Helping the Child with Exceptional Ability* Croom Helm
NCC (1989) *A Curriculum for All* HMSO
Warnock M (1978) *Special Educational Needs* (The Warnock Report) HMSO
Wolfendale S (1987) *Primary Schools and Special Needs* Cassell

## 17 Ensuring equal opportunities
Boyd J (1989) *Equality Issues in Primary Schools* Paul Chapman
Hessari R & Hill D (1989) *Practical Ideas for Multicultural Learning and Teaching in the Primary School* Routledge
Lynch J (1986) *Multicultural Education* Routledge
Myers K (1987) *Genderwatch* School Curriculum Development Council/ Equal Opportunities Commission
Tutchell E ed (1990) *Dolls and Dungarees: Gender Issues in the Primary Curriculum* Open University Press
See also NCC (1991) National Curriculum Guidance on Equal Opportunities

## 18 Working with the community
Docking J W (1990) *Primary Schools and Parents* Hodder
Sallis J (1988) *Schools, Parents and Governors: A New Approach to Accountability* Routledge
Smith D ed (1988) *Industry in the Primary Curriculum* Falmer
Sullivan M (1988) *Parents and Schools* Scholastic
Tizard J et al (1982) 'Collaboration between teachers and parents in assisting children reading' *British Journal of Educational Psychology* vol. 52, 1, 1–15

## 19 Appraising your teaching
Gray H & Freeman A (1988) *Teaching Without Stress* Paul Chapman
Montgomery D & Hadfield N (1989) *Appraisal in Primary Schools* Scholastic
Moyles J R (1988) *Self-evaluation: A Primary Teacher's Guide* NFER-Nelson
Pollard A & Tann S (1987) *Reflective Teaching in the Primary School* Cassell

# GLOSSARY OF NATIONAL CURRICULUM TERMS

| | |
|---|---|
| Attainment targets (ATs) | Objectives for each foundation subject, setting out the knowledge, skills and understanding that pupils of different abilities and maturities are expected to develop within that subject area. Further defined at ten levels of attainment by means of appropriate statements of attainment. |
| Basic curriculum | This comprises the National Curriculum and religious education (RE). |
| Core subjects | English, mathematics and science, and, in Wales, Welsh. |
| Cross-curricular themes | Strands of provision which will run through the National Curriculum and may also extend into RE and provision outside the basic curriculum. |
| Foundation subjects | English, mathematics, science, technology, history, geography, music, art and physical education, and also (for secondary-age pupils) a modern foreign language, and (for pupils in Wales) Welsh. Note: the foundation subjects comprise the three core and seven other foundation subjects. |
| Key stages | The periods in each pupil's education to which the elements of the National Curriculum will apply. There are four key stages: Stage One – ages 5–7 ie the cohorts 5–6 & 6–7) Stage Two – ages 7–11 ie the cohorts 7–8, 8–9, 9–10 & 10–11) Stage Three – ages 11–14 ie the cohorts 11–12, 12–13, & 13–14) Stage Four – ages 14–16 ie the cohorts 14–15 & 15–16) |

| | |
|---|---|
| Levels of attainment | The ten different levels of achievement defined within each attainment target, reflecting differences in ability and in progress according to age. |
| National Curriculum | National Curriculum is the compulsory curriculum laid down by the Government for all pupils in state schools during the period of compulsory schooling (ages 5–16). |
| NCC | NCC is the National Curriculum Council, a body established under the Education Reform Act to keep under review, and to advise the Secretary of State on, matters concerning the curriculum in maintained schools. |
| Profile components | Groups of attainment targets brought together for the purposes of assessment and reporting. |
| Programmes of study (POS) | The matters, skills and processes which must be taught to pupils during each key stage in order for them to meet the objectives set out in attainment targets. |
| Reporting ages | Also known as key ages or assessment ages. These are the four points at which performance against attainment targets and levels of attainment is subject to formal reported assessment. These are at or near the end of each key stage, when most pupils are likely to be 7, 11, 14 and 16 respectively. |
| SEAC | SEAC is the School Examinations and Assessment Council, a body established under the Education Reform Act to keep under review, and advise the Secretary of State on, all aspects of examinations and assessment. |
| Standard assessment tasks (SATs) | Externally prescribed assessments which may incorporate a variety of assessment methods. They will complement teachers' own assessments. |
| Statements of Attainment (SOA) | More precise objectives than the broader attainment targets, which will be defined within statutory Orders. They are related to one of ten levels of attainment on a single continuous scale, covering all four key stages. |
| TGAT | TGAT is the Task Group on Assessment and Testing established by the Secretary of State to advise him on structures and systems for assessing the National Curriculum. |

# END-NOTE TO THE READER

If you wish to share your experiences in using this book or have suggestions on ways it could be improved, please contact:

Robert Fisher
West London Institute of Higher Education
300 St Margaret's Road
Twickenham
Middx TWI IPT

# INDEX